The NEW LANGUAGE of TOYS

Teaching Communication Skills to Children with Special Needs

A Guide for Parents and Teachers

Sue Schwartz, Ph.D., and
Joan E. Heller Miller, Ed.M.

WOODBINE HOUSE • 1996

Photographs by Robert Burke
Cover illustration: Liz Wolf

Library of Congress Cataloging-in-Publication Data

Schwartz, Sue.
  The new language of toys : teaching communication skills to children with special needs / Sue Schwartz and Joan E. Heller Miller.
    p.   cm.
  Updated ed. of: The language of toys. 1988.
  Includes bibliographical references and index.
  ISBN 0–933149–73–5 (pbk.)
  1. Language acquisition. 2. Educational toys. 3. Slow learning children—Language. I. Miller, Joan E. Heller. II. Schwartz, Sue. New language of toys. III. Title.
P118.S293 1996
649'.15--dc20   95–47452
                                                                          CIP

Manufactured in the United States of America

10 9 8 7 6 5

DEDICATION

To our children: Cara, Julie, and Kimberly; Debra, Jeff, and Barry
—for sharing the joy of play with us

To our husbands: Ken and Sid
—for continued support in our endeavors, and for sharing computer time and answering endless questions about computer operations

TABLE of CONTENTS

ACKNOWLEDGEMENTS

Our thanks to:

The staff at Woodbine House for their continued faith in our abilities to help children develop their language skills through play.

The parents and children who agreed to be photographed during their playtime:

Teresa, Meghan, and Natalie Blickman
Aegyung, Sujin, and Adam Cho
Amy Crupiti
Martha Debebe
Michael, Sheila Doctors, and Suzie Dershowitz
Kyle, Jonas, and Lee Epstein
Ben, Francine, and Robert Freid
John, Rebecca, and Daniel Golden
Gabrielle, Needa, and Obed Hoyah
Linda, Broadway the Third, and Chanel Jackson
Julia Korenman
Ken, Joan, Kimberly, Julie, and Cara Miller
Alison and Susan Russell
Leila and Gideon Samara
Debra Schwartz
Deena Shapiro
Dan, Deb, and Justin Snyder
David, Andrew, and Tim Soncrant
Allison and Bradley Stokes
Zachary, Andrew, and Howard Tracer
Birol and Alican Tuncer
Trang Vo
Stacy and Natalie Werther
Karen, Arthur, Jr., Christina and Jonathan Woodward
Thomas and Elisabeth Yackee

Additional thanks to:

Robert Burke for his excellent photographic eye and patience.
Sarah Glenner—for her assistance in typing. You are an inspiration to other young adults and children with Down Syndrome.
Irv Shapell, our publisher at Woodbine House—a man with a vision who has achieved his goal with excellence.
Susan Stokes, our editor at Woodbine House for adding the "little extras" that brought it all together.

Jane Mellon for encouraging Joan's interest in writing and for unwavering support both personally and professionally.

Cece Wett—for lending a critical "special needs focus" to our work.

Sue Petrone—for adding her expertise in visual impairment to supplement our work.

Fran Hunt—for creative and interesting play ideas.

To the entire Miller/Mellon/Heller family for supporting our own family's special education efforts.

All of our friends and colleagues for their advice and encouragement for this work.

INTRODUCTION

Developing communication is as much a basic human need as seeking food and comfort. For many children this is a relatively simple process, while for others there may be significant delays. There are a wide variety of causes for language delay in children. Regardless of the cause, however, the results are usually the same: a child with delayed language development and concerned parents.

These concerned parents want to help their children with special needs learn language skills but often don't know the best way to go about it. Through our years of teaching and raising our own children, we have seen that an amazing amount of language can be pulled from even the most simple toy. Our book, *The New Language of Toys*, shows you how to use toys and other play activities to aid your child's language development.

Our first book, *The Language of Toys*, showed thousands of parents how to use toys and other play activities to aid their child's language development. Since its publication, many new and exciting toys have come on the market and some of the older toys have disappeared from toy store shelves. We therefore felt it was time to offer *The New Language of Toys*. In *The New Language of Toys* we not only added dozens of new toys and activities, but also expanded the age range to include children up to age six. In addition, we added chapters on language-enriching video and computer activities and expanded and updated the Resource Guide at the end of the book. Finally, we replaced all of the old photographs with new photographs of children playing with the toys recommended in the book.

While you are playing with your child, you can be helping him increase his language skills. And you can have fun together at the same time. We know your child can benefit from these times with Mom and Dad. We also know this play/work time is dramatically more important for children with delays in their language development. They will need the extra effort that their parents can give them to help develop their language skills.

When speech and language therapists or teachers work with children with language delays, they usually use toys they think will encourage certain words or sounds. There is no "magic" to the toys they use. Rather, the toys are chosen carefully to be teaching aids. This book will help you to choose and to use toys like the professionals do to enhance the development of language in *your* child. Although we have selected certain toys for this book, we want to assure you that there are many other toys that can be bought or made which can serve equally well.

The New Language of Toys is divided into three parts. In the first part, we explain important background information about language, its sequential development, some of the causes of language delay, the value of play, how play can enhance language development, and your role in all of this. In the next section—which is the heart of the book—we recommend toys that we have found to be useful in stimulating language development and show you how to use these toys in playing with your child. For each toy in the book, we provide sample language dialogues to help you get the most from that toy. We encourage you to use these ideas in your play as well as to go beyond and devise new ways of playing to encourage language development. In the last section of the book, we discuss general issues related to toys and learning that will help you choose and use toys and other language-learning materials wisely.

We have designed this book to be used with *any child who has a language delay, whatever the cause may be.* We have given you guidelines which should help you decide which toys your child would be most interested in playing with and most ready to learn from. Each child has his own unique profile for all developmental areas, including cognition, motor, social, self-help, *and* language. A child may make progress in different areas at different rates. The result is wide variation in the developmental picture for each child, regardless of his chronological age. For example, a three-year-old child with a twelve-month language delay may have "normal" cognitive development or motor skills but speak on a two-year-old level. Alternately, a four-year-old child with "normal" language may have very delayed motor skills.

We have individual suggestions for modifying your play to accommodate the specific learning needs of each child. We are sure that we haven't addressed every possible need but we feel that you will be able to adapt our suggestions to your own child.

The toys and exercises in this book are arranged by language developmental ages. Each section covers several months and presents toys and dialogues that are appropriate for your child's particular level of language development. There are similar guidelines throughout the book to help you pick toys that are the most appropriate for your child's level of language development.

In addition to suggesting toys you can buy, we also include at least two homemade toys for each of our language developmental levels. Many people enjoy making toys, and for children with disabilities, homemade toys can be designed to adapt to their specific needs. There is a lot of benefit in making your own toys—including saving money. In our work, we have found that children and parents treasure these homemade toys long after other toys have been packed away.

Remember, our suggestions are only suggestions. Expand and create. There are many books in libraries and in bookstores that will tell you more about homemade toys. We have included several in our reference list at the back of this book.

Parents often ask, "When should we start?" You can start the exercises in this book even before your child's language delay has been formally diagnosed. If you already know that your child has some special needs, you have to consider the possibility that he is language delayed too. Do not wait until you have a specific diagnosis of language delay to begin. Often your child's diagnosis has to wait until you are able to test him and in many cases that doesn't happen before age two. You can always work on his language skills even before getting a diagnosis. It can only help him in the long run. As you will see in our chapter on language development, you would not expect your child to be talking in understandable language much before one year of age. We want you to enrich your child's language long before that time.

If your child is an older preschooler and you have just gotten the diagnosis of a language delay, then you can start this book at whatever level your child is placed and work from there. You might even be working with a therapist or school at this time. Show them this book and explain how you want to integrate our ideas with your child's specific plan. You will probably find that our examples fit right in with your child's individual education plan.

We do not expect, or want, you to turn into a teacher for your child or to lose your role of being a parent. However, you can combine the two roles in a way that is fun for both you and your child. There is also no need to occupy your child's every waking moment with the exercises in this book. There are times when children should play alone because that is when they build independence and develop imagination. We believe, however, that parents, grandparents, teachers, families, babysitters, and others can enhance the development of richer language by playing with toys with children for *part* of the child's playtime.

Follow your child's lead. If he is interested in farm animals, explore that area in your play. If you see that he has no interest at all in cars and trucks, then put that idea aside for a while. Your play should be fun, interesting, and meaningful. Experience your childhood again and enjoy the time you will spend in playful learning with your child.

Chapter 2

Language Development in Children

As children grow, their physical and mental abilities develop to handle more complex skills. You can see this in an infant absorbed with a rattle, a two-year-old playing with sandbox toys, or a five-year-old building an intricate structure with blocks. Each is playing within a different range of abilities that is appropriate for his growth at that age.

Language ability also develops over time. From a child's first "mama" or "dada" through complete phrases and sentences made up of several words, an amazing amount of language development occurs. Like other areas, language development varies tremendously between children.

Parents of children with special needs often ask, "What is considered 'normal' language development so I can gauge my child's progress?" Figure 1 shows stages of language development in children. Remember, however, there is a very wide range of what is considered "normal" development. For example, although the average number of words a two-year-old can say is 272, a child could say as few as 50 and still be considered to be developing normally. Or, although some children can say a couple of words by the age of nine months, other normally developing children do not say their first word until fourteen months or later. Likewise, there could be a wide variation in your child's language skills.

Language Development In Normally Hearing Children

Vocal Play ◄──► Babbling ◄──► Jargon ◄──► Imitation ◄──►

0 months	6 mos.	12 mos	18mos.
	1 word	3 words	22 words

Phrases ◄──► Sentences/ ◄──► Paragraphs ◄──► Nearly Correct ◄──►
               Questions   Grammar

24 mos.	3 years	4 years	5 years
272 words	896 words	1870 words	2289 words

Full Command of English
6 years
2568 words

Vocabulary numbers taken from Diagnostic Methods in Speech Pathology, p. 192.
Samples taken from children of average IQ.

Parents, teachers, therapists, and other specialists want to be able to determine the level where your child is functioning so they can target what skills need to be worked on. His development in areas such as fine motor, gross motor, thinking, receptive language, expressive language, and speech is tested to determine his strengths and weaknesses. Extensive studies by experts have established ages where most of the children tested acquired each skill. By comparing your child with these norms, the approximate age at which your child is functioning can be found. This is called a **developmental age.** Since there is great variation among children, most tests will give a range from the lowest age where this skill is acquired to the highest age where almost every child tested had the skill. This developmental range is the accurate way to find where your child is functioning at this time.

For parents of children with special needs, development can be complicated. Often these children are a mosaic of different developmental levels. A child may have six-year-old gross motor skills, two-year-old fine motor skills, and another level in language development. Because of these varying levels, deciding where your child currently is *developmentally* in his language skills can be a little tricky.

The next section presents summaries of different developmental ages that emphasize language development. These descriptions should help you to determine your child's current level of language development. We have also included summaries of physical development so that you can have a clear picture of your child's development overall. Remember, these developmental ages are general outlines only. No two children are alike. Far more important than comparing your child's behavior to other children's within the same range is comparing your child's behavior, accomplishments, and progress with his own earlier achievements. It is not critical that your child reach any given stage by a certain age. Quality of development—not just quantity—should be your goal.

In working with your child with developmental delays in language, use his developmental age and not his actual age to determine what skills to work on. For instance, he may be chronologically twenty-four months old, but his language may have developed to a twelve-month-old level. In your work with him, use the language developmental age of twelve months. He will function best at his developmental age and you do not want to frustrate him by working too far beyond his capabilities.

Developmental Ages

This section summarizes developmental ages of children during the first six years of life. This information will help you decide what language developmental age best fits your child now so you can choose appropriate language activities.

One way for you to decide which toys your child will enjoy is to see which category lists the largest number of skills your child has acquired. This level should be close to his developmental age. Using toys from the category should insure that you and your child will benefit from the activities presented. Our selections should not limit you but should be used as a guide. Choose any toy that you think he will enjoy playing with and learn from.

BIRTH TO THREE MONTHS

A newborn is primarily interested in his most basic needs for food, comfort, and love. He spends most of his day being nourished, being kept clean, and being loved. During this time he is developing an understanding of trust and warmth from those who care for him.

Language Development

During his first weeks of life, your baby is most likely to communicate only through crying. The people taking care of him will soon be able to tell what his different cries mean. Is he hungry? Is he wet? Is he tired? Does he want company? Each of these cries has a different tone to it which can be understood easily in a short time. In a few

weeks your baby adds cooing, squealing, and gurgling to his repertoire. You can see that he enjoys making all these different sounds as you talk to him, tickle him, and make those favorite silly faces that we enjoy making with little babies.

The little noises that infants make in these first months are called vocal play. Most infants, even deaf ones, will engage in vocal play. The sounds are vowel-like and can vary in loudness as well as in the pitch of high and low sounds. In these first few months babies often make sounds that are heard in languages other than their own. An American baby might produce an inflectional tone of an Asian language, a guttural sound from a Germanic language, or a tongue click from an African dialect. Because these sounds are not reinforced by the sounds he hears around him, he quickly stops playing with them and focuses more on the sounds that are reinforced in his own language. It is in this way that babies begin to learn to speak their native language.

Physical Development

During the first three months of life, you may see that your infant is developing an awareness of his sense of touch. You can get a response from him by rubbing his hands, arms, legs, and feet with smooth, scratchy, fuzzy, and soft materials. By the third month, he will be able to hold onto objects and will enjoy rattles and stuffed animals.

THREE TO SIX MONTHS

Your baby is now becoming more active and is awake for longer periods of time. He's ready for more play time with you. Instead of spending most of your time just caring for your newborn, now you can increase both the amount of time you spend playing with him and can focus this play more on his language development.

Language Development

Around the fourth month, we begin to hear more of the consonant sounds emerging in a baby's vocal play. He will practice with sounds that use only his lips, such as /m/b/p/, as well as sounds using other parts of his mouth, such as his tongue, which produce /t/g/l/.

Physical Development

Your baby is now able to grasp and hold onto things and will enjoy rattles, stuffed animals, and objects that he can explore with his hands like those textured rattles and animals you bought when he was a newborn. He is able to reach out for things and bring them to his mouth to explore them.

SIX TO NINE MONTHS

Your infant is now on a fairly regular sleep and play schedule. He will be more interested in activities with you and awake longer to enjoy them.

Language Development

You will discover that his attention span is increasing and that he will enjoy longer periods of play and longer periods of looking at books and pictures with you.

Beginning at about six months, your baby's random sounds of vocal play will begin to become repetitive. You'll hear more combinations of sounds that he will repeat over and over again. This is called babbling. You may even hear some combinations of sounds that resemble actual words. They rarely hold meaning for him at this point. Gradually, at around eight months of age, these babbling sounds get more refined and begin to represent words to your baby. Around this time, you may hear his first true word, which will usually be a combination of consonant and vowel sounds that he has played with along the way. For example, he may combine the /a/ and /m/ sounds to produce "mama," or may combine /a/ with /b/ to produce "baba."

Physical Development

He is becoming more physically active and may be ready to crawl very soon. By the end of this time range, he may well be crawling along. He can sit up by himself, which makes him more available for different games that you can play. His fine motor skills are becoming more refined and he is able to pick up things using his thumb to help him. He'll be able to pick up blocks and help you in stacking them and in knocking them down! He'll enjoy stacking rings, but at first he will be more interested in taking them off than he will be in putting them back on.

By the end of this time period, he will probably be pulling himself up to a standing position, so be sure to raise the sides of the crib and put away that crystal vase!

NINE TO TWELVE MONTHS

Language Development

As he moves along toward his first birthday, you will see a dramatic rise in your baby's comprehension (receptive language). He will enjoy playing games of "Show me." "Show me your eyes." "Where's the kitty?" "Can you find your ball?" He will enjoy showing off how much he understands and may even try to imitate some of the key words he hears you say.

His attention span is still increasing and he will enjoy listening to books, records, and tapes. He may even be able to point to some known objects in the books as you tell him the names.

Physical Development

By now you've noticed how very physically active your baby is. He will be holding on and walking around furniture. He may even strike out on his own and walk by himself. He will enjoy active outdoor play. Make sure that his play area is fenced in or that you are with him all the time. He may be scooting around but he has no idea of danger at this time. He is able to roll a ball with two hands and if he is standing alone by this age, he may even be able to kick it as well. Balls are fun and a great way to encourage physical agility.

His fine motor skills are developing and he is able to pick things up, put them into containers, and gleefully dump them out again. We have seen babies do this over and over for incredibly long periods of time. He is able to manipulate small switches, dials, and slides. He is able to clap his hands together and will enjoy imitating you in pat-a-cake type games.

TWELVE TO FIFTEEN MONTHS

Language Development

By now there is much more babbling going on with many sounds strung together into phrase-like and sentence-like series. This babbling will have tone and inflection and many people say, "If I just knew what language he was speaking. . . ." This phase is called *jargoning*. You will occasionally hear a word tossed in among all of his singsong jargoning.

Physical Development

One of the play skills your toddler will find most interesting is turning "dumping" into "pouring." If he has been walking and is steady, he will now be able to walk sideways and backward and will enjoy walking with pull toys as well as push toys.

Up until now you have been rolling a ball to him. Since he is now steadily standing, he will be able to throw the ball to you. He probably will not be able to catch it yet but he will enjoy kicking and chasing it.

His fine motor skills are well developed enough now that he can turn the pages of a book and do other fine motor activities.

FIFTEEN TO EIGHTEEN MONTHS

Your baby's imagination is developing and he will like playing with toys that are representational of his world. He will enjoy acting out many scenes that he sees in his own life.

Language Development

Jargoning continues while words develop. By eighteen months, you'll be able to distinguish more and more recognizable words mixed in the jargon. If you are keeping a list of words for which he has true meanings, you'll probably find that he says somewhere around 22–25 words. These are certainly not absolute numbers—some children may say more and some fewer—but this number is an average for an eighteen-month-old baby.

Physical Development

During this stage, your child is able to climb stairs and expand his world on his own. He now has the physical abilities he needs to indulge his curiosity. He will explore your home inside and out. Be sure to provide a safe environment for him.

EIGHTEEN TO TWENTY-FOUR MONTHS

At this age, your child's interest in books continues and now he is able to "read" the pictures himself. He will enjoy "reading" to you out of homemade books that you may have made for him earlier. He can even help select pictures for new books.

Language Development

At this age, your toddler enjoys imitating your words, tones, and actions. Now is a great time for finger plays and games like peek-a-boo and pat-a-cake. If you check the language development chart, you will see a dramatic rise in the number of words your little one is now able to use. Although there is wide variation, an average number of words a child with no language delay might be using by twenty-four months of age is about 272. We share this number with you so you are aware of the vast number of things he can identify by name. He also will be combining these words into short phrases. You'll hear him say,"Bye bye car" or "Daddy go work." You'll also hear many incorrect grammatical combinations such as "Tommy falled down" or "car go me." You'll begin to hear pronouns being used, although he will still refer to himself by name most of the time. His pronunciation of words and phrases can often be very hard to understand.

Physical Development

Your young child is probably very active at this stage. He is walking steadily, running constantly, and climbing, and now adds jumping to his repertoire.

His fine motor skills are developed to the point where he can open and close containers. He will be able to place puzzle pieces if there is one piece for each space.

TWENTY-FOUR TO THIRTY-SIX MONTHS (2–3 Years)

Language Development

This is a fascinating time for you and your child in many ways. Language development is certainly one of the most exciting things happening during this year. This is the year where the phrases of 2–3 words turn into sentences of 4–5 words. The sentences then turn into questions. This is the year of "why," "what," and "where." Sometimes these questions are really for the purpose of getting information and sometimes your child just enjoys hearing himself talk.

You can expect your child to make many errors in the use of words and how they fit into sentences. He really does not understand the rules of grammar yet. He will also mispronounce many sounds at this age, and for the next few years. Figure 2 shows you when each of the speech sounds usually develops.

Physical Development

By this age he has many of his large motor skills under control. He may be able to pedal a trike, but more likely he will push with his feet on the ground. He will probably discover the low-seated plastic Big Wheels that children enjoy at this age.

His fine motor skills continue to develop and he will be able to play with interlocking block systems to create endless imaginative designs. He is comfortable handling puzzle pieces and enjoys showing off his skills.

Figure 2

Earliest Ages (in years) At Which Sounds Were Correctly Produced, In the Word Positions Indicated, by 75% of 208 Children

Consonants	Beginning Position	Middle Position	End Position
m	2	2	3
n	2	2	3
ng	–	6	3
p	2	2	4
b	2	2	3
t	2	5	3
d	2	3	4
k	3	3	4
g	3	3	4
r	5	4	4
l	4	4	4
f	3	3	3
v	5	5	5
th (uv)*	5	–	–
th (v)**	5	5	
s	5	5	5
z	5	3	3
sh	5	5	5
h	2	–	–
wh	5	–	–
w	2	2	–
y	4	4	–
ch	5	5	4
j	4	4	6

Vowels and Dipthongs	Age
ee (beet)	2
i (bit)	4
e (bed)	3
a (cat)	4
u (cup)	2
ah (father)	2
aw (ball)	3
oo (foot)	4
oo (boot)	2
u-e (mule)	3
o-e (coke)	2
a-e (cake)	4
i-e (kite)	3
oy (boy)	3

* (uv) = unvoiced (using only breath to produce the sound, as in the word three
** (v) = voiced (using the voice to produce the sound, as in the word the)

Figure 2 (continued)

Consonant Blend	Age	Consonant Blend	Age
pr	5	–ks	5
br	5	al	6
tr	5	sw	5
dr	5	tw	5
kr	5	kw	5
gr	5	ngk	4
fr	5	ngk	5
thr	6	–mp	3
pl	5	–nt	4
bl	5	–nd	6
kl	5	spr-	5
gl	5	apl	5
fl	5	str-	5
-ld	6	skr-	5
-lk	5	skw-	5
-lf	5	–ns	5
-lv	5	–ps	5
-lz	5	–ts	5
sm-	5	–mz	5
sn-	5	–nz	5
sp-	5	–ngz	5
st-	5	–dz	5
-st	6	–gz	5
sk-	5		

(Powers, Margaret Hall, "Functional Disorders of Articulation/Symptomatology and Etiology." In *Handbook of Speech Pathology and Audiology,* edited by Lee Edward Travis, p. 842. Englewood Cliffs, NJ: Prentice Hall, 1971.)

THIRTY-SIX TO FORTY-EIGHT MONTHS (3 to 4 Years)

During this year, most young children are involved with other children on a regular basis. Your child will continue to be very active both in and out of doors with playmates and alone.

Language Development

As your child's world begins to expand beyond your doors, new people will be adding to his receptive language. He will begin to have new playmates in the neighborhood and at his preschool or daycare center. He will pick up new and different words and phrases from them.

You will notice that he is able to tell you more complicated stories about things that happen to him when you aren't around. He can tell you about his activities at school and about his play with friends outside.

One disturbing development in his expressive language that may happen during this year may be the occurrence of *nonfluency*. Nonfluency usually happens like this: Your child has many things he wants to tell you. They are all very important to him and often he is overwhelmed with excitement at telling you about them. His thoughts may come so quickly that his oral muscles may not be able to keep up with the speed of his thinking.

Give your child time and attention during these moments. Do *not* comment about his nonfluency. Do *not* suggest that he calm down and slow down. Do *not* give him the words he is stumbling over. The problem will usually evaporate in time if you do not focus on it. There are differing opinions about the subject of nonfluency in young children, but it is our opinion that the less you make of it the better. A note of caution: If the nonfluency continues past age five or if your child develops some other behaviors to go along with it such as a nervous twitch, or stamping his foot as he is talking, or any other involvement of other parts of his body, you will want to have an evaluation done by a speech pathologist, a trained professional familiar with the normal patterns of language development in young children.

It is important for you to note that we call this "nonfluency." You may want to call it stuttering or stammering, but these are loaded terms and do not accurately represent what is happening at this stage. What you actually hear is a nonfluency and this happens for normal reasons.

Physical Development

His fine motor skills are developed enough that he can hold small markers for games. He will begin pedaling his tricycle, may enjoy pulling and being pulled in a wagon, and will use playground equipment such as swings and slides. An outdoor sandbox is a great toy and can be used with his cars and toy people to act out play scenes.

FORTY-EIGHT TO SIXTY MONTHS (4–5 Years)

Language Development

He will be using well over two thousand words by the end of this developmental age. He will be talking in complete paragraphs and you will begin to see that most of his grammatical errors have straightened themselves out. He may still make a few errors in the speech sounds themselves but if he is generally easy to understand by you and others outside your family, you do not need to concern yourself with these few errors. Complete sentences and phrases continue to proliferate.

Physical Development

By the time your child is five, he will be able to walk on a line, hop on one foot for about ten seconds, jump over a rope, and catch a large ball when you bounce it to him.

SIXTY TO SEVENTY-TWO MONTHS (5–6 YEARS)

Language Development

By the end of this developmental period, your child may be able to comprehend 13,000 words: five times the amount of receptive language from the year before. He is able to use pronouns consistently, understand opposites, and can answer questions beginning with, "What happens if . . . ?" He is now able to understand time concepts such as before and after, a.m. and p.m., yesterday and tomorrow, now and later, this month and last month, and days of the week. The average length of his expressive language is 6.6 words, and his *syntax* (the ability to put words together in the right order) is more refined than one year ago. He enjoys beginning printing when copying from a model, although letter reversals and inaccuracies in writing abound. A desire to read begins to emerge at this time as well. Your child begins to recognize numbers one through ten, letters of the alphabet, and written words such as his name and other very familiar words like Mom, Dad, cat, dog, up, and go.

In a nutshell, your child at this stage makes the leap from the spoken, signed, or cued word to the written word, and then to reading words. The play activities in this section will give you many, many opportunities to enrich your child's blossoming language skills. Be sure to offer lots of praise and encouragement for effort, and, overall, remember to keep the fun in your child's language-learning toys and games.

Physical Development

By the end of this developmental age, your child's physical abilities, both large and small, are greatly improved from one year ago. His better-developed fine motor skills allow him to grasp a pencil and print with a nice degree of legibility when copying from a model. He can color inside the lines of a picture quite well, and can copy a simple shape accurately. He can also learn to tie his shoes, although he may need a lot more extra practice in these days of Velcro shoes. He can also button his own buttons, dress himself, and comb his hair.

Your five-year-old loves to use his large motor skills. He loves to jump and hop longer distances. He loves to run fast, skate fast, bike fast. Speed is a big part of this age. His eye-hand coordination has also greatly improved, and now your child can throw and catch a ball with greater accuracy.

Five-year-olds are interested in learning rules to help organize their play, and they like the idea of being part of a club, group, or team. Belonging to a group outside the family will help foster your child's self esteem. This also explains their newfound interest in participating in team sports such as soccer and tee-ball, either as a player, coach's assistant, or a spectator. Do not expect perfect adherence to rules. Fives like the idea of rules, but have been known to sway from playing by the exact rules when it is to their advantage. Great language learning opportunities arise directly due to this moral conflict. Playing fair, emphasizing teamwork, and cooperation versus competition are key elements necessary to govern the play of five-year-olds.

No time of life is as full of as much development and growth as the period from birth to age six. It is almost magic for parents—including parents of children with developmental delays—to observe as their children grow, change, and learn. But parents of children with a delay in language development need to know what may cause this. The knowledge of language development that you have learned is your foundation for understanding problems that may occur in this area.

Possible Causes of Language Delay in Children

We have talked about how receptive language, expressive language, and speech evolve in a child who is moving along the developmental milestones in a typical fashion. How does this differ if there are developmental delays of one kind or another? There have been volumes written on this subject and it is not the intent of this book to focus in detail on specific disabilities. We do, however, describe a variety of developmental disabilities that may have an effect on language development and offer adapted teaching techniques for individual special needs.

In reading about each of these disabilities, bear in mind that each child is unique and his abilities are unlike any other child's even if he shares the same generic label of a particular disability. We have seen children with profound mental retardation who were not expected to walk or talk, do both under guidance from professionals and parents who believe in their potential. But while we need to keep our expectations high, we should not close our eyes to the obvious. In spite of our greatest efforts, some of our children may never achieve the level that we would like to see for them. Reach for the stars but make them stars you can see, not just hope to see. Rejoice in what your child is able to achieve, in the potential he is able to realize.

Cognitive Delays

The relationship of intelligence to language development is a most complex issue. Once again, it should never be assumed that a "low IQ" is an absolute predictor of language development. Many articles have been written about the accuracy of IQ measurements and there is no clear-cut evidence that an IQ is a very good predictor of anything, especially language development. When we speak of an average IQ, we do not mean that a child with an average IQ should only be expected to acquire average language development. We know that experiences and exposure to interesting and exciting vocabulary, as well as personal motivation, can enhance anyone's language development.

If, however, we are talking about children who have been diagnosed as having specific disorders such as Down syndrome, brain injury, or other conditions that can cause mental retardation, then we know that language development will be slower than for children of the same age without these conditions. This does not mean, however, that we stop speaking to this child or stop giving him enriching language experiences. Just the opposite is true; this child needs more language stimulation than other children. Remember that receptive language must come first, and if he has nothing to talk about, it is certain that he will not have expressive language.

The child with mental retardation will acquire language at a slower rate than a child of average or higher intelligence, but in most cases, he *will* acquire language. Remember that language need not be "spoken" to communicate with another individual. He may use a form of sign language, a communication board with pictures, a computer, or other assistive devices to help him express himself. It will be necessary for you to work at the developmental level of your child rather than at his chronological age. When you read our chapters on toys, find a toy that fits with your child's developmental age rather than his chronological age. You will both derive more pleasure from playing this way than if you try to interest him in something that is beyond his abilities.

Physical Disabilities

A child who has severe physical disabilities may be delayed in his language development because so much of his time is spent working with his physical limitations that he simply doesn't have the time to spend enriching his language. He may require many hospitalizations, reducing the amount of time that he is in his own home. This can produce stress for him as well as for you. Neither of you may have much energy left for playing with toys or games. Additionally, he may not have the physical ability to manipulate toys in ways that will facilitate playing. If the physical problems that your child has interfere with the small muscles that are necessary for the production of speech, he may have excellent receptive language and yet be physically unable to produce the sounds necessary for speech. It is at this point that you must find alternative ways of communicating: sign systems, communication boards, computers, and other new technology.

Today's technology allows people who are unable to verbalize to communicate. As discussed in Chapter **6**, computers have voice synthesizers as well as the ability to communicate visually with another person. Although speech is the goal for every child, remember that it is only one form of expressive language.

Sensory Deficits

Children who have sensory deficits in the area of vision and hearing are sometimes at a disadvantage in learning language. Visual impairments limit what the child can actually experience for himself but in no way limit the input that an adult can supply to overcome that deficit. It is important to remember also that not all children with visual impairments are totally blind. Many partially sighted children can see bright colors as well as high contrast colors such as black on a white background. Colors, though difficult to describe to someone who has never seen them, can be adequately described in terms of how they relate to objects the child knows or can learn about that remain constant. For example, a lemon is yellow, apples are red, and potatoes are brown. Use consistent color references often with your visually impaired child. There is a wonderful book called *Hailstones and Halibut Bones* by Mary O'Neill which uses poetry to describe colors and is appropriate for preschoolers ages 3–5. Using other senses can help children with visual impairments to understand, if not entirely know, the concepts of things they cannot see.

Hearing impairment, on the other hand, almost always produces a deficit in receptive language. Without the ability to hear a spoken language, it is very difficult to build a receptive base of language in the critical language-learning years. Many volumes have been written on the "best" way to convert spoken language into visual language. There is no clear "best" way. You will have to explore to find the best way for your child. To help you make that decision, you may want to consult the book *Choices in*

Deafness: A Parent's Guide by Sue Schwartz (published by Woodbine House).

Environment

Your child's language-learning environment is one final factor to consider in unraveling possible causes for language delays.

Studies have compared how children are raised in families with how they are raised in institutions. Looking at families, it is often, but not always, found that firstborn children begin to speak sooner than their siblings. This is probably because parents may have the time for more interaction when they only have one child. Subsequent children may be given less parental time. On the other hand, there are equally as many studies that have shown that children in large families talk early as well because they have many more people to interact with and often learn more from their brothers and sisters than they do from their parents. The key, of course, is that someone must be talking to the child so that receptive language can be built.

By contrast, children who are raised in institutions where there are more children than adults are often delayed in language development. These findings have had a profound impact on modern daycare centers. More and more centers are making it a priority to have low adult-child ratios and to encourage language development among the children through stimulating activities. These studies underscore one important point: It is essential to language development to provide children—particularly children with special needs—with a rich receptive language environment.

The language a child hears in the environment should closely resemble the language that will be used in the school he attends. This has raised questions about bilingual families. Current research shows that children can learn both languages—the native family language and the one he hears in the environment. It is true that these children may have more catching up to do when they enter the school environment than those children who speak the same language as the instructional one. In no circumstances, however, should parents who speak a different language speak no language to their child for fear of him having problems in school. If the child has a rich receptive language background, regardless of the language, he will be more successful than if he has no receptive language at all.

Whatever your child's special needs may be, it is important that you determine the nature of his language delay as early as possible. The earlier you find out how he is delayed, the earlier you can begin to help him catch up.

Use the following checklist to help you determine if your child has a problem in his language development.

Recognizing Speech and Language Problems Early

If your child exhibits any of the following fifteen problems, you should consider consulting a speech pathologist to evaluate your child's language development.

1. Your child is not talking by the age of two years.
2. His speech is largely unintelligible after the age of three.
3. He is leaving off many beginning consonants after the age of three.
4. He is still not using two- to three-word sentences by the age of three.
5. Sounds are more than a year late in appearing in his speech according to their developmental sequence.
6. He uses mostly vowel sounds in his speech.
7. His word endings are consistently missing after the age of five.
8. His sentence structure is noticeably faulty at the age of five.
9. He is embarrassed and disturbed by his speech.
10. He is noticeably nonfluent after the age of six.
11. He is making speech errors other than /wh/ after the age of seven.
12. His voice is a monotone, too loud, too soft, or of a poor quality that may indicate a hearing loss.
13. His voice quality is too high or too low for his age and sex.
14. He sounds as if he were talking through his nose or as if he has a cold.
15. His speech has abnormal rhythm, rate, and inflection after the age of five.

(This was reprinted from *Teach Your Child to Talk*, by David Pushaw, published by CEBCO Standard Publishing, 104 5th Ave., New York, NY.)

Assessment

If you have been concerned that your child has a delay in language development, you will want to have an assessment done by a trained speech pathologist. An assessment is a complete evaluation of the speech and language skills that your child has acquired. His strengths and needs will be determined, which then will be used in planning how to help him.

You should ask your pediatrician if she can recommend someone to do this assessment. If she doesn't know of a speech pathologist in your area, you can contact a national organization such as the American Speech Language Hearing Association (ASHA) at 10801 Rockville Pike, Rockville, MD 20852. You can call collect to the Helpline at ASHA by calling 1/301/897–8682 (Voice or TTY). This association will be able to give you names of certified speech clinicians in your area. If you are unable to make this contact for any reason, try your local college or university and ask if they have a department which trains future speech pathologists. They will be able to refer you to someone for an evaluation. Additionally, every school system has an early identification program. Call your local school district and ask for the program that helps to identify young children with special needs.

Taking a History

When you come for your child's assessment, the speech pathologist will want a complete history of your child's growth up to now. If you have kept baby records, bring them with you to help you remember important milestone events in your child's life. If you have medical information about his special needs, you will want to bring this along with you as well. The more information you can provide about your child, the more the clinician will be able to help you determine where your child might be in his language development.

Testing

Clinicians use a variety of assessment tools and tests to help determine where your child's language development is. Some tests will ask you for information about your child, while others directly ask your child to respond to various questions which will indicate his understanding and expression of language.

Testing Receptive Language. Your child's receptive abilities will be tested by asking him to point out objects or pictures when they are named or to choose between sets of pictures in response to a word or group of words that is presented by the therapist. In one test, for instance, your child will be shown a small doll and will be asked to point to various facial and body parts. "Where is the dolly's nose, eyes, ears, etc.?" His responses will be recorded on a testing sheet which will later be used to determine his language development level. If your child is unable to point to the object because of visual impairment or physical disability, he can be given two or more objects to explore with his hands and then touch or hand you the object requested.

In all of these tests the questions get increasingly more difficult, and your child will begin to be unable to respond. The clinician will keep testing to reach the level where your child is no longer able to respond. This will indicate the upper level of his understanding. It will let the clinician know what level to focus on when working with him later on.

Testing Expressive Language. Almost all of the language tests that are used with young children use objects or pictures to encourage children to respond in certain expected ways. For example, on the Structured Photographic Expressive Language Test (SPELT), your child will be shown pictures of modern everyday situations. He will be asked questions such as "What is the girl wearing?" The expected response is "A dress" or "A red dress." These items are structured so that all the parts of language are tested. Single nouns, plural nouns, possessive nouns, possessive pronouns, and so on are all tested. This and other language tests will give the clinician a good idea of areas where your child might need help and where his strengths are.

Oral Mechanism Exam. The speech clinician will want to check inside your child's mouth. She will want to check the roof of your child's mouth (palate) to see that everything is formed correctly. She will check the size and movement of your child's tongue and see the alignment of his teeth, lips, and jaw. All of these parts of the mouth area are involved in the production of speech. Your child's ability to control drooling will be examined, as well as the tone of the muscles in the mouth area.

Speech Sounds. If your child is talking at all, the clinician will want to systematically check to see which sounds he pronounces correctly and which he has difficulty with. Again, pictures will be used for the stimulus. The pictures will be of objects that show the sound wherever they generally occur in words. For example, for the sound "B" the pictures might be:

beginning: bed

middle: baby

end: tub

Your child may have some substitutions or omissions of sounds. For example, he may say, "fum" for "thumb" (substituting "f" for "th") or "cah" for "car" (omitting the "r"). The significance of these errors will depend on your child's age.

To ensure a complete picture of your child's language development, be sure to tell the clinician of your child's language experiences at home. Your input is important for a complete assessment.

Immediately after the evaluation of your child, the speech clinician will be able to tell you a few specific things that she noticed. Usually, however, you will need to wait longer for a final and more complete report. Be ready to return to review the findings and to follow through on the suggestions that the clinician will make.

Conclusion

Children with language development delays are still like other children. They go through most, if not all, of the language development stages that all children go through. You may need to spend more effort, however, helping your child achieve language skills.

Understanding language development in children is essential to understanding where your child might have a problem. Knowing what some causes of language delay are can help you understand your own child's particular problem. Finally, an assessment by a speech and language pathologist can identify the type of language delay your child has and help you get to work to overcome that delay. That play is, in reality, work for your child, and understanding how your child will approach that work/play is vital to teaching him language skills. The next chapter explains this fascinating world of child play.

Chapter 3

Playing and Learning

Why Play Is Important

In our technological society where we are busy trying to cure cancer, solve problems about nuclear energy, and live in harmony with countries of clashing political viewpoints, can we allow our children to relax, have fun, and play? Of course we can! More than that, we *should* encourage them to play. Why? Because play is important for children—it is a way for them to learn and be creative.

It is through play that children learn about the world around them. While playing, children test ideas, ask questions, and come up with answers. For instance, in playing with nesting blocks, your child learns about size relationships—she learns that smaller blocks fit inside larger ones. She learns cause and effect as she builds her blocks higher and higher until they come crashing down. When her blocks come tumbling down, she can link that to the world of experiences and ideas by using the language we are teaching her.

Play begins in infancy. There are simple games you and your baby play as you interact during feeding time. Your baby sucks on the bottle or breast and if you pull the milk source away, the baby will suck harder, wiggle her toes and fingers, and give you the message that she wants her bottle back. Trading smiles and fake coughs is another early game played between infants and parents. Through these basic games, your baby learns that her actions have an effect on the people around her. She learns early basic ways to control those larger people in her life.

As your baby gains more and more control over her environment, her idea of who she is and what she can accomplish develops in a positive way. She learns self-confidence as she sees that what she does influences what happens to her. She can use this vision of herself as the sturdy foundation from which she can explore what life has to offer. She can try new experiences without being overwhelmed at the prospect of failure. Yes, she will fail sometimes, but sometimes she won't. Without self-confidence, she wouldn't try at all.

The Value of Play

Play time is more than just "fooling around" time. Playing with toys with your child can help her develop emotionally, physically, socially, and cognitively. We'll look at how you can help her grow in each of these areas through play.

Emotional Development

If your child has a language delay, she may have some frustrations to work out. It is emotionally difficult for children not to be able to adequately communicate their needs. The inability to communicate is hard on any child, but when you add a disabling condition with its special needs, the frustration level can be almost intolerable.

By carefully watching your child play, you will be able to see areas of frustration that she may have. She will give hints by the way she handles her dolls, the actions she has play-people perform, or her reactions to stories you read her. For example, through play your child can work out some of her feelings of anxiety or concern. If, for example, she sees a physical therapist twice a week and these visits cause her discomfort, you might want to structure a play situation with her where the toy "therapist" comes to the house to help the little girl feel stronger in her legs, arms, or wherever the difficulties are. Your child can then work out some of her feelings during this play time and you can point out what is positive about what the "therapist" is doing.

In a similar way, if your child had a disagreement with a friend a little while ago, you might want to structure a play situation where you help her work out a solution to the problem. This will keep you from interfering when the friend is there, yet give you a way to show your child what to do the next time she is in a similar situation.

You can encourage positive emotional growth in your child when you interact through play. She will see that you are interested in spending time with her and that you respond to her needs. Children need to feel loved and valued in order to grow. The time you spend with her reinforces her vision of herself as a person who is worthy of your time and love.

As your child gets older, she does not lose her emotional need for some control of her world. By playing with your child, you can allow her to have the control in play that she may not be able to have in real life. If we go back to our example of the physical therapist, you can allow your child to have one of her toy people refuse to see the "therapist," whereas in real life she cannot refuse. She will learn that she can control some areas of her life but not others.

Physical Development

Your child may be language delayed, but it is possible that her physical skills are right on par. This will be very encouraging to you as well to her. She can do things with her hands and feet that perhaps she just is not able to do with language. She will feel confident if you pick up on those physical strengths that she does have and encourage language development around them. For example, you can ask her to shake her rattle. As she does this, you can say, "Good! You are doing a great job of shaking the rattle." You can emphasize specific sounds like "sh" and encourage her to imitate you.

You can stress how well she plays with her toys. You can remind her that she is getting so big that now she can hold the block in one hand. Toys can be a way to give her a sense of pride in what she can accomplish physically.

If your child also has physical limitations, you will want to make sure to use toys that she can handle and to encourage her by making adaptations in the toys. For example, if she has small motor difficulties and loves to play board games, you might want to add Velcro to the board and the bottoms of the markers so that she can easily move her marker along and play the games.

Social Development

The social play of children passes through three stages. At first, the very young child plays alone. She does not like to interact with playmates her own age, although she will interact with you. Gradually, she will move into parallel play and play nicely alongside a friend doing similar kinds of things but not involving each other. In the final stage of social play, the children play together with each contributing something to the play situation. If your child has a language delay, this could be the stage that presents some difficulties for her. By the time children are ready to engage in social play, they need language to communicate ideas. You will then see that you can use your play time to give her the vocabulary that she will need in order to play with her friends.

Your child learns from you that sharing her toys is a fine way for you to play together and that each of you can take a turn. She learns that when her friends come over it is okay to share with them and wait her turn. These are difficult skills for children to learn, but you can practice with her when you are alone. Through imaginative play, you can play out situations that your child may need some help understanding. For example, you can re-enact a scene in the park in which another child was not being very nice to your child. You can show your child how to be sensitive to another person's feelings through this kind of pretend play.

Many more children today are exposed to men and women in nontraditional career roles. They will see more women doctors than you did when you were growing up. They will see more men in jobs that previously only women seemed to perform. Your daughter can use toy cars and trucks to play mechanic, while your son is using the play kitchen to fix lunch. Playing with these toys in nontraditional ways encourages your child to accept society's move away from stereotyping. This is another example of the way that toys can represent our world to our children.

Cognitive Development

There are four stages of cognitive development in children. How does knowing them help you interact with your child and her toys? Your child's ability to think, understand, and eventually reason things out is a dynamic process. With each new toy, game, or experience that you introduce, your child is taking in all the information and knowledge her brain is capable of assimilating depending on her level of development. Although each stage is separate, they are all dependent on each other for success. With the exact same toy, game, or sample dialogue provided in this book, your child can extract from it what she is capable of understanding at any given developmental point in time. Later on she will derive something different from the same toy. As a parent you can help challenge your child's ability to her potential within each stage as well as looking ahead to what comes next.

The first stage of cognitive development is the **sensorimotor stage.** It lasts roughly from birth to two years of age. Your child will be learning about her environment through her muscles and her senses. By watching, hearing, touching, and feeling, she will learn about things around her. You will be giving her language for things that she sees in her daily life such as water, spoon, and ball. She will experience them by touching, seeing, and physically interacting with them.

The second stage, which is the **representational stage,** occurs from two to seven years of age. Your child will begin to be able to represent things by using symbols (pictures, objects, words) instead of the real thing. For example, she can use a play farm and plastic animals to reenact a visit to the farm. It is during this stage that her receptive language will increase rapidly and you will begin to notice a big leap in expressive language at this time as well.

The third stage, the **concrete operations stage,** occurs from age seven to eleven. During this stage, your child is able to think through a situation without having to actually act it out. She is able to see the consequences of her actions and think about what may happen before it actually happens.

The fourth stage, the **formal operations stage,** begins around age eleven. Children who have reached this stage are really able to do serious problem solving. They are able to reason with abstract thoughts and do not need to depend on concrete observations.

As a child progresses through these stages of cognitive development, her ability to play will become increasingly sophisticated to the point that it ceases to be merely "play" and begins to resemble concerted problem solving, exploration, and analysis. Let's look at how play with a ball might change through each of these stages.

In the earliest sensorimotor stage, a parent would want to expose his child to the idea that the toy they are playing with is called a ball. "Look Tyrone, this is a ball. It is round. It is hard. Can you hold it? Can you roll it to Mommy? Look. Mommy can catch the ball. Now Daddy will help you catch it. Let's see if we can throw it way up in the sky."

At such an early stage in infancy, a child might not understand any of the words Mother is saying. However, the child is receiving an invaluable language learning experience. Through Mother's words, Tyrone can begin to understand what the word ball really means—what a ball feels like, how it can be thrown and caught, that it is round and smooth, that it moves apart from his hand when he lets go of it, and that it can land in his lap when someone throws it to him.

In the early preoperational stage, the child would understand the game even better based on his earlier, sensorimotor experiences. Tyrone would now begin to understand that when Mom asks, "Do you want to play ball?", it is a give-and-take, back-and-forth arrangement that involves the two of them playing together. When Mom asks, "Can you roll it?" or "Can you throw it?" or even "Can you bounce it?" each word means something different and has a different action associated with it.

Finally, an older preoperational child has often developed enough logic to know that after Mom throws the ball into the air and yells, "Heads UP!", he can go scurrying after it, trying to follow its course so that it will fall straight down into his hands. Although Tyrone would understand this once he enters the preoperational stage, at the younger sensorimotor stage he would not have understood that "what goes up must come down." That's why we don't play a hearty game of catch with a nine-month-old still operating at a sensorimotor level. But that doesn't mean we shouldn't play ball with an infant at all. Earlier action experiences and the language a child learns set the stage for more complex actions and later learning.

It is easy to see that to a child—especially a child with special needs—"play" is very important. It helps her express herself, develop a positive image of herself, and learn to interact with the rest of the world. But how can you as her parent involve yourself in her play effectively? The next section discusses using toys to help with language development.

Playing with Toys to Help Develop Language

With toys, we can teach our children about our world and how to live in it. We can teach them how to interact with other people and their environment. And toys can substitute for the world while they are learning how to interact. Playing with toys is particularly important for children who have problems in adjusting to their world.

Since one of the primary goals of play is to teach your child about her world, you need to understand how toys can help her with this goal. When she is young, you represent the world for her. If she can learn to interact with you, she can take those learning experiences with her when she begins interacting with the rest of the world.

Toys Are Interactive

You, the significant adult, are your child's first plaything. She reaches out and touches your body as she nurses. She grabs at your nose or Uncle Sonny's glasses. These could be called her first toys. When she grabs you and you respond with a kiss as you remove her hand, the

two of you are interacting. She is learning that what she does can have an effect on you. You begin giving her language for her use of these toys.

"Be careful, those are Uncle Sonny's glasses. Let's give them back. You touched Daddy's nose—where is your nose? Ouch, it hurts when you pull Daddy's hair. See how gently I stroke your hair . . . ."

Because you want to encourage interaction but not at the expense of your nose or glasses, you can substitute toys. You can play with stuffed animals and talk about noses and other facial features. You can hang toys in your child's crib and when she is ready, she can reach out and touch and play with them. The toy will "respond" back as it swings or a small bell rings.

Toys Are Representational

The most significant value of toys may be the way they represent a wider world for your child. Although we encourage you to go on many outings with her to see and experience real-life situations, toys can bring these things into your home. You can use toys to prepare children for experiences that are about to happen and then use the toy again after the experience to reinforce what she saw. Let's use the Fisher Price Farm as an example. You have decided that tomorrow you and your family are going for a ride out to a farm. You can use the Fisher Price Farm to talk about all of the animals, buildings, and people that you *will* see on the farm. At the farm, you can remind her that the cow is the same color as the toy cow at home or that the real horse is certainly much bigger than the toy horse at home. Later, when you have come home from your outing, you can go back to the toy farm and talk about what you *saw*. Did you know that you are also teaching verb tenses?

Children with special needs usually spend a lot of time seeing doctors, therapists, and specialists of one kind or another. They are *very* busy children. We don't want you to become one of those parents who is always pushing his child to do one more task; yet you need to spend time to help her develop her language. You can do this through play. You can pick toys that are both fun and can be used to develop her language. The toys in this book are both amusing and educational. It is easy to capitalize on the natural and pleasurable activities associated with toys to help your child with her language development. Just remember that no child learns well under pressure. If you feel that your child has had enough for one session, quit! You can always play with her another time.

Conclusion

In the next section of the book, you will be taking all the information you have just read and putting it to good use as you try the dialogues we have written for you. Remember to pick the developmental age that best describes your child, then gather some toys that will work with the dialogues you want to use, and start talking and playing.

Chapter 4

Toy Dialogues

Maintaining our children's interest in learning is one of our primary jobs in teaching language. We want to send our children off to school well-prepared *and* as excited about learning as they were as infants when they loved our first imitation games. Many an educator has said that if we could maintain the enthusiasm that young children have for learning before they come to school, many of our educational problems would be solved. The dialogues in this section have therefore been designed to teach basic language in a variety of interesting ways.

How to "Teach" with the Dialogues

As you read the dialogues, you may wonder why there are so many repetitions of key words and concepts. Did you know that a baby must hear thousands of repetitions of a word before he can produce it? As you play with your baby, most of this talking will come naturally.

We have noticed that some people don't talk enough to little children and other people talk on and on, never really giving the child a chance to absorb what is being said. As you speak with your child in the short little sentences described in the dialogues, you will want to pause ever so slightly between sentences so that he will have the chance to take in what you are saying and then to respond. If you keep talking on and on, he will only be processing a jumble of meaningless words.

As your child gets older, you can increase the length and complexity of your sentences, but still make sure you give him enough time to understand what you are saying. It just takes a little extra time and patience to learn to talk this way to a young child. Realize that the brief phrases we have written in our toy dialogues are only examples of what you could say to pull language from any given toy. Feel free to substitute other similar words or ideas that feel comfortable for you.

Children, particularly children with language delays, will benefit more from toy play carried out in a repetitive fashion. It may take days, or even weeks, for a child to grasp the concepts of *up* and *down* or *back* and *forth*. Repetition is not boring for your child and can be of tremendous benefit for your child's learning.

We have included a number of *single concept* dialogues in each developmental age grouping. These focus on one idea at a time and give you the repetition you need to work with your child, stressing just that one idea. The single concept dialogues are of special help to children who may need intensive emphasis in one area.

There are ways to vary the repetition necessary to teach your child. When you are working on the concepts of *back* and *forth*, vary the type and size of the ball. Change the location. With this type of varied repetition you and your child will have the advantage of new play activities within the structure he needs in order to learn.

If you want to make play time something your child will look forward to, then you need to be very careful about how you interact with him when the two of you are playing. If your child's tower falls because he has put too many blocks on it, try to be positive instead of giving him negative criticism. Toy play should have the same goals as other interactions with your child—the goal of helping your child develop a good self-image. "Josh, this time you built the tower higher. Isn't it fun to watch all the blocks tumble down when it gets too high?"

Another way to make sure that your child looks forward to his play time with you is to instill in him the joy of learning. This really isn't very hard to do because children are born curious and eager to learn—if the learning is fun. It's up to us to make sure it is. If you sit down with your child and say "OK, Josh, today we are going to talk about colors. There are three primary colors. Now repeat after me . . ." Josh will probably be halfway out of the room before you finish the sentence. Our dialogues are specifically designed to avoid that regimented teaching style. When you use the dialogues, put some enthusiasm into your voice; move around and use gestures. If your child sees that you are having a good time, he will enjoy himself more and find learning fun.

Focus on one toy at a time. Imagine doing a special type of crossword puzzle designed so that all the clues must be examined simultaneously. It would be impossible. This is how your child would feel if you overwhelmed him with a variety of toys and activities all at the same time.

When your child is very young—say, under two—we suggest that you have as much of your language playtime as you can with him in a high chair. We like to use a high chair because there is a tray to put toys on and the children are at eye level with us. Additionally, this helps your child focus on one toy at a time so that he doesn't become distracted by other toys around him. If you can, you might want to have two high chairs in different rooms so that one is associated with eating and the other with playing. If you have only one, that's okay. Some people also like to use the Sassy Seats™ that attach to the table. These are fine.

Also make sure that you spend time on the floor with your child. That is the natural play environment for a child and you can get down to his level with him. This is particularly important for some of the toys that we will discuss further along in this book. The key is to be at your child's eye level. That way, he is getting additional cues about language from your face. This is particularly important for a deaf or hard of hearing child.

As your child's receptive and expressive skills continue to improve, use the actual names of things as much as possible rather than generic terms such as "cars." Talk about station wagons, convertibles, vans, or campers. With repetition and developmental maturation, your child will learn to *generalize*. He'll learn that each of these vehicles, for example, fit under the broader category of "cars."

The richer the language that you put in, the richer the language your child will use later on. It is not necessary that he have perfect or even intelligible speech to use rich and powerful language. With the increasing use of computers today, even the most severely disabled child can communicate his thoughts. With a computer he can use a head stick as a pointer, eye gaze, and voice commands. We will talk more about computers later on.

Try to play for a few short periods of time each day to try out the dialogues. A good time is right after a nap or after snack time when your child is refreshed. Begin with five- or ten-minute sessions and gradually increase the amount of time as your child is able to handle it.

While playing with your child, there will be many times when you will want to "test" his comprehension by asking him to hand you various objects or name them for you. You know your child and you will know when he has had enough. Even though we are talking about play time as "teaching" time, it still must be fun and your child must think of it as *play* or he will not stay interested for very long.

SPECIAL CONSIDERATIONS

There are a few things to keep in mind for children with different special needs. If your child is deaf or hard of hearing, keep the toy near your mouth so that he can see your lips as you speak to him about the toys. If he has visual impairments, have him hold the toy with you while you describe it and move his hands to each part as you talk to him about it. Add Velcro and other textures to different parts of the toy so he can begin to associate that texture with that particular part. If your child is physically not capable of holding a toy on his own, hold it with him as you describe it to him. Present challenging opportunities to improve motor coordination at the same time

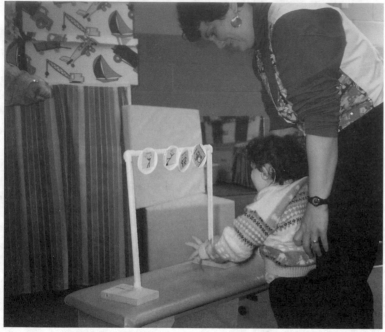

you are choosing toys that are set into action with easy-to-press switches, buttons, and dials.

If your child's speech muscles are impaired, or if he has a disability like Down syndrome that is associated with significant speech delays, you may want to teach him sign language. This will give him a way of expressing his needs and wants to you. Your speech clinician, audiologist, or pediatrician can direct you to an introductory sign language course. You may also want to begin teaching him to point to items on a communication board. Another way of having him demonstrate to you that he understands what you are asking is to have an "eye gaze frame" so he can simply shift his eyes to indicate the object or picture of an object that you are referring to.

An eye gaze frame can be made with simple materials obtained at a hardware store. Buy three lengths of plumbers pipe called PVC pipe in whatever size you choose and however long you want it to be: 12–18 inches should be about right. Then purchase the equivalent elbow connectors that fit the size of pipe that you bought. Buy or make two blocks of wood about 3" by 5". Purchase stickyback Velcro strips and cover the pieces of pipe with the fuzzy part of the Velcro. Hot glue two round pipe connectors to the wood base. Fit the three pieces of pipe together with the elbow connectors and then fit the entire structure to the connectors on the wood base. (Instructions provided by the Center for Technology in Education.)

To use this eye gaze frame with your child, you can put Velcro on pictures or small objects and attach them to the Velcro-covered pipe. At first you may want to put only two objects or pictures on it at opposite ends so the child is very definite in his eye gaze as to which object or picture he wants.

These types of nonverbal communication will still help your child build language skills. More importantly, they will help him to communicate with you. Be assured that learning a nonverbal system first will not inhibit the later development of speech.

Summary of Teaching Techniques for Any Child with a Language Delay

- **START WITH SIMPLE WORDS AND PHRASES**—A strong receptive language base must be built first as a foundation for expressive language which emerges later.
- **USE ACTUAL NAMES OF THINGS WHEN TEACHING LANGUAGE**—Say "bottle" not "ba-ba."
- **USING VARIED REPETITION OF KEY WORDS AND SINGLE CONCEPTS IS CRUCIAL**—This is one of the best ways to pour in all of that extra language that is necessary for learning and is a great tool to aid memory.
- **SPEAK IN SHORT SENTENCES**—Increase sentence length and complexity of meaning as you see your child's language skills improve.
- **PAUSE BETWEEN PHRASES**—This allows your child to process the meaning of each word in the phrase.
- **FOCUS ON ONE TOY OR ACTIVITY AT A TIME TO PREVENT DISTRACTION**—Keep other toys out of sight and keep background noise and activities to a minimum.
- **PLAY WITH YOUR CHILD AT HIS EYE LEVEL**—Sit your child in a high chair or at a table or sit or lie down on the floor when playing with your child and his toys.
- **PLAY FOR A FEW SHORT PERIODS OF TIME**—Five to ten minutes a day. Increase length and frequency of sessions as your child's attention span increases over time.
- **KNOW WHEN IT IS THE BEST TIME FOR INSTRUCTIVE PLAY**—After naptimes or mornings are the times when children are generally the most refreshed and eager to interact with you.
- **KNOW WHEN TO END PLAY SESSIONS**—If your child grows restless, stops paying attention, or becomes fatigued, it is time to take a break.
- **OFFER PRAISE AND ENCOURAGEMENT**—Children love verbal and physical rewards. Saying "Great job!" or giving a big hug works wonders.
- **MOST IMPORTANT—KEEP THE FUN IN LEARNING! BE ENTHUSIASTIC!**

Behavior Management

Behavior management is a major issue for all children but especially if you have a child who is developmentally delayed in any way. You may feel that your child has enough to handle anyway without making his life more difficult with a lot of rules. If you look further down the road toward raising a responsible and independent young adult, however, you will realize that catering to his every whim will not help him in the long run. We encourage you to establish consistent guidelines for his behavior and to expect him to abide by them.

During this time, one of your most important roles as a parent will be to teach your child how to behave properly. We've heard parents say how much easier it is just to let their three-year-old walk out of the grocery store with the small package of Lifesavers™ he's picked up off the shelf than to have a big discipline scene in public. Similarly, it is easier to buy two of every toy for your two children to prevent fighting than it is to teach them to share. We agree wholeheartedly that it is not always pleasant or fun to teach discipline to young children. In many instances, it would almost be easier to become invisible and let your child carry on with his antics until he finds a way to resolve things himself.

The fact is, children do not like it either when they misbehave, particularly if their parents value and encourage good behavior. It's a frightening feeling for them to be out of control and they need you to set limits for them when they are upset. Believe it or not, deep down inside, your child wants to be the sweet little angel that you know he can be. If you praise your child as many times for good behavior as you scold him for bad behavior, he will try his hardest to be good. Everyone likes praise.

When he does misbehave, there are many disciplinary methods that work. If you have found one or two which work for you, then simply stick with them. Many parents of three-year-olds, however, are still groping for suitable ways to manage misbehavior. We offer a couple of specific techniques for you here.

One key to good discipline is consistency. This is true for all children, but especially true for children with special needs. If your child has a condition which hampers his understanding, you may have to go over concepts many times before he has a clear understanding of what you mean.

Be firm and clear about which behavior you expect and be as gentle as you can. "Karen, do not grab that toy from Sarah. If you do this again, you may not play together."

If she does grab the toy again, you must stick with what you said and remove her from the play area. She can sit in your designated *time out* area until you feel she is ready to rejoin the other children. Repeat this technique again and again until you feel she understands the situation.

The theory behind the time out method of behavior management is that a child is disciplined when he cannot demonstrate pro-social behavior. Specifically, children must be taught that it is a privilege to participate within a group. The inherent reward for behaving in a pro-social way is being able to stay in the group and play. If the child cannot play nicely in the group, even after one or two verbal reminders, then the adult must ask the child to sit outside the group. Children should feel permitted to re-enter the group again whenever they feel they can act nicely. If you are alone with your child, the same theory applies and he must sit in his special time out spot until he feels that he is ready to be cooperative again.

Another technique that we like is called the *wait technique*. Here's how it works: Let's say that Karen is playing with her friend Rachel. Karen looks over and sees Rachel playing with a Barbie Doll. Of course this looks like more fun than the book that she has been reading. She grabs the Barbie Doll and as they fight over the doll, she hits Rachel. It's time for you to step in. Karen needs to hear the cardinal rule: "There will be no hitting." Under no circumstances should you, the parent, come in and hit your child for hitting the other child! Firmly and gently state the rule, "no hitting," and insist that your child not play until she returns the doll. You can say, "Karen, I'll wait until you're ready." Once she returns the doll you can then help the two youngsters with the notion of taking turns or trading toys so that each gets a chance to play with the doll.

Social Skills

Many parents of children with special needs feel that neighborhood kids don't want to include their child. One way that you can help bridge that gap is to invite the children to your house and for you to involve yourself some of the time in the play. This way, you can help smooth the road if language gaps get in the way. In these situations, a good rule of thumb is that the maximum number of children who can comfortably play together should equal your child's age in years. For a three-year-old—two playmates, which would be three in total.

We encourage you to start your child in some kind of organized play group or nursery school. This is not to advocate the concept of the overly programmed "hurried child," which the child developmentalist David Elkind warns us aginst. Instead, it is to expose your child to larger social situations than he would normally be involved in at home. For the language delayed child, play groups and nursery schools are excellent learning situations because the children they come in contact with can provide good speech and language models. You must be cautious, however, not to place your child in an environment where he has no possibility of being involved. If his impairments are so severe that he cannot interact in any way with this group of children, then he will only experience frustration and your expectations will not be met as well. Be cautious and realistic when you look for a peer group with whom he can interact.

Toy Selection

Just about anything can be a toy! Cardboard boxes, leftover ribbon, spoons—almost anything you can think of. In putting together our list, however, we had to consider several important factors.

The first consideration for us in selecting toys was safety. Each of the toys that we suggest for a particular developmental age is safe and has been approved by the United States Consumer Product Safety Commission. A list of their criteria is found in Chapter 6 of this book. Then we looked for the toy's suitability for our dialogues. Finally, we considered how easily available they would be to consumers around the country.

The toys we recommend are divided into developmental age categories. Once again, these categories are not absolutes. Many of these toys fit into several age groups and can be enjoyed by children beyond the ages mentioned here. Children will often use an "old" toy in new and creative ways as their world enlarges and their imaginations develop. In general, the lower age limit is the age where your child can begin to physically and mentally handle the toy, but the upper limits have no bounds.

Each toy has been selected so that you can interact with your child for the purpose of encouraging and developing expansive and exciting language. This does not mean that your child should not play with toys alone. He will need time to practice the language skills you have taught him. He may also find new ways to play with the toys that he can show you the next time you play together.

When you first use a toy to "teach" language, it's a good idea not to leave it around to be routinely played with. If you do this, your child may lose interest in your "teaching" activities sooner. Put the toy safely in a toy chest or on a shelf.

A word here about toy shelves and toy boxes. We recommend shelves for two reasons. One is a safety factor. Often toy boxes have hinged tops, which can close on a child who has crawled inside. Or the lid can slam shut accidentally and perhaps injure your child's head or fingers.

The second reason is that toys become lost in a toy box. The ones on the bottom are never seen again as they become buried under layers of other toys. Additionally, they do not have an orderly appearance when they are thrown into a box. We encourage you to use a toy shelf that is sturdy and not very tall. We want your child to be able to reach the shelves himself and not have it topple over on him. The toys should fit easily on the shelves and there shouldn't be room for too many. This way, you can have a few toys accessible and keep the others packed away. If you rotate the toys that are on the shelf, your child will maintain his interest in them for a longer period of time.

Homemade Toys

We have included at least two homemade toys in each developmental age group. These tested, easy-to-make toys will provide your child with great language learning opportunities. Often, they are more fun and interesting to play with than many store-bought toys. They can also be less expensive!

Homemade toys give you the opportunity to create and adapt toys to meet your child's own personal needs and preferences. For instance, your child may have a visual impairment in addition to a language delay. You can meet his special needs by printing letters and pictures in extra large, extra bold type or adding texture to them. Additionally, you will want to simplify the picture by eliminating extra pieces of information like the background. You can cut out one object from the photo or the picture instead of using the whole thing.

Conclusion

We hope that you will enjoy using the toy dialogues we have designed and that you will try out the language experiences we suggest. Remember, the toys, dialogues, and techniques you will be using are like the ones professional teachers and therapists use. You will find that as you use the dialogues, you will come up with some new ideas of your own that you can expand on from here. Enjoy your play with your child. This is a precious time of sharing experiences and of helping your child grow.

The First Year

Birth to Twelve Months

BIRTH TO THREE MONTHS

During your baby's first three months, many new things will be happening. Your whole lifestyle will undergo a change. Your sleeping patterns will change and you may find that you are exhausted. We would like to suggest that you sleep when your baby sleeps and play when he is awake. Save the housecleaning and other chores for another time. Believe it or not, the dirt will still be there waiting for you! Try to avoid getting overtired. You need rest so that you can be available to your baby when he needs you.

If you have learned that there is some delaying condition in your newborn, you will especially need this time for your own rest and care. The emotions associated with this discovery can be very exhausting. You may need to add visits to the doctor or special therapists to your daily routine. Try to add in time for yourself too.

Once you are no longer feeling quite so overwhelmed, you will be better able to concentrate on information that will help you optimize your newborn's early development. Researchers have spent a lot of time with young babies, studying how they learn and develop. For now, we will just summarize research about what the newborn is most interested in focusing on. First of all, you should remember that for the first 3–6 weeks, the optimal focusing distance for your baby is from 7–9 inches from his face and slightly to the right. Babies look to the right more than 90 percent of the time. Some studies have found that the newborn is most interested in bright primary colors such as red, blue, and yellow. More recent research has found that young infants focus best on objects that are black and white. Try them both and see which *your* baby likes the best.

Mobile

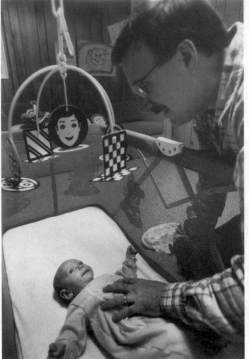

A mobile is a fascinating toy to hang over your baby's changing table, over the crib, or over the kitchen table. We talk about one type of mobile here, another type in the next age category, and a third type you can make yourself in the homemade toy section.

Mobiles are available with many different features. Some just swing in the breeze while others have music boxes attached to them. For our first mobile, we suggest the one made by Wimmer-Ferguson, the Infant Stim-Mobile.™ It is constructed so that the interesting black and white patterns are where the baby can see them, both on the underside and the top. The designs are varied in complexity and provide limitless gazing and focusing opportunities for the newborn infant. A second set of cards is available when the baby is ready, a few weeks later, to also enjoy color. Remember to place the mobile 7–9" from the baby's face and to the right side of his crib. One of the black and white patterns is that of a woman's face. It has been shown that babies are fascinated by faces. In fact, when you are holding and feeding your baby, make sure that he is positioned so that he can see your face. He is most interested in you!

A mobile over the changing table gives the newborn something to focus on at a time when he may be feeling uncomfortable and acting fussy. While you are changing him, you can talk about the various things that he is looking at.

"That's a circle—can you see the lines go round and round? Round and round they go. Let's see another one—hmmm, this one has squares that look like a checkerboard. What happens if I blow on this mobile? (blow on the mobile). Look they are all spinning around. . . . Some of these lines are wavy. They are all black and white."

Notice that your sentences are short with long pauses in between to let the baby focus on what you are saying. You are not trying to teach specific vocabulary at this point but just to show him that what he is looking at has words associated with it and more importantly that you are interacting with him.

Stuffed Animal

One of the first toys that newborns usually get as a gift and enjoy interacting with is a stuffed animal. There are so many on the shelves today that any one that is safe and appeals to you will be just fine for your baby to have. We know many children who have so many stuffed animal friends that it is hard to find room in the crib for the baby!

Stuffed animals offer many new ideas to a newborn. They are very soft. They are usually made of fuzzy materials and infants enjoy the stimulation of this texture. Many stuffed animals today are made in black and white. Again, research has shown that infants enjoy faces and there are always facial features on stuffed animals. We suggest one that is made in a "face-front" style so that all of the features can be seen at one time. A conversation with your newborn about a stuffed panda bear may go as follows:

> "Here's your bear. It's a panda bear. Pandas are black and white. Look, can you see its eyes? It has eyes just like you do. These are your eyes. Can you see the panda's eyes? Its eyes are black but yours are blue. Jake has blue eyes. Oooh, feel how soft the panda is. . . ."

Stroke your baby's arms, legs, face, and stomach with the bear. Point out all of the features of the bear—his arms, legs, and facial features—and relate them to your infant. Remember from our discussion about language development that he does not understand all of the words that you are using, but he will enjoy hearing your voice, and, over time, begin to focus on the meaning of what you are saying. You are the person who "puts in" the language at this time. Without that input, he will not have the vocabulary to use later on.

If you are looking for specific suggestions of stuffed animals, try Wrinkles Giraffe™, made by Dakin. The giraffe stretches out and as it recoils to its former position, it plays a soft tune. This might be very comforting to a newborn who is trying to drift off to sleep. It is in face-front position, so you can talk about the facial features of the giraffe. It is colored like a giraffe in brown and tan and is very soft and cozy to hold. We know your newborn will enjoy it.

> "It's time to go to sleep now, Scotty. Look, I'll stretch out your little giraffe and he will play music for you while you drift off to sleep. Good night, Scotty. . . ."

Rattles

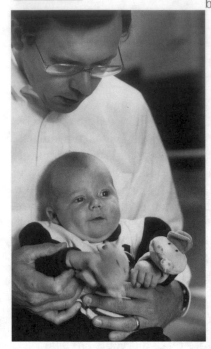

You may receive many rattles as gifts for your newborn. They are generally inexpensive and friends enjoy tying one to the outside of their gifts. It is interesting that this is such a popular toy for a newborn, because babies do not have the coordination to hold a rattle. Nevertheless, *you* can make use of the rattles that you receive as a source of sound and sight stimulation for your infant. Rattles vary in intensity of sound; some are very soft with tiny little beads and others have wooden parts which clap together and are louder and lower in tone. Experiment and see which ones your baby responds to best. During the first month, if there are no other distractions in the room, you may see him respond to the sound of the rattle by blinking his eyes. Later, toward the end of his second month, he will begin to search for the sound of you shaking the rattle off to the side of his head. If you do not notice him searching for the rattle, move it slowly around to the front until he does focus on it. Then talk to him about the sound and try it again from the side. He may need to play this game a few times before he understands what it is that he is listening for. If he still does not respond to this sound in a quiet environment, ask your pediatrician about the possibility of a hearing loss. You will want to check this out as soon as possible.

To stimulate your baby visually with a rattle, you can hold it in front of his eyes and then very slowly move it off to the side. Talking about the movement of the rattle will help him to focus on it as it moves. At this early age, remember to keep the rattle 7 to 9 inches from your baby's eyes.

"Here's your rattle. Watch, here it goes. Can you follow it? There you go. Here it comes back again. . . ."

If, after a few weeks, your baby is unable to track the rattle visually when there are no other visual distractions in the room, you will want to check this out with your pediatrician. You should have a visual exam done just to make sure everything is okay.

As we have said, there are many fine rattles on the market today. One style that we suggest that you look for is a wrist rattle. The one we will discuss here is made by Eden Toys and is called Hot Tots Baby Shakes™. The wrist rattle has Velcro that allows you to attach it to your child's wrist or ankle. As he moves about, the rattle will shake and he will be stimulated auditorily by the sound it makes. By the end of this three-month period, your infant will be moving his hands and feet so that he can see them and the wrist and ankle rattles will stimulate his sense of vision as well as his hearing. Infants often will curl up just as they were in the womb and it is stimulating to them to have their legs and arms gently stretched and massaged during play time with them. Having the wrist and ankle rattles adds to the stimulation.

"What do we have here, Andrew? Let's put this rattle on your little wrist. There it goes. Can you hear that little rattle when you move your arm? That's your arm and you're making that sound. Listen carefully. I'm going to streeeetch your arm. See how nice that feels. Now I'm rubbing your arm and listening. Your rattle makes some noise when I do that. . . . "

Texture Toys

Toy manufacturers know that infants enjoy stimulation by different textures. Almost every manufacturer has a type of texture toy on the market. We will also tell you how to make a couple of texture toys later in this chapter. The one we will discuss here is call the Cock a Doodle Zoo Shake Me® made by Eden Toys. There are three different animals represented and they have black and white bodies as well as splashes of color. The rooster has a red crown, yellow beak and feet, and white hands, all made out of soft plush materials. There is a rattle in the head of the doll so that auditory and visual stimulation are provided. Your infant may be able to grab onto the soft body and hold on as he shakes it back and forth. Your language play may be:

"Christina, here is your little rooster doll. Can you grab it? Hold it tight and shake, shake, shake. The rooster doll has very soft feet and hands. Ooooo—feel how soft they are. . . ."

In the Car

Today's babies are on the go—running errands with Mom and Dad, or off to daycare or Grandma's house. It is the law that a young infant sit in the car seat facing the back of the seat. Imagine how boring that must be! There are, however, many products on the market today that can be attached to the car seat to amuse your baby.

Because newborns enjoy black and white patterns and faces, we recommend the Car Seat Gallery by Wimmer-Ferguson. This "gallery" attaches to the upholstery of the car with Velcro or sticky-back tape. The gallery has four plastic pockets and the set comes with twenty different designs to put in the pockets. For the newborn, there are

black and white patterns and for the older infant, there are more complex color patterns. To begin with, you only want to put one picture in at a time. This keeps your baby from being overwhelmed with too many images. If you have him in the front seat with you, you can change the picture every so often. They are very easy to handle. Remembering which pictures you have in the gallery, you can talk about them as you drive along, adding language input to the visual stimulation that he is getting. Perhaps it is the picture of the woman's face:

> "Look at the picture of the lady, Gideon. She looks just like Mommy. You see she has a nose, and eyes and a mouth just like Mommy. She's smiling because she's looking at you and thinking that you are the most wonderful baby in the world."

This gallery is so versatile that you can add different pictures as your child grows and you are working on specific vocabulary for the week— perhaps farm animals or members of the family. The basic frame can be used for any number of different pictures that you can make and put in.

HOMEMADE TOYS

Texture Blanket

For a homemade toy for this age group, we suggest that you make a texture blanket. Often we put a blanket down for our baby to lie on to protect him from dirt, dog hairs, or small particles embedded in the carpet. You can protect him with your homemade texture blanket and stimulate him at the same time. If you don't know how to sew or don't have a sewing machine, why not suggest this to one of your friends to make for you as a gift?

To make this blanket, visit the local fabric store and look through their remnant basket. Choose a variety of different textures. You should only need one-fourth to one-half yard of each fabric you want to use. We suggest that you not use wool for this project. Although the texture of

wool is wonderful, it is possible that your infant could be allergic to it. Also, you will want to be able to wash the blanket frequently and you cannot always wash wool.

Take your materials home, wash each of the fabrics, cut them to the shapes that you want, and sew them together. You will enjoy putting your baby on this blanket and allowing him to experience each of these textures. When you have play time, lie down with him and talk about each of the different materials that you used. What a treasure for you to keep for your infant as he gets older and can understand that this was made just for him.

> "Oh, would you like to lie down on this nice blanket? Look over here. This is a nice soft blue piece of fabric (take his hand.) Can you feel how soft it is? It feels so nice and furry. Ooooh, soft! Look at this red part over here. This is corduroy and it feels bumpy. Can you feel how bumpy it is?. . . ."

Continue with each of the textures that appear on the blanket. Choose words that accurately describe the feel of the material. Don't be afraid to use the actual names of the fabrics when introducing the various textures to your child. Remember, he needs to acquire language receptively before he can expressively communicate back to you. When you label the corduroy "rough" as opposed to the satin "smooth," your child gains an understanding of these words as he feels the textures. This kind of sensory impression will help him understand the concept and remember it the next time you use the words "rough" and "smooth."

Ribbons on a Hoop

Towards the end of your baby's first three months, he will begin reaching out with his hands and feet and can make things go by himself. This toy that we suggest you create will be fun for him to swat at with his hands and kick with his feet. It is also appealingly colorful.

Once again, we take you on a trip to a fabric store or perhaps a store such as KMart, Wal Mart or similar types of stores. You are looking for ribbon in several different colors and an embroidery hoop.

To make the toy, simply tie the ribbons to the embroidery hoop. You can hang the embroidery hoop on a piece of elastic waistband material across the bars of the crib.

Your language time with this toy might go something like this:

> "Look at all the pretty colors! See, there is blue and a bright red. The red ribbon looks like your sleeper. It's the same color. Can you kick the ribbons? See how they flutter."

For a younger infant in this first three months, you can place a small fan so that the ribbons blow in the breeze, creating a beautiful visual picture for your newborn to focus on.

🖐 **A NOTE ABOUT SAFETY:** Don't use this toy after the age of three months, because your baby will be able to reach it and pull it down and he may get tangled up in the elastic or the ribbon or put it in his mouth and choke on it. This toy is only for very young newborns who can only gaze at it or gently bat at it.

Plate Designs

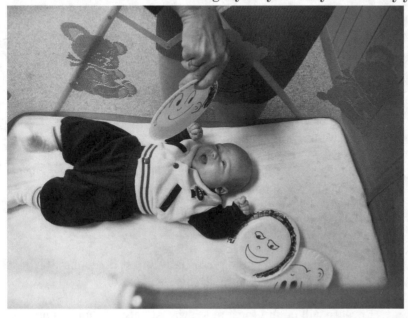

A simple paper plate can be a fascinating and stimulating toy for your baby at this very young age. Take a plain white paper plate and draw black and white designs on it. If drawing is not for you, then cut pictures or designs from newspapers (black and white) or magazines (color). You may also want to paste some pictures of faces on a paper plate. Remember that babies at this developmental age enjoy looking at different faces. You can just put the plates in the crib with your child or you can make a mobile with them.

To make the mobile, tie a wide piece of ribbon tightly across the side rails of the crib or playpen. Attach another ribbon to the paper plates and then tie this to the wide piece of ribbon. You may want to hang two or three of these at a time. They can be changed as frequently as you wish.

> "Look, I made you some new designs to look at. Can you see the black lines on this plate? They go swirl, swirl, swirl around and around. Where is the plate? Can you find it? Good! You are looking at the plate. . . ."

If you put faces on the plates, you can talk about the facial features as described earlier.

> "Here's a woman. She is looking at you. Do you see her eyes? Her eyes are brown just like yours. Look at her nose. Sniff, sniff. What do you think she is smelling? Maybe she smells her dinner cooking. . . ."

THREE TO SIX MONTHS

By the time your infant is three months old, you may be into an established routine. You will be feeling better after the adjustment in your schedule. You will have longer periods of sleep at night, and, in fact, your infant may be sleeping through the night.

She will be more alert and interested in playing with you during these three months of her early life than when she was a newborn. You can continue with some of the activities that we have already talked about and add the new ideas in this section.

Although your baby may not be quite ready to imitate *you* at this time, it is fun to imitate *her*. If she starts cooing, try to say back exactly what she says. You may be surprised to see that she'll wait for you to make your silly sound and then she'll make hers. This is the very beginning of imitation and turn taking and is a fun way to spend diaper changing time. It is also a good way to teach language since imitation is the way that we learn language. Therefore, the more that you and your child can play these babbling imitating games, the more practice she will have making the sounds of our language.

It's important that she have time alone to play around with different sound combinations. It is also important that she have you around some of the time to reinforce those sounds and to play babbling games with her. When you reinforce her "talking," she learns that she is communicating with you. It's up to you to provide the correct model for the word that she is saying. If you imitate back to her, she will enjoy beginning to play an imitating game with you. It is a good idea for you to reinforce her accidental combinations of sounds that sound like real words. This gives her a sense of competence in communicating something to you. Remember, she really doesn't know exactly what she is saying nor does she attach real meaning to your words.

Let's look at an example of how your reinforcement of her accidental combinations of sounds might happen. She's babbling away and accidentally latches onto the vocal combination of "mamamamama" You will want to jump right in with "You're right little one, here's mama. Mama. I'm your mama." She may look at you quizzically and respond back with "tata." But rest assured, you have done your part. Each time she gets reinforced for saying a new combination that is meaningful, you will encourage her to vocalize more and more. She is just playing with sounds, but she is aware when she's listening to what you are saying.

Mobiles

You may want to talk about sharing mobiles with a friend who has a baby the same age as yours. By this time you and your baby have looked at and talked about the same mobile for three months. You both are probably pretty bored with it and it has become something that is just hanging there. If, however, you and your friend have different mobiles, now would be a good time to exchange them. This will give you both a boost.

The mobile that we will talk about during this age range is made by Dakin and is called the Panda Domino. You can use this interchangeably at the earlier age level as well. It has beautiful black and white stuffed pandas. Each of the pandas is resting on a colorful star and the music plays, "Twinkle, Twinkle, Little Star." Most importantly, the pandas are facing your infant as he looks up at them and not facing you as you look down on them. Too many mobiles are made with the adult in mind and the infant cannot see anything that is very stimulating to him.

You can begin naming the mobile's colors for your child as language stimulation, knowing, of course, that he is not really going to associate color names with what he is seeing. But the lyrical tones of your voice intrigue him at this age.

> "Let's look at your Panda Mobile while we change your diaper today. Look at all the pandas playing on the stars. They are such pretty colors: there's purple. Can you reach the purple one? There's green—stretch out and touch the green star. Wow—you kicked the yellow star. See the panda spin around on his yellow star. . . ."

On this mobile, you can turn the music on or off. If you have the music on, you may want to use your language stimulation time to sing the song to him. Don't worry if you don't sing very well—your infant loves the sound of your voice.

"I'm going to turn the music on. Listen. It's playing Twinkle, Twinkle, Little Star. How I wonder what you are. Up above the world so high. Like a diamond in the sky. . . ."

Mirrors

There is really no special age category for this wonderful and unique learning toy. You can put a mirror in your baby's crib on the day that you bring her home from the hospital. We are not sure exactly how much of what she sees she understands in those first few weeks, but we do know how much she likes to focus on faces—and what better face than her own or yours! Looking in the mirror and pointing out her body parts is a lot of fun.

"Hi there, Jill. Look at you there in the mirror. I can see your nose. Up, right there. Where are your eyes? Those are your eyes. . . ."

Continue in that way, pointing out all of the baby's body parts and watch her giggle with glee as she watches you touching her body and sees the same thing happening in the mirror. It is your baby's first mystery! How does this happen to me and that baby in the mirror?

The mirror also helps your baby to recognize herself as separate from you. Early on, infants do not know that they are separate from the people around them. This is something they need to learn. As you play with the mirror, she can begin to see that there are two separate people there. One of those people is touching her and *she* is the other one. It is an interesting thing to think about when you're playing with her in this way.

Introducing your baby to body parts early helps her develop a self-identity—an identity as an individual apart from you—as well as labeling that vocabulary for her. Almost every test of early infant cognitive abilities has sections that test whether she knows where her body parts

Special Considerations

You may think that you cannot play with a mirror if your child has a visual impairment. Remember, however, that not all children with visual impairments are totally blind. There are many children who are partially sighted and will be able to see to varying degrees. You will want to touch your child's body in the places that you are talking about. Touch her nose when you talk about noses. Touch her nose while you point to the baby in the mirror and talk about seeing the baby's nose. Use a lot of expressive language to describe body parts. Use words to describe the feel of hair or the shape of noses, mouths, and eyes and even a totally blind child can learn to understand these differences through words and not necessarily touch.

Blind children often want to touch another person's face or body to explore and understand. Children as young as two years of age can be taught to ask before exploring another person's body. Be sure to teach your child which parts are okay to explore and which parts are not. You can also use dolls and stuffed animals to allow her to explore through touch.

are. These are part of the development of intellectual skills.

Many of the infant toy manufacturers make mirrors. We recommend two that are made by Wimmer-Ferguson. One is a crib mirror that offers a very clear and bright reflection back to the baby and you. It is shatterproof, scratch-resistant, and washable. It comes with ties that are only 11" long (the recommended length for safety) to fasten the mirror to the crib or playpen. The corners are rounded and the edges are vinyl to keep it from slipping. A bonus is that on the reverse side of the mirror are the black and white patterns that baby so enjoys looking at. These patterns vary from simple to more complex designs, which gives the toy a longer life. This is one you will want to keep around for a long time.

The second mirror that we recommend, also made by Wimmer-Ferguson, is good entertainment for your child when you are out running errands or at home during playtime in the crib or play pen. It is called Peek-a-boo-Play and is made like a book. You open the doors and there is an unbreakable mirror. Of course, as the name implies, you can play baby's favorite game of peek-a-boo with this handy little mirror. In the beginning of this time period you may have to open the doors for your baby, but by the time she reaches six months, she will be able to open them herself and be the leader in the peek-a-boo game. The language you might want to use here is:

> "Where is Meghan? Can you find her? Where is Meghan hiding? Open the door—PEEK-A-BOO!! I see Meghan. You are right there in the mirror. Look at that pretty little baby girl. Can you close the doors and we'll look for Mommy."

You will be amazed at how long this activity will keep your baby interested. Babies are just fascinated by their own faces and yours.

✋ **A NOTE ABOUT SAFETY:** Make sure that the mirror you purchase is made of an unbreakable material and provides an accurate reflection. Some mirrors that we have looked at have a very distorted image. Another nice feature of most baby mirrors is that they can be attached to the crib or playpen. A freestanding mirror might be hazardous if your infant were to reach out and knock it down on himself. Check for these features before you buy.

Gymfinity™

This is one of the most versatile toys we have seen. It can be used with a newborn infant and continue to fascinate a stand-alone toddler. Gymfinity is made by Today's Kids and distributed through the Hand in Hand, One Step Ahead, and other catalogs. We'll talk about how to use it at this age level.

Gymfinity stands on its own with an activity center on the top for the toddler and as many as seven hanging toys for the infant who is lying on his back. You can hang one object at a time so that you don't overwhelm your baby and gradually add more according to his tolerance and interest in the toys. Each of the objects is in black and white with a touch of red on some. Your infant can practice his reaching out and hitting or kicking with his feet to make the objects move.

We'll describe each of the objects and then focus on one to give you an idea of the language possibilities. The two hanging objects are a black and white panda with a red bow tie hanging from a red swing and a black and white puppy with a red tongue and a red heart on his chest spinning in his red dog house. These objects are three-dimensional and have raised features, which can help a visually impaired child explore the toys as you talk about them. These two objects can hang from the frame or be removed and played with alone.

The other five pieces can be hung from the frame or can be used on the table top for a standing toddler. Two are puzzle pieces. The black and white cat has raised triangles on the back and the black and white rabbit has raised circles on the back. These raised spots would help a visually impaired child identify the correct piece. The last three pieces that can be used on both sides of the toy are gears. Each of them has a different raised pattern on the back and two of them have a black and white picture on the front: a penguin and a zebra. The third is a small mirror.

On the top of the frame are four shapes that fit similar shapes on the four corners of the table. Three of the shapes can drop through similarly shaped spaces on the top of the table.

For our language sample, let's talk about the dog. You can adapt your language dialogue for all of the other toys in the same way.

"Kyle, look what we have for you to play with today. It's a dog and he has a red doghouse. Watch him spin. He can spin around in his doghouse. Can you make him spin? Push him and around he goes. Around and around. (The dog spins easily so that a child with motor impairments should be able to activate.) Kyle, can you find the dog's ears? Here they are—they're black and floppy ears. The dog also has black spots. What shall we call this puppy? How about Spot? That sounds like a good name for a dog with black spots. Mommy's going to hang him from your gym table. Now you can play with him. You can reach out and push him round and round. Now you are using your feet to make him spin around and around. Good job, Kyle."

Pattern Pals®

Earlier, we talked about how much babies enjoy textures. Now that your baby has more grasp and hand control, we'd like to recommend Pattern Pals® made by Wimmer-Ferguson. Your baby can grasp these shapes, mouth them, and generally explore them. There is a lot of language learning opportunity for you to supply for them.

Three shapes come in this set. One is a gold fish that has a bright yellow satiny side and a black and white bullseye on the reverse side—if you squeeze the bullseye, the toy makes a squeaky sound. The second is a red corduroy sailboat which has a more complex checkerboard pattern on the other side—when you shake the boat, it rattles. The third toy in this collection is a fuzzy blue caterpillar which has a wavy black and white design on the other side—when you squeeze it, it has a fascinating krinkly sound that babies love. All of these toys are washable and nontoxic, which is important for babies who are beginning to bring their hands to their mouth and put things in their mouth. The toys are sturdy and will not come apart.

"Let's play with this fuzzy blue caterpillar. Doesn't it feel soft? It feels good against my face. Do you want to feel the fuzzy side on your face? Ooooo, that feels so nice and soft. Listen—it makes a krinkly sound. Can you squeeze it and make that sound too? You did it! What a strong baby you are!"

Dolls

Dolls are the toys that are most often associated with childhood. Dolls today are available with different complexions so that all children can identify with them. The one we suggest is made by Playskool and is called My Very Soft Baby™. This washable doll has no features that can come off. The face is vinyl and the features are molded into the face. Its arms and body are soft and a squeeze on the body produces a happy giggly sound. This doll can be mouthed and explored without worry about any loose parts coming off and injuring your baby. You can use this doll for talking about body parts and facial features just as we used the stuffed animal in the age grouping of newborn to three months.

Let's use a bedtime scene to illustrate how to use this doll to teach behaviors you want your baby to follow. It seems that this night is one that your baby has decided to be fussy about going off to sleep. You can get the doll and have a conversation like this:

> "Well, BJ, it's time to go to sleep now. Your dolly is tired and wants to go to sleep, too. (Yawn) Wow, Dolly is really sleepy. Did you see her yawn? Let's put Dolly to sleep now. She can sleep right in here with you. You need to be quiet now so that Dolly can go to sleep. Shhhhh. Good night now. . . ."

You can use this doll when you are playing with a mirror as well. She can be another person whose facial features and body parts can be compared. You can do exercises with the doll that your baby needs to do every day and may find uncomfortable. This becomes an especially valuable tool as your child gets older and perhaps resistant to some of the things she needs to do for her therapy sessions. In addition, you can make the doll "talk" in language learning sessions. Put the doll in front of your face while you imitate and babble along with your infant. This gives your baby something to focus on while you do the babbling from behind the doll. This also gives your infant an opportunity to listen carefully, since your face is not visible to her. For a child with a hearing loss, this will provide valuable auditory learning time.

We're sure that you will think of many other ways that you can play with a doll. Until your child is older, try to resist getting the dolls that wet, cry, eat, and do all sorts of other things. Your baby is not ready for so sophisticated a doll and it will not fill any need for her at this time.

HOMEMADE TOYS

Ball Bounce

One homemade toy that we suggest for this age group is a lightweight ball (like a beach ball) that is attached to a plastic Slinky™ and suspended from a hook in the ceiling. You can use a plastic-coated twist tie to connect the beach ball to the Slinky. Make sure you bend the edges of the twist tie over so there are no sharp ends. When you're not around, hook the Slinky and ball up high on the hook so that your baby doesn't accidentally get all tangled up in it.

When you're in the room with him or when you're playing with him, have it suspended so that it is just out of his reach.

When you first introduce this toy to your baby, demonstrate how it moves when you hit it with your hands. Encourage him to reach out and bat the ball with either his hands or his feet. If he needs help making the Slinky move, you can hold his hands or feet and help him bat or kick. He will be able to see the results of cause and effect and will enjoy making this activity happen all by himself. (You could also suspend the ball from a string, but the Slinky is more fun because it adds bounce to the activity.)

> "Look, Jonas, can you make the ball bounce? See, you just bat at it with your hands. Watch and see how it bounces. Now *you* try it. Can you make the ball bounce? It can go up high and bounce down low. Good boy, Jonas, *you* did that! I see you can make the ball bounce. Now try kicking it—you are a strong boy—you can kick the ball with your feet. Good job, Jonas."

Peek-a-Boo Board

We talked earlier about peek-a-boo being a favorite activity of this age. The toy we describe here combines peek-a-boo-type play with learning about textures. Your baby should enjoy it for a long time to come.

Buy a plain-colored vinyl placemat from a linen store, grocery store, or general purpose store such as KMart. Cut pieces of texture material that you have left over from your texture blanket into four-inch squares. Use a pinking shears so there will be no edges to fray. Use hot glue or regular strong glue to fasten the top edge of the squares to your placemat. Leave the other three sides unglued. Once the placemat is covered with different textured materials, put a small square of sticky-back Velcro under each textured square. (You can purchase Velcro in any fabric or arts and crafts store.) Next, cut out pictures of objects from magazines or catalogs or choose small objects that will fit beneath the textured squares. Fasten the other half of the Velcro square to the back of the picture and attach the picture to the Velcro under the textured square. Now you are ready to play with your infant.

> "Stephanie, where's the doggy? Can you find the picture (or object) of the doggy? Where is it? I think it is under that red scratchy square. Can you find it? Look, here it is. You found the picture (or object) of the doggy."

Sometimes, your child may be more interested in just feeling the different textures on the mat. Take this opportunity to give your child language for the different textures she is feeling. That's what gives this toy varied play opportunities. At this age, she may not be able to find the object or picture you asked him for, but you can show her where it is and reinforce the language of the activity.

SIX TO NINE MONTHS

At this developmental age, your baby is able to do more and more things that he could not do before. If he has no physical limitations, he will be able to sit alone for long periods of time, which will give him a whole new perspective on the world and also make it easier for him to play with you. He is able to pick up and hold objects, which will allow him to be more involved in playing with you. You will begin to see more play that involves both of you, including times when he will initiate the fun.

During this age span, your baby should be able to sit in a high chair comfortably. If he has physical limitations, he may be able to sit in a specially constructed chair with support. On the floor you might get a baby-sized swim ring and seat him in the middle. This will give him support all around yet allow his hands to be free to interact with you.

A word is in order here about "baby talk." It is our opinion that baby talk on the part of the baby is cute, but on the part of the parents, unnecessary. It is cute when a one-year-old asks for his "baba," but when the same child does this at age five, it is less appealing. When your baby asks for his "baba," you can respond with, "Sure I'll get your bottle." You are telling him that you understand his communication but this is what it really sounds like. If you start doing this now, you will have less correcting to do when he is older.

While your child is beginning to communicate with you by crying and cooing, keep in mind that he is also on the receiving end of the communication. Talk to him about your everyday activities and things you are doing with and for him. "Hmmmm, looks like you need your diaper changed. Shall we go and get you a clean one? Okay, off we go." Remember, receptive language must come *before* expressive language. He'll enjoy hearing your voice and begin to understand what you are saying months before he will be able to say any intelligible words.

Soft Blocks

Blocks are very versatile toys, and your baby can enjoy block play at different levels for many years. He can begin playing with them now and continue into his early school

Single Concept

Now for introducing the concept of *up*. Take the blocks and show him how you can stack one on top of the other.

▼ "Here's one block. Now I can put one *up* on Top. See it go *up* on top? Here's another one—*up* it goes. Can we do one more? *Up-up-up-up* on top. See, we made the block go *up*."

Single Concept

This toy also lends itself to teaching the concept *down*. We suggest that you do not introduce this concept at the same play session when you introduce *up*. Otherwise, your child may be confused by the two concepts.

▼ "Do you want to make the blocks fall *down*? It's fun when they all crash *down* to the ground. First let's make a tall tower. Let's make it as high as we can. Great—now let's knock it *down*."

Gently take your child's hand and knock down the tower.

▼ "Here they come *down*. Wow—they all fell *down*."

years, when he will build elaborate roads and structures which will be the basis for a lot of his imaginative play for many years.

At this developmental age, your baby will be able to stack two or three blocks on top of each other. You will be able to teach the concepts of *up* and *down* with blocks, and we give you examples of dialogues for each concept.

We suggest that your first set of blocks be the one made by Battat called Soft Cubes. There are four soft blocks in this set. One block has pictures of pets, another farm animals, another zoo animals, and another sea animals. The pictures are colorful and very interesting to look at and present a wealth of information for you to talk about. Although the concepts we are going to discuss here are *up* and *down*, remember to talk about each of the animals during another time in play.

As you stack the blocks, you can take the new one, start at the bottom of the stack and say *"up-up-up"* as you pass each block that you have already put down.

The most exciting part of this game for your baby is when they all tumble down. He thinks that is great fun and you will hear him chortling with glee. This kind of fun will carry over to the times when he builds his own structures and watches them tumble down. He will remember from his infant days that tumbling down is half of the fun.

Fold N' Go Play Around™

This wonderful portable play environment by Playskool can be used at home or when you are out visiting family and friends. It is nice to be able to take along some of your child's favorite things to play with. This toy is so portable and provides lots of opportunity for play. You can also use it for the baby to nap in, as she will be protected all around with soft bumpers.

On the sides of the bumpers are play activities for your child. There is a turtle with a corduroy body whose head pulls out on elastic so you can talk about the turtle sticking his neck out as he moves along or hiding in his shell when he wants to sleep or be quiet. The soft, furry rabbit has a rattle carrot to eat, which can be stored in a pocket on the bumper. There is a teddy bear that makes an interesting crinkly sound when it is squeezed. On the back of the bumper is a set of plastic keys that your baby can rattle and teethe on. And to make it easy for Mom or Dad, the whole toy folds into itself for carrying.

"We're going to Grandma's house to-day for lunch. Let's take your Play Around toy. You can play with the toys while I talk to Grandma and then when it's time for your nap, you'll have your favorite toy to nap in. You can play while I get our other things together. Where is that green turtle? Can you pull his head way out? A turtle likes to stick his head out when he crawls. Where's the furry rabbit? Ummm, that feels nice and soft, doesn't it? What a funny sound you're making with the teddy bear. Crinkle, crinkle. I like that sound. I think it's my favorite. You're doing it again. You must like it too. Okay—I'm all packed up. Let's fold up your toy and off we go to Grandma's. . . ."

Easy Touch Tape Player™

A tape player for a baby? What an interesting idea! Actually, you can use this tape player in your baby's crib right from the beginning. This model made by Mattel has a "parent controlled lock out design" so that little fingers cannot get into the controls. When your baby is a newborn, you can put it in his crib with soothing tapes as an

aid to falling asleep. At this developmental age of six to nine months, you can put in a tape of you talking or singing to your little one, which might give you an extra few minutes of precious sleep in the morning since he will be able to activate it himself.

An intriguing feature of this tape recorder is that on the front of the player are two large buttons—one green with musical notes on it (start) and the other red (stop). They are very easy to activate, so that even a child with severe motor difficulties should be able to turn the player off and on. If your child has visual impairments, you can use different textures on the two buttons. For example, you can put a piece of sandpaper on the "on" button and felt on the "off" button. Be consistent when you use textures so that your child learns what the textures mean. One expert says that a child with visual impairment who doesn't have any cognitive delays won't need these cues for very long as he develops spatial awareness.

The teaching opportunities of the tape player are limitless. At this age, you will want to talk about the green button which turns the music on and the red button which makes it stop. You can put in tapes (the baby is unable to reach the tapes himself) that have lullabies or your baby's favorite songs. As we mentioned earlier, you can put in tapes of you talking, which your baby will easily recognize. During these taped "conversations," you might be able to direct his attention to things around his room that he can look at while you're not there. Perhaps you have put pictures of family members in plastic protectors around the crib. You can say, "Where's a picture of Uncle Bobby? Can you find Uncle Bobby? Where is Aunt Fran? Look in the corner and you'll see a picture of Aunt Fran."

One of the most important skills that this toy will teach is cause and effect. When your baby pushes the green button, the tape will go on and when he touches the red one, it will go off. Using the off and on buttons is also a very important skill for children who have developmental delays to learn because they may need to operate many switch toys and devices later in life.

As a toddler later on, your child can carry this tape player around with him and use it to listen to stories on tape as he turns the pages of a book. It is a toy that will span many age ranges. We know you will enjoy it.

Humpty Dumpty Comeback Roller

During this developmental age period, your child will be getting more and more mobile as he learns to crawl and roll to get to the places he wants to be. One toy we have found that encourages this movement is the Humpty Dumpty Comeback Roller by Ambi Toys. This colorful little rolling toy rolls away from your child, encouraging him to come after it and then rolls back to him. Since your child will be sitting well by now you can roll it back and forth to him. A little motion on his part will set the toy moving. It works best, however, on a smooth, non-carpeted surface.

"Here, David. Here's a new toy for you to play with today. I'm going to give it a little push and off it goes. Can you get it? Hurry or it will come rolling back. Hurry and go get the Humpty Dumpty toy. Can you crawl real fast and get it? Here it comes. It's coming back to us. Hurry and catch it. . . ."

Pat Mat

Pat Mat is made by Rainbow Mountain, Inc. and distributed through the Hand in Hand Catalog. This toy brings a whole new dimension to the idea of sensory exploration. The mat fills with water and has many sponge objects representing things that live in or go in the water. The first thing you will want to do is allow your child to touch the mat and explore how it feels to squoosh the mat and to see the objects swim around inside. Of course, it feels cool to the touch and somewhat like a waterbed, which is very soothing to some children. Your language can be something like this:

"I filled your mat with water. Can you see all of the animals floating around? Let's feel the mat, Natalie. Doesn't that feel cool and squooshy? If you push on it over here, all of the animals will float to the other side. Let's try that. I like to see them go back and forth, back and forth. They're swimming around. I see a fish. Can you touch the fish? I see another fish—where Is the other fish?"

There are two of each of the animals: fish, starfish, octopus, seahorse, crab, turtle, and duck. This means you can introduce some number concepts, which, of course, are only receptive language at this point.

✋**A NOTE ABOUT SAFETY:** The toy is well constructed and shouldn't leak, and your baby shouldn't be able to get to the water directly. It is best, however, to be overly cautious—especially around water! Stay with your baby while she is playing with this toy. Be especially careful that your child does not lie face down on this mat if she is unable to get up on her own.

Household pets will be fascinated by this water toy. When you are not playing with the Pat Mat, put it safely out of reach of pets, especially cats. They think it is their own private fish bowl!

You will also want to change the water frequently as it might get discolored and emit an odor.

HOMEMADE TOYS

Where's the Cheerio™?

Babies in this age range love to play disappearing games because they are beginning to understand that when they cannot see something it does not mean it is gone. For this game use unbreakable plastic cups that you can't see through. Put a Cheerio™ or other piece of cereal under a cup. (Start with only one cup at a time—as your baby gets better at this game you can add a second cup and perhaps even a third.) Let him watch you put the cereal under the cup. Then ask him, "Where is the Cheerio? Where did it go?" He will gleefully pick up the cup and find the Cheerio. Of course, the ultimate reward is that he can then eat the Cheerio or other food you may want to use.

From this game, your baby is learning to build trust and understanding that when something is gone, it will usually come back (the Piagetian concept of object permanence). He is also learning to show you what he understands by looking for an object that you name. Later on, when he hands you a certain object, it will indicate that he understands the language you are using.

Magnets on a Cookie Sheet

There is actually nothing to make for this toy. You just need to gather the materials together, which can really be fun. Pick out some interesting refrigerator magnets—perhaps depicting animals and foods or other objects that you want your child to be able to name. Then get out a cookie sheet or a cookie tin that holiday cookies come in. Teach the vocabulary to your child and then stick the magnets to the cookie sheet. Next, ask your child to give the appropriate magent back to you as you name it. Your child will delight in pulling them off the cookie sheet. Of course, she doesn't understand about magnetism at this point, but the early learning is there. Let's use animals for our example.

"I have a dog here. Look, I can put it on the cookie sheet and it sticks there. It's a magnet dog. Now what's this? Ummm, a cat—can you stick the cat to the cookie sheet? Good job—you did it. Let's see what this one is. Oh, it's a little mouse. Let's stick that to the cookie sheet also. Now listen very carefully. Give me the dog. Nope, that's the cat—here's the dog. Now can you hand it to me? Good, you did fine. Let's see—where's the little mouse? That's right—you found the little mouse. Give it to me. Great. There's one more animal—it's a cat. Hand it to me. Good job—you gave me the cat."

NINE TO TWELVE MONTHS

If this is your first child, you will be astonished at how active your baby becomes in this last part of her first year. You will look back in amazement at all that she has learned. You should also be pleased at how interested she is in playing with you. Her attention span is longer and she understands more and more of what you say to her. If she has started to walk, she will soon be running more than she will be walking.

If she has a visual impairment, she may not be as comfortable in another house as she is in yours. Don't hover over her, but help her adjust to this new environment. If she has never been there before, you can take her on a tour of the place and tell her where certain things are. For example, "You are standing in front of the couch and there is a small table next to you." Obviously, these directions are more than a child of this age will be able to understand, but you are giving her the language at the same time you are giving her a general feel for where things are. She may not understand "small," but "table" will alert her to a possible obstacle. Tell her where you will be and that she can call you if she needs you for any reason.

The toys we suggest in this section are ones that your child will enjoy for many months to come. They include activities that will use many of her new skills and capture her attention.

Rock-a-Stack™

Similar toys—consisting of different-colored rings on a cone—are made by different companies. The one we describe is made by Fisher Price, Inc. This toy has many different play possibilities. We will talk about five different concepts you can teach with this toy. You will not want to talk about all of them at this age. However, we'll give you all the language here and you can add it to your play when it is appropriate for your child.

Motion Concepts

Your child will be interested in pulling the rings off before he is physically able to put them back on.

Single Concept

This is the simplest activity to do with this cone of rings.

▼ "Look at this new toy that we have to play with. Watch it *rock* back and forth. Can you *rock* it? Good! You can *rock* it back and forth. *Rocking, rocking, rocking.*"

Continue taking turns rocking the cones until you see that your child is tiring of this activity.

Single Concept

▼ "Here's our cone of rings. Let's take them all *off*. Can you pull the red one *off*? Great, you took the red ring *off*. Let's take the blue one *off*. *Off* it comes. Now comes the yellow one. Pull it *off*. Good work, we've got all of the rings *off*."

"All right, Danny, let's take the rings. Can you pull it off? Pull. Pull. Good for you! You pulled the purple one off. Can you give the purple one to me? Thank you. Let's pull the next one off. That one is yellow. Pull it off. Pull. O.K. Now we pulled off two rings. . . ."

Continue until you have them all in your lap. Because he doesn't know the sizes yet, you can hand him the appropriate sizes in order to put the rings back on. Then give him the language for this activity.

"Put the red ring on. Do you need some help? Put it on. Good! You put it on. . . ."

Continue until all the rings are back in place.

Color Concepts

In these early months, talking about colors will be only an introduction to them for your baby. He probably will not understand all the color words. However, we encourage you to use the color names because, as we have said before, he will need to hear thousands of repetitions before he understands or uses those words.

"Look at all the pretty colors on this toy—red, green, yellow, orange, blue, purple. This ring is red. Here's a green ring. This one is blue. . . ."

At this age, you are naming colors, but later on you might want to see if your child can choose between colors, which would show his understanding of the words. Children can usually match colors by age two, point to them by age three, and name them by age four. However you will want to use the vocabulary early and often to expose your child to the names. To play this way, you would put all the rings in your lap. Then take two different colors and put them in front of your child and say, "Which is the red ring? Can you find the red one? Good for you—you picked the red ring."

If your child chooses the wrong color, tell him the correct name for the one he chose and then hand him the correct one.

"That color is blue. Here is the red ring. Can you give
the red ring to me? Good job. . . ."

As your child begins to understand the colors, you can
add one at a time until he has all the colored rings in front
of him and can pick the one that you ask for.

In another year or two, when he can say the names of
the colors, your play can go like this.

"What color is this ring? Can you tell me the name?
That's right—it's red. . . ."

If your child's articulation is not clear, remember
what we said about modeling. You don't want to become a
speech clinician and correct his speech all the time. Instead, restate what he said using the correct pronunciation.

Size Concepts

As with colors, your child is not ready to learn size differences now. However, at a later time, you can use this
toy to teach size differences because the rings are graduated from large to small. You would do this in the same
way as you did with the colors. The difference is that the
colors are distinct from each other but one size is only rela-
tive to another size. We suggest you save this concept until he is two or three years old. If you are using a sign
system, be sure you are signing these concepts as you introduce them. Here are some ideas for introducing size
concepts.

"Let's take off the smallest ring first. The smallest
ring is purple. The next ring is a little bigger. . . ."

Compare the two to see that one is a little bigger. Continue in this way, comparing each ring to the next larger
size. When you put them back on, you'll be comparing
smaller and smaller sizes. Eventually you should be able
to have all the rings in front of your child and have him
put them back on from largest to smallest.

Balls

We have talked about balls before and will talk more
about them at later ages. A very fine ball to have at
this time is a beach ball. It is light, very colorful, and easy
for your baby to catch and hold onto because of its size.
We suggest that you not blow it up all the way so it is easier for your child to grasp. You can use the beach ball and
another ball like a Nerf ball to compare sizes with your
baby:

Single Concept

▼ "Look, these balls are *round*. (Stress the shape with your hands.) The beach ball is a big *round* ball. The Nerf ball is a little *round* ball.

Point out the colors of the balls to your child to help familiarize her with the concept of colors.

▼ "Look, your ball is red and yellow. It has stripes on it. Here is a red stripe and here is a yellow stripe."

"Come and get the big ball. Which is the big beach ball? Good job, you found the big beach ball. Can you roll it to me? Good work. . . ."

Aside from teaching the concept *big*, you can use the balls to teach the concept *round*.

Of course, you would not want to introduce all of these concepts at one time to your child. Just remember that this is language associated with ball play and use it when it is appropriate and she is interested in that particular activity.

Now that your baby may be up on her feet, it is easy to teach action words involving balls.

"Can you *roll* the ball to me? I'll *roll* it to you. Let's *roll* it to Henry. Boy, that ball can really *roll*."

"Can you *push* the ball? Take two hands and *push* it. *Push* it hard. Great job! You *pushed* it."

"Now can you *kick* the ball? *Kick* the ball with your feet. You *kicked* the ball a long way."

"Now let's practice *throwing* the ball. Take two hands. Way over your head. Hold onto the ball real tight. Now let go. *Throw* it. Great. You did it. You *threw* the ball."

"Can you *catch* the ball? Hold out your hands like this. Now you are ready to *catch* the ball. Here it comes. Fantastic! You *caught* the ball."

"Now let's *bounce* the ball. *Bounce* it on the ground. Now, *bounce* it high in the air. You can *bounce* the ball very well. Good for you."

Hide Inside®

This beautiful toy made by Discovery Toys is soft, colorful, and washable. Your child will spend hours putting the little objects in the fabric box and dumping them out again. There are five textured objects that can be hidden in the box. There is a terrycloth bunny, a squeaky duck, a satiny heart, a krinkly fish and a textured bumpy flower.

Special Considerations

When you are playing with this toy with a child who is blind or visually impaired, allow him to hold onto the rim of the soft box and explore with him as you move your hand with his around the edge of the box and then slowly into the box to take out the small textured toys. Putting your hand over his as he explores toys is called hand-over-hand exploration.

This toy can help to reinforce the concept of object permanence we introduced earlier. That is, just because something is out of sight does not mean it is gone forever. Your child is beginning to learn this about you as well. When you are out of sight in the next room, you will reappear when he cries or calls for you. Some language play you might do with this toy is:

"What's hiding inside your little box? Can you pull one out? What's that you found? A bunny! Right—you pulled out the white bunny. Hop, hop, hop. The bunny can hop over to the table. What else can you find? There's a yellow duck. What sound does a duck make? Can you make that sound? Quack, quack, quack. You sound just like a duck. Can you make him waddle over to the bunny? Now the bunny and the duck are waiting for us. What else is hiding in the box? Wow—you dumped the rest out!"

Bead Frame

Everywhere you go where there are children, you see bead frame toys—Doctor's offices, children's book stores, children's play areas at shopping centers. This intriguing toy appeals to young and old. We have seen a six-month-old slowly moving the beads up and down the curvy, metal frame and we have seen adults idly fingering the beads as they watched their children play. Some of the many benefits to be reaped from this versatile toy include eye-hand coordination as the child moves the beads around the frame, color recognition, math concepts as the child counts the beads as they flop to the other side of the frame, and, of course, many opportunities for teaching language. Bead frames range in size from small three-pathway frames to very large and complicated mazes.

The one we will describe here is made by Playskool and uses transportation objects as the beads that can be manipulated. These transportation objects give us the opportunity to talk about specific types of transportation as well as the math and color concepts mentioned previously. On this bead frame, there are cars, trains, and hot air balloons. Your play dialogue might go something like this:

"Here's a train, Alison, and a car. And what is this over here? Those are hot air balloons. They can take people way up in the sky. You're moving the trains—one, two, three trains. Around and around the frame they go, all the way over to the other side. There are two left. Can you move those over with the other trains? Great. Now all of the trains are together on the other side. Let's make a noise like a train as we move them back to the station. Choo choo—there goes the first train. Choo choo—here comes the second one. Choo choo—now the third one. Can you make the sound for the fourth train? Great, Alison, I heard you say choo choo. And now the last train. Let's say it together—Choo choo. Here comes the last train down the tracks."

One child in our neighborhood suggested that as children get older they can pretend that they are going on vacations via train. After the train stops at a certain city, they take a car to their hotel. Imaginations can run wild with this very simple toy. Enjoy your child as she goes from simple manipulation of the toy to complex story telling.

Books

We have not talked very much about books yet, but you will want to expose your child to books from his very early days. You will find an annotated list of books at the end of every developmental age section. Making reading part of your life and part of your child's will help him to develop his love of books as he gets older and can manage them himself. We know one young mother who read the complete original version of *Peter Pan* to her infant as she nursed her in the very early days of her life. Perhaps it is only coincidental that this little girl was reading by herself at the age of three. We do know, however, that early and consistent exposure to books is important for young children because it instills an interest in reading, shows that you value reading, and is an excellent vehicle for expanding language experiences and vocabulary.

There are several books on the market today that are interactive and allow the child to play with the items in softsided books. One that we will share here is made by Discovery Toys and is called *Snuggle Time*. This would make a wonderful bedtime story book for children at this age.

On the first page of the cloth book is a Teddy bear that fits under the sheet on his bed. You can talk about Teddy getting ready to go to bed but first he wants to visit with his friends in the book. The first animal is a sheep which has a fluffy lambswool coat on. You can talk about how this feels and that this is what the sheep's coat feels like. On the opposite page Teddy can visit his elephant friend, who has a lovely crinkly ear and a pebbly body. The next page features a yellow fish that can be pulled out of his bowl. The fish is made of shiny satin and makes a crinkly sound when squeezed and the fishbowl is mesh, which has an interesting texture. You might want to share with your child that the fish can only breathe in the water so he has to be put back very quickly. The next page has a picture of a queen with wonderful facial features for you to point out and show your child that she also has eyes, a nose, and a mouth. The queen's necklace features three small beads that can be moved along the necklace. A bright yellow sun is next and when you flip his smiling face up, there is a small mirror underneath, so you can play a game of peek-a-boo.

Special Considerations

If your child has a visual impairment, books such as Pat the Bunny and Pat the Cat can provide different textures to explore. For older children with significant visual impairments, there are "twin vision" books that have both braille and print so that you can read to your child and he can follow along with the braille version. At this age, your child is certainly not reading braille, but early exposure to his reading medium is as important to him as exposure to print is to the sighted child. The source for these books is listed in the reference section at the end of the book.

If your child has a hearing impairment, hold him to the side so he can see your face and signs or cues as you read. You can also have him sit on your lap facing you or have sit him on the bed or sofa watching you.

The last page features a bear driving a car. The door of the car can be opened and closed with an accompanying rattle sound. You might say, "This is your little Teddy bear's Daddy. He is coming home from work to put your little teddy to sleep. Let's close the book and put Teddy back under his sheet so he can snuggle up and go right off to sleep—just like you."

HOMEMADE TOYS

Stacking Cups

Your child is on the go at this age and loves to be with you in the kitchen. Let her have a set of your plastic bowls that nest inside one another. She will have great fun stacking them up and taking them apart. You might also save the plastic cups that single-serving pudding and Jello™ come in, as well as other plastic containers. These are also fun to stack up together. In a way they are similar to blocks but they are unlikely to tumble down unless you try to stack a whole bunch of them. Stacking them is good for eye-hand coordination skills and you can talk with your child about them as you are fixing supper or cleaning up afterwards.

> "You're stacking the cups. Put one in—now another. You have two cups stacked together. Now you're putting in another one. Now you have three. Your stack of cups is getting taller. Are you going to put in more? No—now you are taking them apart. Pull—ooooh, it's a little hard to get them apart. But you're doing a good job with them. Keep pulling. Now you can put them together again. I'm glad you're in the kitchen with me. It's nice to have company while I am fixing dinner. You're playing so nicely with your cups."

Danielle's Story

This would be a good time to make a book about your child. Take actual photos of your child doing her daily activities: in her crib; at nap time; eating breakfast; taking a bath; playing outside; going in the car; at a therapy session. Whenever. Put these pictures in a sturdy book such as a photo album with easy-to-turn pages or a looseleaf notebook which can be added to over time. You will find these books to be a treasure as a chronicle of time and your child will enjoy looking at them over and over again even as she grows older.

If your child has a visual impairment, use high contrast "mug shots" (faces only). Use pictures that are taken against a solid background and show only a closeup of the face. Start with pictures of family and friends. Connect the person or object with the picture and use the language to describe who they are. If you cover the pictures with clear contact paper or photo album pages be sure to hold the book so that the light doesn't make a glare on the pages. Also look for books in the library that have high contrast pictures of everyday objects. Examples include *Black on White* and *White on Black* by Tana Hoban.

As you talk with your child about the picture, paste it into the book and then write a sentence about it. We know that she is not reading words yet, but exposing her to print early gets her thinking about the printed word.

> "Look at this picture, Danielle. This is a picture of you upstairs in your crib. Are you sleepy? There's your rabbit. Time for a nap. Danielle is taking a nap in this picture. Let's paste it in your book. Can you help? I'll put the paste on and you can turn it over and pat it down. Now let's see—we'll write 'Danielle is taking a nap.' Okay. Let's see Danielle's other pictures. . . ."

Continue in this way as long as she stays interested in what you are doing. Add pictures of relatives so that they are available when these people are about to visit. Preparing your child ahead of time allows her time to think about unfamiliar people coming into her life. If she is going to therapy, be sure to take a picture of her therapist so that on the days when she is going to see her, you can refer to this picture. You can even have a second picture to put up on the calendar on the days when she will be going so that she can see the relation of the calendar to her activitiy. Again, remember, this learning is at a receptive level. We do not expect her to be at all aware of days of the week at this age.

Summary

Here we are at the end of the first developmental year. Can you believe how many things your baby is able to do for herself? This is a time of rapid growth and all of the months of building her receptive language will start to pay off. She'll probably be saying or signing at least one or two words by now and soon this number will increase dramatically.

TOY SUMMARY THE FIRST YEAR

The following is a list of the toys we have worked with in this developmental year. Asterisks indicate homemade toys.

Infant Stim-mobile
Panda Bear Stuffed Animal
Hot Tot Shake Me Rattles
Cock-a-Doodle-Zoo Shake Me
Car Seat Gallery
*Texture Blanket
*Ribbons on a Hoop
*Plate Designs
Panda Domino Mobile
Mirror
Peek-a-Boo Play
Gymfinity
Pattern Pals
My Very Soft Baby
*Ball Bounce
*Peek-a-Boo Board

Soft Blocks
Easy Touch Tape Player
Humpty Dumpty
   Comeback Roller
Pat Mat
Play N' Go Round
*Magnets on a Cookie
Sheet
*Hide the Cheerio
Rings on a Cone
Hide Inside
Bead Frame
Snuggle Time Book
Balls
*Stacking Cups
*Picture Book

VOCABULARY AND CONCEPTS

The following list will give you an idea of the vocabulary and concepts that your child has been exposed to during this first year:

- action words (push, turn, slide, dial, fly, flutter, fill, pour, roll, kick, throw, catch, bounce, fill, dump, crawl, walk, jump, run)
- animal names (sheep, horse, kitty, puppy, rabbit, bear)
- baby's belongings (cup, bottle, high chair, playpen, crib, spoon)
- body and facial parts (eyes, nose, mouth, head, tummy or stomach, arms, legs, fingers, toes)
- child's name
- clothes (pants, shirt, hat, sweater, shoes, socks, mittens, coat)
- colors (black, white, red, green, blue, yellow)
- common familiar objects (fruit, toys, foods, instruments, balloon)
- daily activities (play in crib or playpen, riding in a car, going to the doctor or therapist, taking a nap, taking a bath)
- descriptions of animals (fluffy, has tail, hops)
- emotions (happy, sad, laugh, cry)
- familiar television characters (Big Bird, Ernie, Barney, Baby Bop, Thomas the Tank Engine)
- family members' names
- goodbye
- hello
- lullabies
- materials (corduroy, satin, felt, plastic, cotton)
- more animals (cow, duck, fish, squirrel, goat, owl, bird, turtle)
- more colors (orange, purple)
- names of everyday activities (change diaper, bath time, meal time)
- opposites (up/down, in/out, on/off, back/forth, sleeping/awake)
- shapes such as round and square
- size discrimination (small, smaller, smallest, big, bigger, biggest)

BOOKS

It is never too early to introduce books as a quiet activity before bedtime. Usually bedtime is not a problem at this age, but it is a nice ritual to begin.

You will find that your child is much more interested in sitting still for a quiet session of book reading now than when she was younger. She will not be able to follow a

complicated story, but will enjoy pointing to pictures and perhaps naming a few in some of the early picture books.

A word here about the format of books for this age. If you are reading to your child, then any kind of book will do. However, if you want her to participate in the activity, you might want to use books with sturdy cardboard pages that are easier for her to turn. These are also nice for her to explore on her own.

ABC: An Alphabet Book. Thomas Matthieson. New York: Platt and Munk. 1966.

Photographs of common objects that will be familiar to a young child. A is for apple, B for Balloons, G for guitar. The photos are clear with only one to a page. The facing page has the letter and a brief paragraph using the word.

Animal Alphabet Book. Bert Kitchen. New York: Dial. 1984.

Large letters match with corresponding animals.

Animal Picture Book. New York: Platt and Munk. 1968.

A board book with large photographic pictures of familiar animals, one to page. The animals are a squirrel, goats, ducks, rabbit, kitten, owl, puppies, parrot, fish, cat, and turtle. The pictures are labeled with the word. Lots of opportunity here for talking about the animals' features.

Animal Signs. Debby Slier. New York: Checkerboard Press. 1993.

Sturdy board pages show 14 animals and the sign language equivalent for each one.

Babies. Gyo Fujikawa. New York: Grossett and Dunlap. 1963.

Board book showing babies being washed, changed, eating, laughing, crying. Babies enjoy seeing pictures of others just like themselves.

Baby's First Cloth Book. George Ford. New York: Random House. 1970.

Cloth book which your baby cannot rip, with pictures of everyday objects.

Baby's First Words. Lars Wile. New York: Random House. 1983.

Board book of photographs of clothes, objects, and actions in a young child's life.

Baby's Things. New York: Platt and Munk. 1978.
Photographs of familiar objects.

Baby Talk: A Pillow Pal Book. New York: Platt and
Munk. 1982.
A soft plastic book that can be chewed, put in the bathtub, and played with. Opens up into one long mural
showing pictures of babies at play.

Black on White. Tana Hoban. New York: Greenwillow
Books. 1993.
Beautiful photographs of everyday objects in black, sil-
houetted against a white background. Babies love this
book.

Board Books by Sandra Boynton. New York: Little Si-
mon/Simon Schuster.
This set of board books, which includes *Horns to Toes*
and *In Between,* introduces your child to animals, colors, parts of the body, and daily objects.

Early Words. Richard Scarry. New York: Random House.
1976.
Cardboard pages with little clutter. The objects are
easily recognizable. The objects are of daily activitIes
of waking up, washing, dressing, eating, playing, and
bedtime.

Faces. Barbara Brenner. Photographs by George Arizona.
New York: E.P. Dutton. 1970.
Pictures of many faces showing features that are all
the same but illustrating that we all look different. Introduces the senses that we use with the facial features.

Family. Helen Oxenbury. New York: Wanderer Press.
1981.
This is a board book that talks about members of the
immediate and extended family.

Goodnight Moon. Margaret Wise Brown. New York: Harper and Row. 1977.
A classic tale for young children in which the little
mouse says goodnight to all the objects in the bedroom and also to the moon. An all-time favorite with
children.

Hush Kittens. Emanuel Schongut. New York: Little Simon Books. 1983.
Two little cats making different sounds, such as crack-
ling leaves, popping balloons, breaking dishes, ripping
paper.

I Hear. Lucille Ogle and Tina Thoburn. New York: American Heritage. 1970.

> Same format as the *I Spy* book with these pictures showing sounds that different things make. Some sounds may be out of a young child's realm of experience but the sounds are fun to practice for speech sounds.

I Spy. Lucille Ogle and Tina Thoburn. New York: American Heritage. 1970.

> Clear photographs of familiar objects such as toys, food, pets, clothes. A fun book for naming, guessing riddles, and playing "I Spy."

Let's Eat. Gyo Fujikawa. Japan: Zokeisha Publications, Ltd. 1975.

> Shows children of various nationalities eating different kinds of food—peanut butter and jelly, pizza, a drumstick, an apple, whatever.

The Me Book. John E. Johnson. New York: Random House. 1979.

> A cloth book that names different parts of the body. Baby will enjoy pointing to his own parts as you show them in the book.

The Me I See. Barbara Shook Hazen. Illustrated by Ati Forberg. New York: Abingdon Press. 1978.

> In a lovely, rhymed text, parts of the body, senses, and functions of each are shown.

My Animal Friends. New York: Grossett and Dunlap. 1981.

> A board book with pictures of familiar animals.

My Back Yard. AnnE and Harlow Rockwell. New York: Macmillan. 1984.

> Shows pictures of objects in the yard such as trees, birds, laundry drying, sprinkler, sandbox, and swing.

My Feet Do. Jean Holzenthaler. Photographs by George Ancona. New York: E.P. Dutton. 1979.

> Photographs of a small girl's feet showing left and right, walking, running, and hopping.

My First Soft Learning Books. New York: Nasta.

> These are plastic tub books. One talks about numbers and the other about letters of the alphabet.

My Hands Can. Jean Holzenthaler. Illustrated by Nancy Tafuri. New York: E.P. Dutton. 1978.

> Shows the different things that hands can do. They can button, zip, do good things, can hurt, and can show others how we feel.

My Picture Book. New York: Platt and Munk. 1968.
> This is a board book, showing pictures of cups, spoon, zipper, gloves, house, umbrella, telephones, clock, balls, cookies, pencils. Some of the pictures are a little old-fashioned, but they are good for expanding baby's knowledge.

My Shirt Is White. Dick Bruna. New York: Methuen. 1984.
> A simple book about color. There is one item of clothing and one color on a page.

My Toys. Dick Bruna. New York: Methuen. 1980.
> A board book that folds out to show toys that will be familiar to baby.

Pat the Bunny. Dorothy Kunhardt. Racine, WI: Western Publishing Co., Inc. 1968.
> A hands-on touching book with activitIes for babies to do: play peek-a-boo, pat the soft cotton on the bunny, look in the mirror, feel daddy's scratchy face, read a small book, put a finger through a ring, and wave bye bye. A long-time favorite that will interest young children for many years.

Pat the Cat. Dorothy Kunhardt. Racine, WI: Western Publishing Co. 1984.
> A brother and sister play with their cat, shop with Daddy, eat snacks, and prepare for bedtime. Scratch and sniff labels, textures to feel, flaps to lift, and things to move.

Playing. Helen Oxenbury. New York: Simon and Schuster. 1981.
> Simple pictures of babies with different toys such as a block wagon, drums, books, teddy bear, and sitting in a box.

Say Goodnight. Helen Oxenbury. New York: Macmillan Publishing Co. 1987.
> Gorgeous pictures and lovely rhyming text to accompany pictures. Will help lull your baby to sleep.

Spot's Toys. Eric Hill. New York: Putnam. 1984.
> Vinyl book that can go in the tub with pictures of the little dog Spot, playing with toys.

Touch Me Books. P. and E. Witte. Illustrated by H. Rockwell. Racine, WI: Golden Books. 1961.
> Different textures such as sponges, wood, and furry things on each page.

What Do Babies Do? Debby Slier. New York: Random House. 1985.

> A board book with pictures of babies doing everyday activities such as sleeping, eating, looking in a mirror.

What Is It? Tana Hoban. New York: Greenwillow Press. 1983.

> Excellent photographs of everyday objects in a baby's life.

White on Black. Tana Hoban. New York: Greenwillow Books. 1993.

> Horse, baby bottle, sailboat, on a black background.

Word Signs. Debby Slier. New York: Checkerboard Press. 1993.

> Objects babies are familiar with are pictured along with the sign language equivalent for each one.

SUMMARY OF YOUR CHILD'S FIRST YEAR (0–12 MONTHS)*
LANGUAGE

Developmental Milestones	Date Achieved	NOT YET	PROGRESSING
cries to express needs			
makes vowel-like cooing sounds			
responds by smiling to friendly faces			
turns to sound			
laughs out loud			
vocalizes when spoken to			
uses her voice to express needs			
babbles several consonants			
"talks" to toys			
"talks" to mirror			
responds to name			
stops action when "no" is said			
waves bye bye			
nods head for "yes"			
responds to "yes/no" questions			
enjoys music and rhymes			
one or two words			

* *This chart lists skills acquired by babies who have reached the **developmental** age of twelve months. Children who have developmental delays may be chronologically several months to several years older before they acquire these skills.*

PHYSICAL

Developmental Milestones	Date Achieved	NOT YET	PROGRESSING
follows a moving person			
follows a moving object			
focuses on hands			
brings hand to mouth			
can hold on to rattles			
plays with fingers			
plays with hands			
can move object from one hand to another			
can crawl			
can sit alone			
can clap hands			
can drink from a cup			
can roll a ball			
can creep upstairs			
can walk with one hand held			
can walk alone			
moves body to music			
can build a tower of blocks how many?			
can put objects into containers			
can dump objects out of containers			
can pick up small objects			

COGNITIVE

Developmental Milestones	Date Achieved	NOT YET	PROGRESSING
responds to visual stimulation			
responds to touch stimulation			
responds to sound stimulation			
focuses on faces			
discriminates between family and strangers			
enjoys being with people			
raises arms when told "up"			
responds to name			
discriminates between friendly and angry voices			
understands bye bye			
can follow a single direction 　　"come here" 　　"stand up"			
has exposure to colors 　　red 　　green 　　blue 　　yellow 　　black 　　white			
has exposure to facial parts			
has exposure to vocabulary 　　of textures 　　smooth 　　scratchy 　　bumpy 　　rough 　　soft			

The Second Year

Twelve to Twenty-Four Months

TWELVE TO FIFTEEN MONTHS

During this developmental period, you will begin to see your play with the dialogues pay off. Your toddler understands more and more of what you say. He should be able to go and get an object that you ask him for, such as his ball or doll.

> "Bring me the doll. Good! I'll put the doll on the shelf. Now get the big giraffe with the long neck. He goes on the top shelf because his neck is so long. Can you reach the top shelf or shall I lift you up? Oooooo, he's tall and so are you. Up it goes. Now, we have all of your nice toys ready to go to sleep and ready to play with you tomorrow. Let's choose our story now. . . ."

It is fun to listen to a child of this age with a toy telephone because you will hear him using your tones and your inflections. Once you have realized how easily your child can imitate tones and inflections, you will want to pay attention to how you use your voice with him. Your tone and your inflections carry a lot of meaning for him. He will need to learn to understand your tones of love and caring as well as the tones you use when you disapprove of his actions. While he is learning to communicate, walk, and interact with you, he is also learning about his feelings. You can teach him about his feelings by telling him how you feel at different times. Repeat in meaningful ways how much you love and care for him, your pleasure in him, and your joy in being with him. Communicating feelings of love will help him to grow with confidence and self-esteem.

Physically, your child will be on the go all of his waking hours. Be sure to encourage his participation in cleanup time. Make this a ritual before bedtime or whenever it is convenient for you. If you join him in the clean up and make it a language-learning time, it will be enjoyable for both of you.

Push and Pull Toys

This is an active period for your toddler. If he is physically able, he will be up on his feet during this time. He probably will be able to push toys forward before he will be able to pull them with a string. If he has physical delays, however, pulling may be much easier than pushing. You can ease things for your child by adding a large bead or ring to the string to enable him to hold the string.

A fine push toy that most toddlers enjoy is a toy lawn mower. We do not recommend that your youngster follow you along as you mow the lawn because it is too dangerous. However, he can pretend to cut the lawn either before or after you do. There is good language that can be learned from this chore. You can introduce the concepts of "before" and "after" by talking about how tall the grass is before you cut it and how short it is after you cut it. Talk about the need for sun and rain to make the lawn grow. During the week, you can talk about the weather and the effect that it might have on the grass. Your toddler will not have a very good grasp of all of this scientific data, but remember you are building receptive language skills all the time and these are always ahead of his expressive skills.

Your toddler can also help you in the house by pushing the vacuum cleaner with you around the living room. You may have to go back later to actually get the job done but he will feel big and important in helping you with this household chore. Once again you can talk about the carpet being dirty *before* you vacuum and how nice and clean it is *after*.

There are many push-type toys on the market today for your toddler, but one

Single Concept

▼ "It's time to cut the grass because the grass is too *tall*. What makes the grass grow *tall*? The sun makes the grass grow *tall*. The rain makes the grass grow *tall*. The grass is *tall* before we cut it. Now let's get the lawn mower and cut the grass. Will the grass be *tall* after we cut it? No. But the sun and rain will help the grass grow *tall* again."

that we like incorporates three toys in one: The Fisher Price Activity Walker. It can be a push toy for a new walker to hold onto as he begins his first tentative steps; it can fold down and become an activity table; and it can be converted into a stroller for the proud junior Dad or Mom to take a little baby doll for a walk. Since the stroller is the most unique part of this particular push toy we will talk about some language you might use with your child as he plays with this activity walker in this way.

> "Oh, I see you are going to take your little girl for a walk today in the stroller. She likes to ride in the stroller just like you do when we go shopping in the mall. Where are you going today? Really? You're going to the mall also. What do you think you will buy? Some new shoes for your little girl? What a good idea! Bye bye—you push her in the stroller—see you later. . . ."

Remember that whenever you are playing with your child—whether you are following his lead or initiating your own play— you want to allow enough "wait" time to give your child a chance to talk. Sometimes, we are so enthusiastic about putting language in or perhaps even frustrated at waiting for language to emerge that we talk and talk and never give our child a chance to speak. At this developmental age, your child may be beginning to say a few words—be sure to give him a chance to use them! You need to take turns in speaking just as you took turns when he was an infant and you played peek-a-boo with him. All of these turn-taking activities build the idea of reciprocal conversation for your child.

Pop Up Farm

Our children and children we know have always enjoyed pop-up surprise boxes during this developmental age. There are several varieties on the market, featuring different characters underneath the pop-up lids. The one we will share with you is the Pop Up Farm by Fisher Price. Your toddler can carry it about with him with the handle and play wherever he wants. The manipulatives are the same that you find on most toys of this type. There is a dial to turn, a wheel to push, a lever to pull down, and a lever to turn. They each release a box which holds the farmer, a rooster, a cow, and a sheep. Everything is housed in a tractor and barn frame.

This toy provides a lot of language to talk about, as well as good practice for fine motor control with the easy-to-manipulate switches.

One of your first activities might be to see if your child can manipulate each of the switches. If he has a visual im-

pairment, let him gently hold the top that pops up with his non-dominant hand. That way, when he manipulates the switch, the cause and effect will be clear, even if he can't see the toy popping up. If your child is not able to physically manipulate the switches himself, put your hand over his and guide it to the appropriate action.

"Look at the tractor's tire—you can turn it—can you put your finger in and turn it around? Yup—there it goes— around and around and. . . POP! Look who's there. The farmer. Let's see, what's next? How does the wheel work? I see—you can push it and POP up comes the rooster. How about this lever? Can you make it work? That's right—you pull it down and POP up comes the cow. Now there's a latch on the gate— how does that work? You turn it and POP up comes the sheep! You really can work all of the switches— good for you. Put the tops down and you can play again. . . ."

Of course, the animals and the farmer also give you plenty of opportunity for language learning.

"Look under here—this is the Farmer. He's in charge of everything on the farm. Let's see what he is wearing—a big yellow hat—wow! Which animal is this? A rooster—you're right. Can you make the sound of a rooster when he wakes everyone up in the morning? Cock-a-doodle-do! Who's next? You're right. That animal says Mooooo—that's a cow. Look, he's got a little bell. And the last animal is the sheep. Can you make the sound that he makes? Baaaaa. . . ."

Now that you have introduced all of the actions and some of the vocabulary concepts, you can play a game with all of the characters. With your toddler watching, you push down the lids of each character one by one. Say "Bye-bye Farmer, Bye-bye Rooster." All the way down the list of characters. When all of the lids are closed, you can cover all of the lids except one and ask:

"Where is the Farmer? Do you know where he is? Right, he's under this one. Can you wake him up?"

After your toddler turns the dial and the Farmer pops up, you can say:

"Hi, Mr. Farmer. Were you sleeping? Wake up time. Now I wonder who's under this next one. . . ."

Continue until you have all of the characters up again. In this way, you have repeated the words, "hi," "sleeping," and "wake up" four different times as well as action words and the names of the characters. That's quite a bit of language for about five minutes of play time.

Once you have all of the characters up, you can proceed one by one to put them back to sleep.

"Oh, the Farmer looks sleepy. Let's tell him bye bye and put him back to sleep. Bye bye, Mr. Farmer. . . ."

If you control each character by covering the others with your hand, you will be encouraging your toddler to wait for your direction and to curb his impulsiveness. He will also be learning to take turns, which, if you remember, is a very critical part of communication.

You can teach a tremendous amount of language with this simple toy. You'll think of even more fun things to do with it as you go along.

Sesame Street Tub Puzzle

Bath time is a fun opportunity to play and expand language. There are many toys you can find to play with in the bathtub. Often there is hardly room for the baby in the bath because of all the toys. A handy item to have is a net bag to hold all of your child's toys when she is finished with her bath so an adult can have a leisurely bath or shower without tripping on one of her playthings.

The Sesame Street floating Tub Puzzle made by Tyco Toys and distributed through Hand in Hand catalog and many stores is a language-rich activity for you and your child to play with in the tub, in the sink, or in a wading pool. There are five Sesame Street characters that are in different floating devices. Big Bird sits in the middle and centers the float, Bert is in a canoe, Ernie is in an inner tube, Elmo is in a boat, and Cookie Monster is lying on a raft. Each of these objects fits into a corresponding space on the float, making it a shape-sorting kind of puzzle. Each of the pieces can be played with independently.

First of all, you will want to help your toddler learn the names of all the characters. She probably has begun to watch some of them on

Sesame Street so it will help her to remember if you name them for her. After you have told her the names, you may want to ask her to hand you specific figures.

"Can you find Ernie? Where is Bert? Can you give me Elmo?"

Then you will want to talk about what they are sitting in or riding on. This will probably be new vocabulary for her.

"Bert is riding in a canoe. Float Bert in the water in his canoe. See how he floats on the water. Let's get Elmo now. He's in the blue boat. Can you put him in the water? Elmo can float in the boat also. Do you remember where Ernie is? That's right—Ernie is in the white inner tube. Watch how that floats, too. Cookie Monster is lying on a raft—he's just floating around and around. Can you put him in the water with his other friends? Now there's one left—who's that? Big Bird—yes, that's Big Bird. Wow, everyone is floating in the water now."

As you get ready to clean up after the bath, you can have your youngster put the objects back into the float and challenge her fine motor skills with the puzzle portion of this toy.

Balls in a Bowl™

Another toy that can be enjoyed in the bathtub as well as out is the Balls in a Bowl™ by Early Start Child Development Toys and distributed through International Playthings. Filling and dumping is an enjoyable activity for this developmental age and this toy provides endless opportunity to do this over and over. The opening of the Bowl is wide enough to allow the balls to go in easily but not wide enough to pose a safety hazard. You will surely find that this Bowl occasionally has other toys in it as well.

Each of the balls that comes with this toy is an activity in itself. They each have a colorful spinner inside and the slightest movement will create a visual delight for your toddler. He will enjoy playing with the balls alone. If he is walking during this developmental age, he will delight in throwing the balls and then toddling after them. The balls are large enough not to create a safety hazard.

We'll talk more about ball playing in the next section but remember these Balls in a Bowl because they will be used again and again.

Since dumping and filling occupies such a large portion of your child's play time at this developmental stage, let's use that activity for the language for this toy.

"Hi, Ken—let's see what you're doing with that bowl. You're putting the balls into the bowl and whoops—here they come out again. One, two, three—in they go. You're good at putting those balls in. Boom—here they come out again. One's rolling away—hurry, go and get it! Wow—you got that runaway ball and in it goes. In and out—you put the balls in and out. You really like putting those balls in and out of the bowl. . . ."

Push N' Go Train

For your "on the go" toddler, there is nothing more fun then making an object move and then chasing after it. This little train is easy to operate. There are no batteries and no strings to pull. You simply push down on the head of the conductor and off he goes. Your toddler will love

pushing and chasing and pushing and chasing. We did find when we were playing with this toy that it goes further on hardwood or tile floors than it does on carpet. It will go forward on carpet but not as quickly as it does on the smooth surface floor. Tomy also makes this toy as a dump truck and a plane. Any of them will be fun for your youngster.

"Watch me push the conductor's head down—off he goes. "Choo Choo"—there goes the train. Quick—run and catch it! You got it! Push his head down and make it come back to me. Here it comes—choo choo—here comes the train. I got it. Now it's my turn to make it go. I will push the head down and OFF it goes—run quickly—go and get it!"

If your child is not up and about yet, she will still enjoy crawling or rolling to get it. It will encourage her to want to move on her own to get that train. If she is not able to crawl at all, you can still engage in the play with her and move her to where the train goes and hold her hand as she pushes the head down and makes it go herself. If your child has a visual impairment, tie a string to the toy so that she can keep track of where it goes and she can go and retrieve it.

HOMEMADE TOYS

Large Boxes

When you watch your child unwrap his gifts at holiday or birthday time, you may have been amused to see that he loved the boxes the gifts came in almost as much as the gifts themselves. We suggest that you keep some large boxes around for your toddler to play in, on, under, and anywhere else he can get himself into. Our favorite has always been the boxes that refrigerators come in. You can usually check at a new home construction site and talk with the site manager. He can let you know when they will be delivering the home appliances. Your child will enjoy making his box into a play house, boat, car, airplane, and whatever else his imagination leads him to. Your play with him might be like this.

> "Do you want to play in your huge box today? What shall we make it? An airplane? Okay. Do you want to be the pilot or a passenger? Okay, I will be the passenger then. Wait a minute and let me get my suitcase. (This can be pretend or real.) Okay, I'm ready now. I will sit in my seat and put on my seatbelt. Are we ready for take off?"

Encourage revving-up noises in your youngster. He should be able to imitate these sounds. If you have more than one child or a playmate over, you can have other roles to play, such as the co-pilot or attendant. At this age you will be providing most of the dialogue for this play, but remember to pause when you think your child can supply some words.

Hats Galore

Youngsters in this developmental age are just beginning to notice more and more of the world outside of themselves. They enjoy seeing the firefighters, postal carriers, construction workers, and other people in their occupational uniforms. Many toy companies make children's versions of these kinds of play hats but you can start a collection of your own. Start asking around and visiting different places where people work and ask them if you can have one or buy one of their hats. The fire department often has a fire safety awareness day in the Fall and gives out junior-sized fire hats. Have these hats in your dress-up corner and let your youngster pretend to be different people. Also, any hats that you, your friends, and family no longer want will be great dress-up and pretend fun for your child.

"You're wearing your firefighter hat today. Are you off to fight a fire? Will you save the little doggy that's in the house? What a brave firefighter you are!"

FIFTEEN TO EIGHTEEN MONTHS

You will notice your active toddler becoming even more active during these few months. She can climb now, so you need to be careful of dangerous things, not only on the floor but at any other level as well. There is no place that she cannot get to at this time. Safety first. If you think she can't, she will. She is also walking well by this time. She rarely falls. When she is running, she still may fall because her feet tend to get ahead of her. She enjoys moving in time to music.

Your child will also enjoy scribbling with crayons and markers. When buying crayons and markers, get the kind that are rather fat. These are easier for her to hold. At this stage, she will be holding the crayons in her fist rather than as you would hold a pencil. That is fine for this developmental age.

You will want to keep crayons under your control. They often end up being used to decorate walls and furniture. We do not recommend coloring books at this age since your child is most comfortable with scribbling and may be frustrated because she cannot color within lines. She will be able to color within lines by the time she is five. For now, large blank pieces of paper or rolls of white shelving paper are perfect. She may go off the paper, so make sure the surface that she is coloring on is washable or covered with a layer of newspaper.

You will notice that she is interested in helping you when you dress her. She can be most cooperative. She is also very capable of taking off her shoes and socks even though she will not be able to put them back on. Encourage these self-help skills. After all, your goal is to turn your toddler into a full-fledged adult one day. These early signs of independence should be encouraged.

You are still the main source of receptive language building for your child. You'll want to begin to use more specific and descriptive words for things. Talk about how things taste, how they feel, and the sounds that things make. You'll want to talk about shapes, sizes, and colors. Remember that her receptive language is more highly developed than her expressive lalnguage. You can feel comfortable using words like "fuschia" for "pink" and "huge" for "big." Talking about foods in a positive way gives your little one the idea that all foods are acceptable and may prevent some of her "I hate spinach" attitudes. For example, say, "These peas are a glowing green color." Using exciting and descriptive words doesn't mean that you want to bury your toddler in an avalanche of words, however. Keep your phrases directly related to objects and activities around your child.

At this age, you will see a great increase in your child's expressive language. She is making even more rapid gains in her receptive language and you can help her with this by keeping your phrases short. Don't be afraid to repeat the same words over and over; your child learns by hearing the same words again and again. You will probably find that by the time your child enters the next developmental age, she will be understanding and repeating more of those same words back to you.

Listen and Learn Ball™

The Listen and Learn Balls™ by Texas Instruments are a lot of fun for your toddler to play with during this developmental period and later. There are three different balls that all operate the same way. The Farm Animal ball depicts twelve different farm animals and reproduces the sounds they make; the Sounds We Hear ball features twelve everyday sounds in the environment that your child can learn to listen for; the Nursery Rhyme Listen and Learn Ball™ is discussed below.

Nursery rhymes are your child's first introduction to poetry. Children love the rhythm of the lines and enjoy saying the rhyming word at the end of each phrase. We do not suggest that you wait until this age to introduce these wonderful rhymes. You can begin in infancy as you nurse or feed your baby, singing the lyrical tunes of nursery rhymes. By this toddler age, however, your child probably will know some of the words to some of these rhymes and she can sing along with you.

The Listen and Learn Ball™ is easy to operate. Whichever side is facing up, that is the melody that is played. On the nursery rhyme ball, six sides play the music and sing the words to: "Jack and Jill"; "Hey Diddle Diddle"; "Mary Had a Little Lamb"; "Hickory, Dickory Dock"; "Eensy, Weensy Spider"; and "Humpty Dumpty." Additionally six sides play only the music to: "Pat-a-Cake"; "Twinkle, Twinkle, Little Star"; "Rain, Rain, Go Away"; "London Bridge"; "Baa-Baa Black Sheep"; and "Hush Little Baby."

Children with visual impairment love this toy because of the sounds it makes. If your child has some usable vision, you can make the pictures easier to see by outlining them with a black marker. You can also find outline pictures of the objects represented and go over them with black marker to make them even darker. Coloring books are a good source of outline pictures.

Let's use one of the nursery rhymes that just plays music for our language dialogue here. This will give you the opportunity to teach the words to your child and to give her a chance to say the words of the ones she knows. When your child turns the ball, a short melody plays to attract her attention before the actual song begins. This gives you time to see which song it is and to sing the words as it plays.

> "You have your nursery rhyme ball. Let's see which song will play first. Listen, I hear a new song. Can you sing it with me? 'Twinkle, twinkle, little *star*. How I wonder what you *are*. Up above the *world* so *high*. Like a *diamond* in the *sky*. "
>
> Nice singing! You knew some of the words in the song. Let's listen to another one. . . ."

A nice feature of this toy is that when your child does not activate it for a few minutes, it plays a little tune to capture her attention once again. If it still is not played with, a lovely voice says, "Bye Bye" and it automatically turns off.

The Farmer Says—See N' Say

Mattel has remade the classic See N' Say toys. The new ones have an easy-to-pull lever instead of the sometimes frustrating string that was used before. The sounds that it makes are very clear and the reliability factor of it actually saying the one you are pointing to makes it a better toy than the older model. It is an excellent toy for practicing listening skills since it is quite predictable in what you will be listening for. The twelve animals represented on the Farm model are: a sheep, dog, duck, frog, horse, coyote, rooster, pig, cow, bird, cat, and turkey. You operate it by moving the pointer to a specific animal and then pulling the lever. The toy says, "This is a dog. Arf arf." To use this as a listening activity try the following:

> "Here's our See N' Say toy, Carl. Shall we listen to some of the animals? Which one do you want to hear first? The dog? Okay, move the pointer to the dog. Let me show you how. Okay, now it's pointing to the dog. Now pull the lever down. Wow—you are strong! Listen. . . . What did it say? "Arf arf." That's right. . . ."

Continue to play with the toy, supplying the language and having your child listen. Then take turns. First, you take the toy and set it up with the pointer at a specific animal and tell your child to listen carefully and tell you which animal he hears. Then pull the lever down and see if your child can tell you what he heard. If he gets it wrong, turn the toy around and show him what you pointed to and play the sound again.

"Listen, Carl. Tell me which animal you hear. Ready? (Child gets it wrong.)

"Watch, I'll show you—the Farmer is pointing to the duck. The duck says, "quack, quack." Listen again. (Pull the lever with the child watching.) Right, you heard "quack, quack."

Learning to listen for some sounds is not an impossible task even if your child has a hearing loss. It just takes time and patience on your part to help him with this listening experience. Don't continue too long in one session with this intense type of listening exercise. Take a break and just play with the toy while your child is watching and looking and getting lots of positive feedback from you and the toy as well.

Baby Gumballs

Even though your toddler may be up and on the go most of the time, there are still many times when it is fun to sit still for a few minutes and play with an interesting cause and effect toy such as Baby Gumballs (made by Hasbro, Inc.). Toddlers at this developmental age still enjoy the idea of filling and dumping, but this toy requires one more step for the dumping part of the game—the toddler needs to push a lever down to cause the balls to come rolling out of the top. It is not easy to predict which ball will come rolling out so there is an element of surprise as the different colored balls come rolling down the chute. If your child has motor difficulties, this is a great toy for practicing that reaching and pushing motion so necessary for using other toys and, later, equipment.

Baby Gumballs also has the repetitive activity that toddlers enjoy so much at this developmental stage. Your child may put the balls in and out many many times. This gives you an opportunity to put in lots of language. Some possibilities for language learning are as follows:

"All the balls are in the bowl. Push the handle down and let's see what happens. Ooooooo, down comes the . . . YELLOW ball. The yellow ball came down the chute. Push again. What happened ? Yep—now the blue one came down. Down came the blue ball. I wonder what the last one will be? Here it comes—a GREEN one. Look there, Danielle, you have all of the balls now. What shall we do next? I see you putting them back in. The yellow is in, the blue ball is in, and last is the green one."

Your toddler may not remember all of the color names of the balls but your play here is just to put language in and someday it will click and she will be ready to tell you what the different colors are herself. Remember to allow plenty of "wait" time for her to respond with her language or her answers to your questions.

Talking Peek-a-Boo Zoo

There are many electronic toys on the market today and we will talk about some more of them in different chapters as well as in the chapter devoted to computers. This one by Texas Instruments has very good sound reproduction and has interesting activities to engage your child. It is easy to operate so children with motor difficulties may be able to handle the simple levers and dials on this toy. The animals say many different things so it may be difficult for a deaf or hard of hearing child to pick up on all of the language. While you play with your child, however, you can mouth, cue, or sign what the animals are saying.

The animals that are represented on this toy are Emily Elephant, Molly Monkey, Percy Parrot, Barney Bear, Katy Kangaroo, and Terry Tiger. Emily Elephant says, "Peek-a-boo, I see you. I'm Emily elephant. See my big ears." Each of the animals has something similar to say.

Each animal hides under a different-colored hand. When all of the hands covering the animals are up, the toy plays the song, "I went to the Animal Fair." It is only the tune, so if you don't remember the words to sing along, we'll give them to you here.

"I went to the animal fair. The birds and the beasts were there. The old baboon by the light of the moon was combing his auburn hair. The funniest was the monk. He stepped on the elephant's trunk. The elephant sneezed and fell on its knees, but what became of the monk, the monk?"

This is a fun nonsense song that your child will enjoy sharing with you. Remember, if you need to, use signs or Cued Speech along with your singing for your child to get the most of what you are trying to sing to him. Do not stop singing to your child if you discover he has a hearing loss. You would be amazed at what some children are able to pick up from singing. We know many hard of hearing and deaf children who love to sing because they enjoy the rhythm and feel of the music.

After the tune is completed, the voice instructs the child to push the hands down again and the second round of play begins with the voice saying, "She's hiding—can you find her? She's hiding under the (color) hand?" This guessing game is a lot of fun for your toddler. Help him find the right ones if he seems a little confused or frustrated.

An important thing to remember with this and any other toy that may frustrate your child is: don't stay with that toy. Just because it is in a particular developmental age does not necessarily mean that your child will find it interesting at the same time. You can put it away and try it again weeks or even months later.

The visual interest is very high and your child will play with you and this toy for quite a long period of time. It has the same elements of surprise as the Pop Up Farm but adds the electronic speaking feature as well. You can also talk about the colors of each of the hands that the animals are hiding under. This toy adds several new colors such as purple and orange to expand your child's knowledge of colors.

Since this toy operates with batteries, it is very nice that it shuts off automatically when it is not being used.

Bubbles

Bubbles are great fun at any age. They are a wonderful speech practice tool. Toddlers love to chase the bubbles and we have found that it may be the only way to elicit "voice" from some children as they get into the carefree "pop pop" of popping the bubbles. You can buy bubbles very inexpensively at lots of stores. Once you have the container and the bubble wand, you can continue the fun by mixing your own bubble solution in the same container. To make your own bubble solution, mix one cup of water with ¼ cup dishwashing liquid detergent and a teaspoon of sugar. You can also use pipe cleaners and bend them into the shape of a wand.

At first you may want to blow the bubbles yourself. Small children often lack the breath control to do it themselves. They will enjoy running about and popping the

bubbles. Try having your child imitate the word "pop" as she pops the bubble. As in any speech game, accept whatever sound she gives you and model the correct way for her. Give her the opportunity to try to blow the bubbles also. When she blows too hard, take her arm and blow gently on it. She will feel the difference between a gentle stream of air and a hard one. You will just love seeing her face the first time that she is successful at getting a good stream of bubbles out.

We have never seen a child who was not fascinated with this activity. You may also find that your older child will enjoy blowing bubbles with her younger brother or sister.

Besides helping your child learn breath control and to use her voice, you can also introduce the ideas of *all gone* and *disappeared* as the last of the bubbles drifts away. Talk about how the bubbles go "up up up" and then back "down down down." If you blow some bubbles for her she might enjoy blowing them away with her own breath. This is a great exercise for any language delayed child who needs some work on getting more breath behind some of her sounds.

If your child has a visual impairment, blowing bubbles is a good activity to encourage visual tracking. If she has a significant vision loss, however, remember that she will not be able to follow the bubbles much beyond 8 to 12 inches.

✋ **A NOTE ABOUT SAFETY:** Be careful that your youngster does not swallow the bubbly water as she puts her mouth close to the wand to blow it. Do not leave her unattended with the jar of bubbles. You also may want to blow bubbles outside or on a floor that can be mopped. It is inevitable that the bubble mixture will spill! Even if it doesn't spill, if you play for a long time, you will have a soapy film on the floor and furniture.

Blocks

Most children enjoy playing with blocks. We talked about soft blocks in the six-to-nine-month-old section and now your child should be ready to build interesting structures or simply to pile up blocks and watch them tumble down. Because toddlers like to do this latter activity so much, we recommend saving the wooden blocks for later and using easy-to-handle, lightweight cardboard blocks for now. Many companies make these types of blocks and they can be found in most toy stores. They are very sturdy—so much so that even an average-weight adult can stand on them and not break them. At the same time, they are light enough to be lifted easily and, most importantly, will not injure anyone when they topple.

Your child may build a structure large enough to play inside with different toys, perhaps small cars or dolls. The blocks can become a house, a fort, or whatever his imagination wants it to be. Follow his lead and join in the play in whatever direction he wants it to go. Whatever he builds, give him the language he needs and be sure to listen for the language he wants to use himself.

"You're playing with your blocks today, Tommy. Wow—you have them stacked up really tall. Ooooo, down they come. They fell all around us. Can you build them up again? Let's count them—one, two, three, four, five. Can you reach higher? Do you need some help? Here I'll put one up higher. Look out— they're awfully wobbly. Down they come—all around us on the floor. Now you're making a row of blocks. Look, you can make them go around in a circle, then you can sit inside. . . ."

HOMEMADE TOYS

Funny Bath Buckets

Single Concept

▼ "*Pour* some water into this bucket with holes in the bottom. Look what's happening. It's coming out the bottom in little sprinkles. *Pour* in some more. Sprinkle it all over yourself. It feels sort of tickly, doesn't it? Now let's *pour* some in this other bucket. Oooooo—it's coming out the side. I wonder why?"

We have talked about how much fun it is for the toddler to fill and spill. This interest can carry over to the bathtub, sink, or outdoor wading pool. We suggest making buckets that will build on your child's interest in pouring.

Use two-pound plastic deli containers from your supermarket. Make several small pinholes in the bottom of one container—this will make a sprinkling type of bucket. In another, cut a hole in the side of the container near the bottom and your toddler will see that the water comes out of the side! For a third, you could cut a hole in both sides and the water will pour out both sides, amusing the little scientist to no end! Leave the fourth one as it is and just use it for regular pouring and for filling the others.

Styrofoam Boats

Save the styrofoam plates that fruits come on in the supermarket. Wash them well with detergent and let them air dry. Then cut a triangle from a piece of paper, stick a toothpick through it, and stick it into the styrofoam to make a boat.

You can use these boats for practicing blowing skills, which can help teach your child breath control. You can float the boats in a tub, sink, or outdoor small pool. You and your child can have a race with each other, each of you blowing your boat to the finish line. Sometimes, it helps a young child to direct her breath if you have her use a straw to blow through. That will concentrate whatever breath she has in a straight line. Some children find this fun and get better results than just blowing wildly about.

> "Do you remember when we made the little boats this morning, Katie? Let's float them in the sink. I'm going to blow on mine and make it move. Can you blow on yours, too? Let's have a race and see who can get to the other side of the sink first. Ready, set, go!"

EIGHTEEN TO TWENTY-FOUR MONTHS

As your toddler nears the developmental age of two years, you will notice an incredible leap in his expressive language. If you remember our discussion on language development, we talked about how he may comprehend approximately three hundred words and use approximately fifty words by the end of this time frame. All of the hard work that you have put in will be worth it as you hear him come out with more and more recognizable words.

This is where your months of playing imitation games will begin to make sense. You don't want to correct your child when he says phrases incorrectly or uses the wrong tenses of verbs. What you want to do is model the correct way to say them and hope that he will want to imitate you. When he says, "car go me," you say, "You want to go in the car? Okay, we're leaving soon."

Remember that you are continuing to build your child's receptive language at the same time that you're admiring his growing expressive language. Reading books, playing with him and with his toys, and using descriptive and novel words are great activities for this age. While you are looking at books together, involve him in the "telling of the story" by asking him to supply the endings to familiar sentences in a story. We know a youngster of this age who was "reading" the Madeline books because of the rhyme and repetitive nature of the story.

His love of jumping at this age may spell big trouble for your bed and his. Do you have an old mattress? Put it in his playroom and let him jump about to his heart's content. Put his indoor slide next to it so he can slide down onto a soft place. Having an indoor slide gives you a lot of opportunity for language input of action words and prepositions like "up," "down," and "under." He is ready to learn this now and you can count on his love of active play to stimulate his interest in this type of language development.

Outside, he needs a fenced area or you need to supervise him closely. This is the time when you can begin talking about safety regarding cars and setting limits of where he can play. Don't expect him to follow these rules without supervision. He is endlessly curious and may set off in any direction at any time. If you have a driveway, tell him that he can go to the end of the driveway and stop. You may want to put some type of barrier up there to visually remind him. You can line your trash cans up across the drive. If you have a sidewalk in front of your house or apartment, he can play on *your* sidewalk but not the neighbors'. Once again, a trash can at either end of the boundary will help to remind him. If he moves beyond those boundaries, you will be there to gently remind him of the rule.

Take advantage of his energy level and take a trip to the park. There you'll find many physical activity toys such as slides, swings, and seesaws which provide great opportunity for language building. We urge you to use the language that you think of as you push your child up and down on the swings and as he goes way up in the air on the seesaw or round and round on the merry-go-round.

"You want to go on the swing now? Okay, up you go. Let's put this bar down so you don't slip out. Here we go. (If this is a new experience for your child, stay in front of the swing and gently push it back and forth.) You're swinging now. The swing goes back and forth, back and forth. You're swinging. Back you go and foward you come. Back and forth. You're swinging! Do you want to go higher? Up you go. Down you come. Up and down."

"This is the seesaw. When you go up, Johnny goes down. (If this is your child's first time on the seesaw, stay on his side with him. If you have no playmate for the other end, you can make it go up and down by pushing him down and lifting his side up.) Here you go, up in the air. Look how high you are. You are up in the air. Shall we go down? Down, down, down. Now you are back on the ground again. You came down. Do you want to go up again? Up, up, up; way up high. And now it's down, down, down again."

"Let's try the merry-go-round. It goes round and round. (If you're not sure that your child will stay seated, sit with him on your lap and push the merry-go-round with your feet.) Round and round and round we go. Everything is spinning by.We're going round and round and round. Close your eyes. Can you still feel us going round and round? Oooooo, I feel a little dizzy. Sometimes you feel dizzy going round and round. . . ."

Indoor Slides

Many different companies make indoor slides. One word of caution: make sure that the spaces between the steps are either wide enough or narrow enough that a small head cannot get stuck between them. Make sure that it is sturdily built and there are no pieces that could splinter.

The slide we feature here is called the Combo Climber™ by Step 2 Corporation. This company recommends that you use a high bed of mulch under the slide if you use it outdoors and a wide soft mat under it if you use it indoors as an added safety feature.

One favorite teaching activity with this toy is to have a child wait at the bottom of the ladder for you to say "up" as she climbs each step. This is an excellent exercise for teaching your toddler to wait for her turn. When you have done "up" for the steps, have her wait at the top for the command "down." It is fun to expand this game to a stuffed toy or doll. Your child can then give the command to her stuffed friend. This will help her with her expressive language as well as allow her to control the game. When you get to the "down" part of the activity, you can add in a long vowel sound for the sliding part—"ooooo down."

The prepositions "in," "on," "under," "behind," and "in front of" can all be taught using this slide. You can give directions to your child to go under the slide, stand behind it, or in front of it. If your child is afraid to do these activities, you can have stuffed animals go on the slide or in the hole under the slide. You can also kneel in front of the slide and extend your arms to her as she comes down the slide.

If your child is less mobile physically, you can still give her an opportunity to experience this activity. Just make sure you support her as she comes down or under the slide. If your child has impaired vision, be sure to let her explore the slide tactually first. Then she will be familiar with the different parts and feel secure about playing on it. Be sure to give her the language as she does this.

"Do you want to go up the slide? Stand here at the bottom and listen. When I say 'up,' you go up one step. Okay, up you go. Good—wait. Okay, up again. Once more. Up you go. Now you're at the top. Sit down and get ready to slide down. Listen. Okay, down you go. Wheee, down you go. . . ."

It is fun to take small cars or baby dolls and have them ride down the slide also. Matchbox makes many small replicas of different kinds of cars and you can use the appropriate names for each of the cars.

"I have some cars here. Let's put them at the top of the slide. Here's a van and a Chevy. Which do you want? Okay, I'll take the Chevy. Let's make them go down the slide. Are you ready? Go! They went down the slide. Down to the bottom. Shall we do it again? Go and get the cars."

An extra benefit is that the slide is an active toy for a toddler and will help her use up some of her excess energy in a very positive way.

Puzzles

Puzzles range from very simple to incredibly complex. The primary skills that they teach are eye/hand coordination and the ability to visualize abstract shapes. Additionally, for the young language delayed child, they can be used to teach the vocabulary that is on the pieces themselves.

The simplest puzzles have one space per object. Some

are made of wood and have knobs to aid in taking out and putting in the pieces. We recommend the wooden puzzles since they are very sturdy and your child can use the pieces in a variety of other play situations without fear of damaging the pieces. One puzzle-making company, Wind River, deserves special mention. Wind River makes puzzles with children in wheelchairs, on crutches, and using a walker, as well as puzzles featuring multi-ethnic children. The puzzles include a picture of your puzzle with each of the parts marked so that you can order replacement pieces.

Puzzles increase in complexity until you reach adulthood and encounter puzzles with hundreds and thousands of small pieces and very complicated designs. When our children were small, we always had a puzzle out on a table where anyone passing by could add a piece or two. We often sat together at the table and TV was quickly forgotten when we were spurred on by someone finding just the right piece of blue sky. It is a great family activity for people of all ages.

The puzzle we will describe here is made by Simplex. It has nine pieces with one piece per space, and should be manageable by the end of this age category. There are

knobs on the wooden pieces that will help your toddler pick up each of the individual pieces. They have a little dimension to them as well, so they can be stood on end and played with in another play setting as well. This puzzle has pieces that represent various types of transportation. This is excellent for vocabulary building because it will enable us to talk about specific types of vehicles rather than just cars and trucks. The vocabulary in this puzzle is very interesting: a concrete mixer, a dump truck, a cherry picker, a service station with a tow truck, a motorcycle, a van, a four-wheel drive type vehicle, a car, and a sports convertible. You and your child can play with this vocabulary for months to come. He can also use the pieces in his block building to talk about cities and towns and the vehicles in them. Let's base our language lesson on the cherry picker, which is probably the most fascinating and unusual item on this puzzle.

(First name or have your child name all of the various types of vehicles—forming the foundation for your play.) "Dan, let's take out the cherry picker. Which one is that? Good, you found it! The cherry picker can go very high up in the air. See how it expands and goes higher and higher? The worker is going to fix the lightbulb in the street light. Do we have a street light like that? (Go to the window and look.) Maybe one day a cherry picker will come to our neighborhood to fix our lightbulb. Look at the blue supports on the truck. I wonder why they're there. You're right—it gives support to the truck so when the cherry picker goes way up high the truck won't topple over. . . ."

Once you have played with this puzzle a few times and you feel confident that your child knows the names of the pieces, you can line them up and have him choose the one that you say and he can fit it back in the puzzle. Take turns and have him ask you for certain pieces and you put them back in the puzzle as well.

As we mentioned before he can take these pieces out and use them in his construction activities with his blocks and they can be pieces for the city streets.

Puzzles, particularly wooden ones, can last through many months or even years of playtime. We know a little girl who liked to dump all of her puzzle pieces in the middle of the floor, line the boards up, and go around fitting the different pieces into the different puzzles.

Peek-a-Boo Stacker

We've talked about how much youngsters enjoy stacking and knocking down objects. This toy made by Fisher-Price, Inc. provides a more sophisticated stacking opportunity as well as lots of language to be explored with your toddler. It has an element of magic and surprise in it.

There are four colored stackable cups and each has a white face that pops up as you stack the cups. Two of the faces have smiles on them, one has a look of surprise, and the other is winking. What interesting language to share with your toddler.

Language to be explored includes:

- **colors:** red base, orange cup, blue cup, green cup, yellow cup
- **sizes:** small, smaller, smallest; big, bigger, biggest
- **facial expressions:** smiling, happy, winking, and surprise
- **prepositions:** up, down, in, inside, top, on top of
- **action words:** put it on, take it off, disappeared

Your child should be able to stack these by himself because they go together very easily. At the beginning of this developmental age, however, he may not be able to get the order of the stacking exactly right. Let him explore and help him as he figures out the puzzle of how the cups go together. You will both enjoy the new and interesting language you can use to describe this toy.

Form Fitter

> ### Single Concept
>
> ▼ "Let's take the triangle and trace around it. We'll count the *three* sides of the triangle. One, two, *three*. We have a picture of a triangle with *three*."

There are many kinds of shape sorters on the market. This is not surprising, as children enjoy beginning to sort objects and learn the difference between shapes. You can begin with form fitters that only have three shapes: triangle, square, and circle. Later, you can move on to form fitters with many shapes, as in the game "Perfection"™, where players race a timer to get the shapes in. So this learning activity which begins in infancy can continue on for a long while into childhood and even adulthood.

The shape sorter we will talk about here is made by Playskool. There are six sides to this shape sorter and three objects fit into each side. Each side of the box has a different texture, which matches the texture of the objects

that fit into that side. This feature will not only help children learn textures but also aid children with visual impairments in using this toy. A visually impaired child can feel the edges of the shapes and also have the texture of each object to help him fit it into the proper side. The objects store conveniently in the box.

For a young child, you will want to separate the shapes out and only use one for each side. Six shapes is enough to start with. You can gradually add in more as your child is able to handle more. Once you find the proper hole for each shape, be ready to help your child put the shapes in by guiding her hand with yours.

"Look, Emily, this shape is called a square. Feel it—it has four sides. Let's count them. One, two, three, four. Can you count them now? Good for you. Now where does it fit? Let's look for the hole that has the same shape. It will be on this side because they feel the same. See how bumpy that is. Oh, you found it. That's right. Let's fit it in. Wow, you did it. Let's find another shape. . . ."

Little People® House

Toys that represent real parts of your child's life can be used at any of the age levels interchangeably. The house and objects in it will be fascinating to her and by the end of this age period, she should know the use of most items in the house.

The house that we will describe is made by Fisher-Price and has two bedrooms, a living room, and a kitchen. There is also a garage with a door that goes up and down. Each room has appropriate furniture in it and the garage has a car that goes inside. With this toy, you can talk about the furniture and the function that each serves. Let's do a play scene with the two bedrooms and then you can create your own play with the other rooms.

There are many ways to play with this toy. The way we've selected is to name furniture. Help your child match each piece of toy furniture with the real furniture in your house.

"There are two rooms upstairs. What are they called? That's right, those are the bedrooms. Which one is the bedroom for the little boy (girl?) Okay, that looks like the little girl's room. Can you find a bed for the little girl? Good work. Put the bed in her room. That's where she will go when she is tired. What do you do when you are tired? You're right—you go to bed. Shall we put the little girl to bed? Do you think she is tired? Okay, she can stay up and play for a little while. What else goes in her bedroom? I think she needs a bureau (chest of drawers, dresser) to put her clothes in. Do you have a bureau in your room? Let's go and look at your bureau. Which do you think is bigger— your bureau or the little toy bureau? You're right— your bureau is bigger. . . ."

Continue in this way with each piece that you put into the bedroom. Then move on to the other rooms of the house. You will want to name the furniture for your child and have her make the comparisons between the furniture in your house and the furniture in the play house.

Kitten in a Keg

This toy is a seemingly simple one with numerous possibilities for effective language play and learning. It consists of several barrels of graduated sizes that fit into each other with the tiniest one containing a little kitten. Each of the barrels is a different color, which also helps your child with color recognition and naming.

Hand the barrels to your child and help him shake it. If he cannot hear the noise, he will feel the barrels move inside and you can provide the language that tells him what he feels. If he cannot see it, he will be able to hear and feel the shaking of the barrels.

"I wonder what's inside. Can you guess? (Accept whatever guesses he makes.) Maybe. Let's see if we can find out."

Hand the barrels to your child and tell him to open them up. Most likely he will not be able do so and you will need to help him. The language you will use involves action verbs such as *twist, turn, pull, open,* and, later, *close.*

Put the smallest lid back on the barrel and twist it to close it while talking about your actions. Then you need to put the other barrels back together again. It is unlikely that your child will be able to size them properly by himself at this age. One way to help him is for you to pick out one part of the barrel and have him find the one that matches it. He will be matching size and color. Continue to find the bottoms of each barrel for him as he finds the matching tops. During this whole process, you can keep reminding him that the kitty is inside and is

---

Single Concept

▼ "Let me help you *open* the barrel. I'll twist it. There, it's *open*. *Open* the blue barrel. Can you *open* it? Is it hard to *open?* Good for you. You can *open* the barrel."

▼ "Let's *open* all the barrels. You need to turn the top. Turn it. Can you get it *open?* Shall I help you turn it? Oh look, there's another barrel inside. Listen, do you hear that? I think there's something else in there. What could it be? Let's *open* the barrel. Turn it. Turn the barrel. Well, my goodness, there's another barrel in there. Now we have two. Listen! I hear something else inside. What could it be?"

And so on until you arrive at the smallest barrel and say:

▼ "Look at this last wee little barrel. It is so small. Shake it. Well, I don't hear anything. Is there something inside? I don't know. Shall we look? Can you open it? Can you twist the top off? Can you get it *open?* Oh wow—look at that. There's a tiny little kitten inside. Hi, kitten. Why are you hiding in the barrel? Listen, the kitten is talking. She said, 'meow.' Can you say 'meow' just like the kitten? Oh, the kitten is stuck in the barrel. Maybe she likes it in there. Maybe we should let her go back to sleep. Bye bye Kitten. See you later. . . ."

---

sound asleep now. As you put the barrels on, you can make your voice increasingly softer, encouraging your child to imitate varying intensities. He will need this skill when he is in social situations or school. When his teacher asks him to "lower your voice," he will need to know how to do it.

Another activity that you can do with this toy is to close all of the barrels independently and stack them up from largest to smallest on the top. You can talk about stacking the barrels, putting them *up*, and inevitably watching them tumble *down*.

The language concepts that you will get from this toy are:

- color matching

- stacking the toy

- size comparisons

- nesting the toy

- hiding concepts

- inside of the toy

HOMEMADE TOYS

Mini Sandbox

A toy that is fun to have during this developmental age and many to follow is a "sandbox" that can be used indoors on rainy days. You can make one using a plastic shoebox or container for leftovers. We feel plastic is best because it will hold up longer than a cardboard box. You can vary what you use for "sand." You can use sand, dried beans or rice, or packing foam pieces. The material doesn't really matter and, if you want to, you can even have several boxes filled with different materials. Be sure to cover the surface of the space you are using to help with cleanup at the end of your playtime.

The idea here is to provide a toy that your child can use to:

fill	dump
spill	pile
pour	measure
turn over	find
empty	touch
squeeze	

Your play with this toy may go something like this:

"Oh, it's raining out today. Let's play with your indoor sandbox. Let's go find it. Here's a cup. Can you fill it all the way to the top? Good job, Jeff, the cup is full. You want to pour it out? Okay, pour it out—ooooooooo, all gone now. Now your cup is empty. Look, Jeff, here's a funnel. Let's fill up this milk bottle with sand. Can you fill it half full with sand? Whoops—stop there. It's half full now. You dumped it out. Now the bottle is empty. What shall we fill up now. . . .?"

Your role is to provide the language for the activity that he is involved with by cueing words or repeating them.

✋ **A NOTE ABOUT SAFETY:** Don't leave your child alone with this toy unless you are absolutely sure he will not put the sand in his mouth. This could be a choking hazard!!

Bowling Set

Collect ten two-liter soda bottles. When you have ten, you will have a set of bowling pins. Get a tennis ball and you're ready to play. Leave the bottles empty for your toddler and fill them partly with sand as she gets older and is able to knock them down more easily.

Set the "pins" up in a triangle pattern and let your little one have a go at it with the tennis ball. Don't keep score at this age as the best fun is just knocking them down and setting them up again. To give the ball a little head start, you may want to use a ramp and have the ball roll down the ramp in the direction of the "pins."

If your child has a visual impairment, you might want to use a ball that has a bell in it. These can be found in pet stores and are hard rubber balls for puppies to play with. The jingling will help your child sense the direction that the ball is going in. Similarly, you may want to put some bells in the liter bottles so that when they fall over, she can hear the bells ringing. Be sure to put the tops on the bottles so she won't be tempted to put the bells in her mouth.

"Leslie, let's play with our bowling set this afternoon. Can you set up all the bottles? Great, you've got them all set up in the shape of a triangle. Now you go first and see how many you can knock down. Roll the ball. There you go. You knocked down a lot. Go get the ball and see if you can knock them all down now. . . ."

TOY SUMMARY SECOND YEAR

The following is a list of toys that we have worked with in this developmental year. The asterisk indicates a homemade toy.

push and pull toys
lawn mower
vacuum cleaner
Activity Walker
Pop Up Farm
Sesame Street Tub Puzzle
Balls in a Bowl
Push N' Go Train
*large boxes
*Hats Galore
Listen and Learn Ball
The Farmer Says - See N' Say
Baby Gumballs

Talking Peek-a-Boo Zoo
Bubbles
Cardboard Blocks
'Funny Bath Buckets
'Styrofoam Boats
Indoor Slides
Puzzles
Peek-a-Boo Stacker
Form Fitter
Little People House
Kitten in a Keg
*Mini Sandbox
*Bowling Set

VOCABULARY AND CONCEPTS

The following list will give you an idea of the vocabulary and concepts that your child should be familiar with at the end of the second developmental year:

- action words: topple, fall, swing, pop, turn, push, pull, pour, twist, open, close, sleep, hide, float, fill, spill, turn over, squeeze, dump, pile, measure, touch, find
- colors: yellow, green, blue, purple, orange, red
- commands: bring me; find the; where is; get the; get it; give me the; show me the
- community helpers: firefighter, mail carrier, construction workers, farmer, pilot
- expressions: winking, smiling, surprised, happy

- farm animals: dog, duck, frog, horse, coyote, pig, bird, kitten, cat, rooster, cow, sheep, turkey
- farm equipment: tractor, barn, gate
- names of vehicles: Chevy, van, concrete mixer, dump truck, cherry picker, tow truck, motorcycle, four-wheel drive vehicle, car, sports convertible
- nouns: sun, rain, stroller, tire, wheel, gate, latch, lever, inner tube, boat, raft, canoe, balls, train, airplane, suitcase, seat belt, street light, bed, bureau
- numbers: one, two, three, four, five
- nursery rhymes: Jack and Jill; Hey Diddle Diddle; Mary Had a Little Lamb; Eensy, Weensy Spider; Humpty Dumpty; Pat-a-Cake; Twinkle, Twinkle Little Star; Rain, Rain, Go Away; London Bridge is Falling Down; Baa Baa Black Sheep; Hush Little Baby
- opposites: behind/in front of; before/after; in/out; tall/short; up/down; under/over; high/low; dirty/clean; hi/bye bye; empty/full
- playground equipment: slides, swings, seesaw, merry-go-round
- prepositions: inside, top, on top of, over, under, up, down, out, in
- questions: where, what, when, who
- rooms of the house: bedroom, living room, kitchen, bathroom, garage
- self-help skills: getting dressed; going to the potty, brushing hair; eating meals
- Sesame Street characters: Big Bird, Ernie, Elmo, Cookie Monster, Bert
- shapes: circle, square, triangle
- sizes: small, smaller, smallest; big, bigger, biggest
- TV characters: Barney, Baby Bop, Lamb Chop, Thomas the Tank Engine
- zoo animals: elephant, monkey, parrot, bear, kangaroo, tiger

BOOKS

Your child will enjoy books if you spend time reading with him every day. Books that name things are probably still his favorites. Now he should be able to name more and more of the pictures in his old favorites. He also will be able to follow a simple story plot. Some of the picture books that have no words are also fun. Be sure to keep adding books to your child's library and to make sure books are readily available.

Since animals are of great interest to toddlers, we suggest several zoo animal books. You can read these both before and after you go to the zoo. Other titles you might be interested in also focus on animals. Be sure to choose others that you see in the library when you visit.

Remember the language books that you made a while back? You can take pictures on a visit to a farm or zoo and add them to your language experience books. If you have a Polaroid camera, you can have instant pictures and you can make the book the same day. You also could take advantage of the one-hour photo developing that is available today. At this age when you make a language book, have your child give you the language for each picture. For example, "I had french fries at McDonald's today." Then write what he says. It's wonderful to look back at these books as your children get older.

Animals in the Zoo. Feodor Rojankavosky. New York: Knopf. 1962.

> A beautiful alphabet book that features different zoo animals for each letter. A good book to read both before and after a visit to the zoo.

Ask Mr. Bear. Marjorie Flack. New York: Simon and Schuster. 1971.

> An older book that has withstood the test of time. Its repetitive simplicity has appealed to children through the years. A young boy wonders what to give his mother for her birthday. He asks many animals for their suggestions until he finds the perfect solution.

But Not the Hippopotamus. Sandra Boynton. New York: Little Simon/Simon and Schuster. 1982.

> A hippopotamus stands aside and watches as the other animals interact. Finally he joins in. A nice beginning to social interaction language.

Chicka Chicka ABC. Bill Martin, Jr. and John Archambault. Illustrated by Lois Ehlert. New York: Simon and Schuster. 1989.

> A wonderful alphabet chant book for even the youngest child.

Farm Animals. Nancy Sears. New York: Random House. 1977.

> Large, clear pictures of familiar animals.

The Farm Counting Book. Jane Miller. Englewood Cliffs, NJ: Prentice Hall. 1983.

> Colorful picture book that uses animals on the farm to teach the numbers one through ten. A different concept on each page. A nice way to learn and review the animal names. Halfway through the book, pictures of

the animals are represented and the child needs to count them. Photos are simple, brightly colored, and clear. Numbers and words are bold and easy to read.

Gobble, Growl, Grunt. Peter Spier. New York: Zephyr. 1971.

Delightful pictures of familiar and exotic animals and the very strange sounds they make. Great fun for you and your child to read and imitate together. Good practice for the elements of speech that are just vowel-like sounds.

Good Morning, Farm. Betty Ben Wright. Illustrated by Fred Weinman. Morton Grove, IL: Whitman Publishing Co. 1964.

Beautiful photographs showing the farm dog going around to wake everyone up and say good morning. Told in delightful rhyme.

Guess What? Roger Bester. New York: Crown Publishers. 1980.

Photographs of common animals. The text lists three characteristics of each animal and gives your child a chance to guess which animal they may be talking about. Animals included are horse, squirrel, duck, cow, chicken, and pig. A nice follow-up story after a farm visit.

Hi Cat. Ezra Jack Keats. New York: Young Readers Press Inc. 1970.

Archie's new friend is a crazy cat who causes all kinds of trouble, but Willie the dog teaches him a lesson. Another fine book in the offerings from this author.

I See. Rachel Isadora. New York: Greenwillow Books. 1985.

A beautiful cardboard picture book showing a baby responding to all the things she sees.

I Touch. Rachel Isadora. New York: Greenwillow Books. 1985.

A beautifully written and illustrated book showing a very young child responding to the things she touches.

It Does Not Say Meow and Riddle Rhymes. Beatrice Schenk de Regniers. Illustrated by Paul Galdone. New York: Seabury. 1972.

Rhyming riddles are a fun way for children to learn about the animals and their sounds in a fun way. Learning the negative in a positive way.

Let's Look All Around the House. Photographs by Harold Roth. New York: Grosset and Dunlap. 1988.

A lift-the-flap photo book which teaches your child great language about his household.

Little Blue and Little Yellow. Leo Lionni. New York: Obolensky. 1959.

> Talks about the activities of two friends, blue and yellow, and what happens when they are together (they make green). A fun book to read after you do your playdough activity with your child.

Little Red Hen. Paul Galdone. New York: Seabury. 1973.

> A hardworking hen tries to get her lazy friends to help her bake some bread. Young children get the message easily from this charming story of how they must help if they want to benefit.

Millions of Cats. Wanda Gag. New York: Coward McCann. 1928.

> A charming book that has endured for over fifty years. An elderly couple would like just one little cat to keep them company, but making the decision is hard and lots of fun.

Moo, Baa, La La La. Sandra Boynton. New York: Little Simon/ Simon and Schuster. 1982.

> Lyrical verses about what different animals say.

My Day on the Farm. Chiyoko Nakatani. New York: Crowell. 1976.

> A very simple text describing the sights, sounds, smells, and feelings of being on a farm. A nice follow-up to a real visit.

The Napping House. Audrey Wood. Illustrated by Don Wood. New York: Harcourt. 1984.

> A clever and beautiful book for young children. A cumulative rhyme that adds a variety of sleeping people to the bed until the surprise ending at dawn. The lighting on the page cleverly shows the passage of time as the night turns into morning.

Play with Me. Marie Hall Ets. New York: Viking Press. 1955.

> A little girl makes friends with different animals: a frog, turtle, chipmunk. She learns she needs to sit quietly and wait for them to come to her. The illustrations are simply lovely and endearing.

Rainbow Candles. Myra Shostak. Illustrated by Katherine Kahn. Rockville, MD: KAR-BEN Copies. 1986.

> A rhyming book about every child's favorite activity at Chanukah time, lighting the candles. Teaches the concepts of numbers one through eight. Sturdy board book format.

Sam Who Never Forgets. Eve Rice. New York: Puffin Books. 1980.

> Sam is a zoo keeper who never forgets to feed all of the animals promptly at three o' clock until one day. . . .

Shai's Shabbat Walk. Ellie Gellman. Illustrated by Chari McLean. Rockville, MD: KARBEN Copies. 1985.

> A sturdy book that helps a young boy discover that Shabbat is for resting and sharing.

Sleepy Book. Charlene Zolotow. Illustrated by Vladmir Bobri. New York: Lothrop, Lee and Shepherd. 1958.

> In very few words, the text tells about how and where different animals, including boys and girls, go to sleep. A lovely bedtime favorite.

Snake In, Snake Out. Linda Banchek. Illustrated by Elaine Arnold. New York: Thomas Crowell. 1978.

> An unlikely trio of an old woman, a parrot, and a snake demonstrate different prepositions such as: in, out, on, up, over, off, down, under.

Talkabout Bedtime. Margaret Keen. Illustrated by Harry Wingfield. London: Ladybird Books. 1977.

> A lovely book that talks about every aspect of bedtime. Different kinds of beds, different people sleeping—adults as well as children. Talks about some of the noises you might hear at bedtime and jobs that people have who work at night. As in the other "talkabout" books, there are activities for matching and finding similarities and differences.

The *Three Little Pigs* can be found in many collections of nursery tales. One such collection is *My First Book of Nursery Tales.* M. Mayer. Illustrated by W. Joyce. New York: Random House. 1983.

> A classic tale which young children enjoy. They can join on the repetitive part of the wolf when he says, "I will huff and puff and blow your house down." Many of the modern versions have a more humane ending for the wolf than having him boil in the stew pot. Take your choice of many versions of this classic favorite.

The Very Busy Spider. Eric Carle. New York: Philomel. 1986.

> Different barnyard animals try to distract an industrious spider from building its web. Children can chime in with the different animal sounds that are described here.

The Very Hungry Caterpillar. Eric Carle. New York: World. 1970.

> Several language concepts can be built from this book. Days of the week, metamorphosis of a butterfly, different foods, numbers. An eternal favorite.

Wake Up and Goodnight. Charlotte Zolotow. Illustrated by Leonard Weisgard. New York: Harper and Row. 1971.

> A very lyrical and charming story which begins in the morning and continues through the day into the night. A book of daily activities which your child can identify with.

What Do Toddlers Do? Photographs by Debby Slier. New York: Random House. 1985.

> Beautiful, clear photographs show the everyday activities of young children picking flowers, swinging, climbing, and banging on kitchen pots.

Where's My Baby? H.A. Rey. New York: Houghton Mifflin. 1943.

> This little book has a foldover page on each page. Shows the mother animals and then asks the question, "Where's my baby?" The foldover flap shows the baby animal that belongs to the mother. Gives an opportunity to talk about the actual names for the babies such as calf, colt, and lamb.

SUMMARY OF YOUR CHILD'S SECOND YEAR (12–24 MONTHS)
LANGUAGE

Developmental Milestones	Date Achieved	NOT YET	PROGRESSING
uses jargon			
names objects which ones?			
uses nouns with adjectives—e.g. big truck; little car; red ball			
uses subject-predicate phrases—e.g. Daddy go car			
uses two-word sentences			
can say own name			
knows at least one family member by name—e.g., Mom or Dad			
asks for food at the table			
follows one direction at a time			
hums to music			
imitates your words			
listens to rhymes			
uses pronouns which ones?			
comprehends about 300 words			

PHYSICAL

Developmental Milestones	Date Achieved	NOT YET	PROGRESSING
can walk alone			
can turn pages of book			
can climb stairs on all fours			
can walk sideways			
can pull a toy			
can climb onto furniture			
can feed self			
can undress self			
can scribble			
holds crayon in fist			
can run stiffly			
can build a tower of blocks how many?			

Developmental Milestones	Date Achieved	NOT YET	PROGRESSING
can walk up stairs holding hand or rail			
can walk down stairs holding hand or rail			
can kick a ball			
can throw large ball			
can do single piece puzzles how many pieces?			

COGNITIVE

Developmental Milestones	Date Achieved	NOT YET	PROGRESSING
can point to facial features eyes nose mouth			
follows simple directions Give the ball to me Sit on the chair			
can name several nouns that are familiar objects table bed toy car apple			
can point to pictures showing different action verbs			
can match colors without necessarily knowing the names red green yellow blue			
develops imaginative play			
has longer attention span			
can demonstrate understanding of prepositions in out up down			
understands math concept of "one more"			

The Third Year

Twenty-Four to Thirty-Six Months

The developmental period from two to three is the one in which your toddler strives to become more independent. This period is often called the "terrible twos." A few suggestions might help you ease your way through this time with a little less trauma for both you and your preschooler. One simple tip is not to ask a "yes" or "no" question. If you do, you are more likely to get a "no" than a "yes." A better approach is to offer two alternatives, both of which are acceptable to you. This gives your youngster a feeling of control over her life. Let's look at an example of how this might work. Say, "Would you like to have apple juice or orange juice for a snack today?" as opposed to "Do you want apple juice?" If your child responds to the first by saying, "I want a cookie," you can calmly say, "Cookies are not a choice today. Do you want apple juice or orange juice?" If you are consistent in this approach, you should experience fewer problems.

Consistency is another key issue in handling your youngster. Try to establish a daily routine for her. This does not mean that every day is etched in granite never to change, but, as much as possible, give her a routine that she can latch onto. While toddlers are struggling to become children, they also need the stability of knowing what is happening so that they feel they are in control.

Control is one of the key issues that results in misbehavior from children. Often children want to show that they are in control and parents often give up in frustration or tiredness and the children "win" again.

Keep your youngster active. She will be more likely to demand your attention, fuss, and misbehave if she is bored. This doesn't mean that you need a three-ring circus going all the time, but try to arrange some time during each day when you have a trip to the store or the play-ground or a special trip to a museum. This will give her something to plan for and give you some leverage for keep-ing her behavior manageable. When you do go out, keep your trip short and have a definite purpose in mind.

The two- to three-year-old loves to play rhyming games and she will learn how to use different sounds by playing these rhyming games with you. Running errands in the car is an ideal time for these kinds of word games. Just think of words that rhyme—they don't always have to make sense. A lot of laughter can come from silly sound-ing rhyming words. This is great exercise for all of those speech sounds that our mouth muscles need to learn to say.

This is also a good time to begin teaching your child her full name, her address, and phone number. One mother used a familiar nursery rhyme and inserted her child's full name into the rhyme. Another time, she would add her address or phone number to the rhyme. Using this technique makes it fun and easy for your child to be-gin to learn this very essential information. For example, you can insert your child's name in the song, "Mary Had a Little Lamb" so that it would sound like this:

> "Jenny lives on Jessup Road, Jessup Road, Jessup Road. Jenny lives on Jessup Road at 12604. Jenny lives in Mt. Sinclair, Mt. Sinclair, Mt. Sinclair, Jenny lives in Mt. Sinclair, it's in the state of Maine. . . ."

Your child will love having her own personal rhyme.

Where language learning is concerned, you need to continue the same modeling that you have done before. Use the same idea that she has said to you but say it back to her correctly. She says, "wheel falled off." You say, "Oh my, the wheel fell off your car. Do you need help fixing it?"

At this age, your youngster needs even more time to play alone. Many of the toys we select for this age group are perfect for stimulating your child to create on her own. At the same time, you want to remember that you are helping to build receptive language and expand the language she has.

Duplo or Lego Blocks™

These toys are ageless. We know of youngsters into their teens who still enjoy building intricate models with these interlocking blocks.

The beginner blocks are large, easy-to-handle, and fit together well into tall buildings, long roads, or other fantasies created by your child. There are times when you need to leave your child alone with these blocks as he builds creation after creation. Later, you can sit with him and ask him about his creation. Be careful not to interject your own opinions. Do not say, "Oh, what a beautiful house you built," when, if you wait just a minute, he will tell you that he built a hotel and create stories of all of the people who are staying at the hotel. When you want to use these blocks for "teaching" language, the following ideas will be useful.

The most obvious skill to be taught is color matching and color naming. Take one block of each color—start with only two colors—and put them in front of you. Point to the bucket of blocks and ask him to find another blue one. When you first ask him, don't look at the blocks in front of you or indicate in any way which is blue. You are "testing" to see if he knows. If he picks up the red one or just looks at you and doesn't know which to choose, point to the blue block and say, "Can you find another one that looks just like this one?" If you still don't get a positive response, then pick up the blue block, rummage through the bucket, and make a big deal about finding the one that looks just like it.

"This is the blue one. Now we have two blue blocks. Look, they are the same. See, this one is blue and this one is blue. We have two blue blocks. . . ."

Snap the two blocks together and go on to find another red one to match the one in front of you. When your child is always successful at choosing the right color out of the bucket, you can add more blocks to the game. You should be able to quickly get to where you have all of the different colored blocks in front of you and he is able to make tall towers from them.

At another time, you will want to have your child actually name the colors as you build with them. Ask him directly, "What color is this block?" and continue until he can successfully name all of the colors that you have in your set of blocks. He may have difficulty with the naming part until a little later, but asking him for the information lets him know that you expect him to learn this. Children with no delaying conditions can match and point to the correct colors by this age but often cannot "name" them themselves until a little later on.

Both Lego and Duplo block sets are available with pieces that have wheels on them. Lego has some motorized pieces and Duplo now has a pull-back motor that younger children can use to make their creations "go." You can make moving vehicles which give you the opportunity to talk about *stop, go, wait, fast,* and *slow.* You can talk about how many wheels are on the wagon pieces, and when your little builder has completed a structure, he can use it as a pull toy. If it doesn't have a string attached to the wheeled portion, it is easy enough to get a long shoelace and make your own pull string.

Other concepts you can teach with these toys are:

on the block	take it off
on top of	get another
next to	same
under	different

"Shall we build with your blocks? Here's a blue one—can you put it on top of the other block? Good. You put it on top of that block. Here's another one. Put it next to the block. Good, you put it next to the blue one. Here's another one. Put this one next to the blue one. Now it's next to the blue one. Can you get another block? You got another block. Put that one on top of the blue one. Let's see—we have all the blue blocks here. They are all the same color. All of these are the same. Can you find a different color? You're right! That yellow one is a different color. Can you find another yellow one? Good, those two are the same. Put the yellow block on top of the other yellow block. They are the same color. . . ."

Mr./Mrs. Potato Head™

This classic toy made by Hasbro, Inc. has been around for many many years. Originally created out of plastic, it is now available with a soft WASHABLE fabric body. The fifteen different accessories attach to the head with Velcro. This makes it much easier for children with motor problems to handle the toy themselves. Any place the child sticks the pieces on, they will stay!

We have talked often about body parts and facial parts. Until now, perhaps this has only been part of your child's receptive language development. With Mr./Mrs. Potato Head, you can find out which of these parts your child knows while having a great time playing. Let her create whatever features she wants for this toy and then ask her to name the various parts as you or she points to them.

"Beth, you made a Mrs. Potato Head. You put so many parts on the potato head. Let's see if you can tell me what they are. Great—that's her eyes and her mouth and that one is her nose." (You repeat them only after your child has told them to you.)

Waiting for a turn is also an emerging skill at this age level. You might play a game with this toy when you are ready to put it away by having your child wait while you put away each piece.

"Can you take off the eyes, Beth? Now where is the nose? Good for you. Let's put away the hair now. Where is that pretty flower for her hair?"

Sound and Sight Animal Puzzle™

We love toys that have many different purposes and incorporate different types of play. The next two toys we talk about have multiple features that will keep children amused, help them learn new motor skills, and provide practice with new and old vocabulary.

The Sound and Sight Animal Puzzle made by Battat, Inc., features six animals: a sheep, a dog, a duck, a horse, a cow, and a pig. We have played with these animals before, and, again, this may be a developmental stage where your child is ready to show you what she has been learning all along. The first thing to do with this toy is to identify each of the animals and the sounds that they make. They can come out of the form and stand alone as you identify each one. Underneath each animal is a different shaped button that the animal puzzle piece fits onto. When you push this button, the toy makes the sound of that particular animal. The sounds are very realistic and have good clarity. The six animals fit into the six puzzle shapes. The six pieces also fit together onto the form board.

There is a lot of fine motor coordination practice in this toy as well as the listening and learning language op-

portunities. We'll talk about using it as a listening activity, but remember that it also requires your child to recognize the name of each animal and the sound it makes.

Remove each of the animals from its puzzle piece as you talk about the animal, its attributes, and the sound it makes. Set it up in front of your child on your play table. After all of the animals are lined up on the table and have been discussed, have your child listen as you press each of the shapes and make the animal sound. Your child can then find the appropriate animal and fit it back onto its place on the board. You may want to start with only two, then build to three, and so on as your child gets more skillful at listening and identifying the correct animal.

"Oh, Justine, look at all the animals. Can you tell me their names? Right—a cow, a sheep, and a dog. Listen and tell me which one you hear. (Push one of the shapes that activates the sound.) You're right—you heard the cow. Can you put it back in the puzzle? Great, now there are two animals left. The sheep and the dog. Listen, which one do you hear? Good listening—you heard the dog. Put him back in the puzzle. Okay, here's the last one. Listen for the sheep—what will he say? Right, the sheep says, 'Baaaa.'"

Learning Blocks™

There are six different activities that can be played with these blocks, which are made by Battat, Inc.

The twelve blocks can be formed into two different puzzles: one depicting Humpty Dumpty sitting on the wall, and the other, Jack and Jill. Putting them together can be quite a challenge, so your youngster may need help from you. This gives you a great opportunity to talk about these nursery rhymes, however. Try this with your child:

Jack and Jill went up the _____(hill)

To fetch a pail of _____(water)

Jack fell _____(down) and broke his (crown)

And Jill came _____(tumbling after)

Your child may be able to fill in the blanks since you have probably been reciting nursery rhymes for many months now.

A third side of the blocks depicts twelve different silhouettes of common objects for your child to name. These shapes are recessed, which would help a child with visual impairments to identify the different shapes. The vocabulary depicted represents four different categories: 1) transportation: airplane, boat, car; 2) sea animals: whale, fish, lobster; 3) insects: butterflies, dragonfly, beetle; 4) animals: rabbit, elephant, dog. Some of this vocabulary will be very new and interesting to children in this developmental age. The insect category may be particularly appealing to your child at this age. If you can manage it, go outside and look for these and other insects. It is fun for the young scientist to collect a few and put them in a jar with holes in the lid to observe them up close.

The fourth and fifth sides represent numbers 1–12. One side has numbers, and, like the objects above, the numbers are recessed. The other side has recessed dots representing the numbers 1–12. Again, the recessed area helps reinforce these concepts through another sense modality.

The sixth side contains twelve different shapes. These are the only pieces that come apart from the blocks. There is a storage section on the toy that holds these pieces. Some of the shapes your child will already know from previous shape sorting toys that she has played with, but some may be new to her.

We think this toy will hold your child's interest and provide opportunities for new learning throughout this developmental age and perhaps beyond. It is visually attractive and the recessed items are great tactile reinforcement for learning, especially for children with visual impairments or children who learn best through a multisensory approach.

Little People® Fun Park

Representational toys are great fun for children. They can be used to expose your child to an activity that is going to happen, to provide the language for the things that he will see, and then give you an opportunity to review the language after the activity is over.

Most young children enjoy going to amusement parks and some are able to go on the kiddie rides by themselves and some of the other rides with an older sibling, parent, or friend. This fun park toy can not only prepare your child for the experience, but also give you lots of opportunities to work on action verbs and prepositions, which are often difficult to fit into a play environment.

The Ferris Wheel goes *round and round;* the airplane ride *goes up in the air* and *round and round;* and the roller coaster ride sends the Little People *down and around* the loop-de-loop and *out through* the clown's mouth. Your child can *turn the crank* on the Ferris Wheel and *make it go around and around.* He can put the Little People *in* the seats of the Ferris Wheel and watch as they go *up, up, up, and around.*

Your child can pretend to be the Carnival Barker (there is a figure that represents this character) and you can help him with the language:

> "Come one, come all and step up to the Giant Roller Coaster for a thrilling ride of a lifetime. Get your tickets here!!"

You can then be one of the children who gets on the Roller Coaster (two children come with the set) and go down the Giant Roller Coaster.

> "Yes, I want to ride the Giant Roller Coaster. *Two* tickets, please. *One* for me and *one* for my friend. I want the *red* car. Which color do you want? Let's get in our cars at the top of the giant hill. Here we go—Wheeeeee— *down, around,* and *out* we come *through* the Clown's mouth. I want to go again."

The Carnival Barker fits onto a knob on the airplane ride and your child can make it go *round and round, faster and faster.* He can make the Little People *walk up* the steps and *get into* the plane.

This toy will provide you and your youngster many hours of fun and creative play.

Tea Set

The kitchen sets that are available at toy stores are incredible. Many of the brand names that you might have in your own kitchen are available in the toy department. Our young chefs can have the finest in Pfaltzgraff and Revere-

ware as well as micro-wave equipment. At a later developmental age, we will talk about an Easy Bake Oven™, but at this age, we really feel that you can stop with a tea set. We advise you *not* to take your youngster along when you pick out a tea set, as you may end up with more equipment for her than you have for yourself! She will enjoy whatever you provide for her.

The tea set gives you an opportunity to teach your child the vocabulary for the items that you use for your mealtimes. You can also teach her the correct placement of the items on the table with the fork on the *left* and the knife and spoon on the *right*. Napkin rings for the tea set can be made by decorating a paper towel roll and then slicing it into napkin ring pieces. Your child will enjoy decorating the paper towel roll.

Wonderful table conversations can be created while sitting down to a tea with your child. This might be a time when you can discuss other things that went on during his day. Perhaps you had a visit to a doctor or a therapist that day and you can chat about it over tea. If at all possible, have your tea be something that the two of you have cooked together. Cooking and eating together are wonderful activities for sharing thoughts and feelings.

"Yum, these cookies that we made are delicious. Maybe we should save one to give Diane when we go back on Thursday. This morning when we saw Diane you had to do some interesting jobs for her. Do you remember? You were walking on that straight line right down the middle of the room. You did a good job of staying right on that line. Was that tricky for you to do? It was easy? Well, good for you. It looked very tricky to me."

(child) "I liked walking on that line, but I couldn't catch the ball. I'm mad that I couldn't catch the ball."

"Catching balls can be tricky. I saw how hard you were trying. Maybe when we get finished with our tea, we could play with the ball and you could practice. Then on Thursday, maybe it will be easier for you when you and Diane play ball. Would you like to practice with me?" (As an aside: you can make or buy gloves with Velcro on them and put some on the ball, which will make catching a lot easier if your child is physically challenged.)

(child) "Okay, but it is hard for me. Maybe I can't do it."

"That's okay. Practicing will be fun. If you can't do it today, maybe tomorrow it will be easier. Remember, you didn't always know how to walk on the straight line but we practiced and practiced and now it's not tricky for you anymore. . . ."

Your child may not be able to express all of these feelings, but you should be able to keep up a dialogue with her about her feelings of frustration and how you are willing to help her practice. Bringing up successful moments that you observed in the therapy session will help her see that she was successful with some things, even though she had trouble with other things.

Cars, Trucks, Road Signs

We have come a long way from the days when only girls played "cooking," while little boys dug roads and tunnels for their cars and trucks. We encourage you to provide all of these opportunities for your children regardless of their gender. Mattel and other companies make very realistic replicas of cars, trucks, and many other vehicles. You can teach unlimited vocabulary with these toys. Each rescue vehicle and construction truck has vocabulary unique to that item. You can teach road safety with toy sets of stop signs, yield signs, and traffic lights.

Setting up roads with blocks and moving vehicles are great activities for your child and her friends as well as terrific teaching time with you. Be sure to use the actual names of the vehicles. For those of us who grew up not knowing a bulldozer from a crane, most of the toy packages are labelled and you can learn them with your child. We have been amazed at how many of the names our children have learned already. Each of these types of cars and trucks has different attributes that you can talk about. The function of the construction truck, the way the doors open on the van, the way the top goes down on the convertible, why there are numbers on the racing car are all good opportunities for introducing language.

You can make appropriate vocal noises as you drive the trucks along your highways and squeal the brakes as you stop at the traffic light. As with the house, you may want to make up a story of what the construction people are building and how the different machines help them to do their jobs better and easier. Enjoy yourself and get into the play. If you're a Mom, you may find that you get as much pleasure out of these trucks as your child, perhaps because you never had the opportunity to play with them when you were a child yourself.

The large scale version of the Tonka trucks are wonderful for outdoor play in the sand or the dirt. Your child will spend many hours with these large trucks and they are made so well that they will probably last through your grandchildren.

Creative Pegboard

We like it when toys with small pieces have a self-storage feature. This really helps to prevent the frustration of losing pieces. And if you encourage your child to keep the pieces in the storage pocket of the toy, it teaches organizational skills. With this pegboard made by Fisher Price, Inc., the pieces fall directly into the storage bin when you "erase" the board by pulling the lever. The pieces are then ready to play with again or to be put away. This toy provides language learning opportunities, as well as practice with fine motor control as your child puts the pieces into the pegboard and then pulls the lever to release the pieces.

The set includes all the shapes that your child is already familiar with—circles, squares, and triangles—as well as new ones such as arches and rectangles. Let your child play freely with the shapes, creating whatever pictures he wants, while you supply the language when he needs it and encourage him to talk as he plays. Do not predetermine what his picture is; let him tell you what he is creating. Then if he needs help with certain words or phrases, you can supply them for him. This is called expansion of language. For example, he may say: "Train going bye bye," and you might model correctly, "Yes, you go on the train when you go to see Grandpa. We say 'bye bye' to everyone and get on the train. Where is your train going today?"

If your child has fine motor problems, putting the pieces in is good practice. The holes are fairly large and the pieces fit very easily. The lever is also easy to pull down. Your child should have fun being creative with this fine toy.

HOMEMADE TOYS

Flannel Board

A flannel board is a toy that you will use over and over again. It is very simple to make. You need a backing for the flannel. You can use a piece of plywood, a piece of wallboard, a piece of styrofoam, or even a cardboard box. A cardboard box is nice because it is light and can stand on its own. You can keep your flannel pieces in the box when you're not using it for play.

A word about the "flannel." You do not need to use flannel per se. Any material with a nap to it that will allow other pieces to adhere to it will work quite well.

To make the board, all you need to do is cover whatever you have decided to use with your "flannel." If you use wood for the frame, you will need to glue or staple the material to it. With other lighter materials, you can use wide masking tape, glue, or staples.

Once your board is made, you can begin to create materials made out of the same type of fabric—anything with a nap that will stick to it. You can cut out numbers, letters, shapes; just about anything that you would like to teach your child about. If you are not good at drawing, coloring books are a wonderful source of pictures. For example, you can get coloring books that have fairy tales with nice, simply drawn pictures. Trace the picture onto the fabric and cut out the figures. Then you can add the subtle features with magic markers.

Let's assume you're going to do a fairy tale story. You have made all of the story pieces for the story of Goldilocks and the Three Bears. You introduce the story with a book and then take out your characters and you and your child retell the story using the characters you have made. Your child will have great fun remembering the story and imitating the characters. Her retelling may not be exactly as the story goes but she will have great fun acting it out.

The child with partial vision will be able to feel the outline of the shapes, and, with high contrast colors, may be able to see the pieces. Before you tell the story, introduce each of the characters to your child and let her explore the object. Give her the language for what she is seeing and feeling.

Bat the Balloon

You can make a very active game for your child to play with you now and with his friends later. Take two wire hangers and bend them into the shape of a square. (Simply pull down on the middle part of the bottom of the triangle.) Bend the hook part of the hanger down to form a handle and cover with duct tape so that there are no sharp points to hurt your child. Take a knee-high stocking and pull it over the hanger; tape it over the handle with duct tape. Make as many paddles as you have players.

For the ball, get a nine-inch balloon and blow it up. Bat the balloon to your child and have him run, catch it, and bat it back to you.

"Here it comes, Keith. I am batting the balloon over to you. Can you catch it? Get it! Great, you caught it! Now bat it back to me. It's going up in the air and down it comes. Now it's my turn to catch it. . . . "

TOY SUMMARY THIRD YEAR

The following is a list of toys that we have worked with in this developmental year. The asterisk indicates a homemade toy.

Duplo or Lego Blocks	Tea Set
Mr./Mrs. Potato Head	Cars, Trucks, Road Signs
Sight and Sound Animal Puzzle	Creative Pegboard
Learning Blocks	*Flannel Board
Little People Fun Park	*Bat the Balloon

VOCABULARY AND CONCEPTS

The following list will give you an idea of the vocabulary and concepts that your child should be familiar with by the end of the third developmental year:

- action words: walk, run, jump, pull, twist, pour, turn, put, down, eat, erase, open, close
- animals: rabbit, elephant, dog, whale, fish, lobster, butterflies, dragonfly, beetle
- body parts: eyes, nose, mouth, hair, ears
- child's name, address, and phone number
- colors: naming and matching
- expressions: Please, Thank you
- fairy tales
- farm animals: sheep, dog, duck, horse, cow, pig
- farm animal attributes: tail, fur, ears, udders, snout, webbed feet
- farm animal sounds: baa, arf-arf, quack, neigh, moo, oink
- feelings: happy, sad, mad, angry

- mealtime utensils: spoon, fork, knife, plate, glass, cup, mug
- nouns: boat, airplane, car, Carnival Barker, Ferris Wheel, roller coaster, airplane ride, trucks, road signs, traffic lights, balloon
- numbers: one through twelve
- nursery rhymes: Humpty Dumpty, Jack and Jill, Mary Had a Little Lamb
- opposites: up/down; in/out; left/right; fast/slow; same/different
- prepositions: on, off, on top of, next to, under, through, round and round
- questions: what; what's inside; when; where; who
- shapes: square, triangle, circle, five-pointed star, cross, pentagon, hexagon, six-pointed star, heart, arches, rectangle, an "X"
- traffic signals: red-stop; green-go; yellow-wait/slow down

BOOKS

During this time, your child will begin to be more interested in her books. Bedtime reading should be a ritual by now. Many stories she will have heard so many times that she may be able to read them to you. Encourage her participation. Let her tell you the story. You'll be amazed at how accurate she can be. Stories that tell about courage—such as *The Little Engine That Could*—and stories involving a problem to be solved—such as *Corduroy*—are easy for your youngster to relate to.

ABCing: An Action Alphabet. Janet Beller. New York: Crown Publishing. 1984.
> Clear photographs showing kids in action for each of the letters of the alphabet. For example, Dancing, Eating, Jumping.

Anno's Counting Book. Mitsumasa Anno. New York: Philomel Books. 1989.
> A beautifully illustrated book which teaches the concepts of the numbers one through twelve. Each page unfolds to the changing seasons, offering different things to count on each page.

At Work. Richard Scarry. New York: Golden Press. 1976.
> One of a series that focuses on special topics. This one shows various occupations, such as working at home, gardener, tailor, letter carrier, teacher, firefighter, cashier, butcher, baker, carpenter, nurse, dentist, musician, painter, driver, pilot, sailor, airport worker, cir-

cus performer. Great opportunity to introduce a wide range of new vocabulary. Other books in this series are:

> *My House*   *On the Farm*
> *On Vacation*   *About Animals*

The Baby's Catalogue. Janet and Allan Ahlberg. Boston: Little Brown. 1982.

Colorful, detailed drawings point out the numerous objects on each page which tell of the daily lives of young families and their babies. Young children will love looking at the pictures while being introduced to new vocabulary words.

Brown Bear, Brown Bear, What Do You See? Bill Martin, Jr. Illustrated by Eric Carle. New York: Holt. 1983.

A cumulative rhyme that begins, "Brown bear, brown bear, what do you see? I see redbird looking at me. Red bird, red bird, what do you see?"

After several readings of this book, your child will be joining in on the refrains. A few more readings and your child may be "reading" on her own with the help of the pictures and repetitive texts. A favorite with preschoolers.

Caps for Sale. Esphyr Slobodkina. New York: W.R. Scott. 1947.

Classic tale of a peddler who carries his hats on his head and what happens when he falls asleep under a tree full of monkeys. The simple repetitive nature of the story appeals to young children and they shortly know what to say at the right moment giving them a chance to "read" the story too.

Corduroy. Dan Freeman. New York: Viking Press. 1968.

An endearing tale that young children have enjoyed for many years. Tells the story of a stuffed bear who searches through the toy store for its lost button, and finds a friend and a home.

Dear Zoo. Rod Campbell. New York: Four Winds. 1982.

A lift-the-flap book which shows all of the zoo animals who have arrived in various crates. They are different sizes, shapes, and colors, which gives you plenty of vocabulary to talk about.

Great Day for Up. Dr. Seuss. New York: Random House. 1979.

If you ever wanted to focus on a single vocabulary word, this is the book for "up." The catchy and repetitive rhymes make it fun for children to listen to and join in.

Harry the Dirty Dog. Gene Zion. New York: Harper and Row. 1956.

> Harry doesn't want to take a bath. He buries his bath brush, runs away, and gets so dirty that when he comes home, no one recognizes him.

I Can, Can You? Peggy Parish. New York: Greenwillow Books. 1980.

> This book capitalizes on all of the "I can do it myself" feelings of this age. Gives young children an opportunity to imitate simple actions that are shown in the book. For example, wiggling fingers, sticking out tongues, and touching their toes. The pictures of children are multiethnic and help any child identify with someone like herself.

I Can Do It Myself. Illustrated by June Goldsborough. New York: Golden Books. 1981.

> Another example of a book that can help a young child going through the stage of wanting to do everything on her own. This book follows a young child throughout her day and shows all the ways in which she can help around the house and do things on her own.

Is It Hard, Is It Easy? Mary M. Green. Illustrated by Len Gettloman. New York: Young/Scott/Wilson-Wesley. 1960.

> During this stage of wanting to do things on their own, some children may become frustrated with things they cannot do very well alone. This little book pictures children doing things that are easy and some that are hard. It shows that we all cannot do things equally.

Jesse Bear, What Will You Wear? Nancy White Carlstrom. Illustrated by Bruce Degen. New York: Macmillan. 1993.

> This charming story is written in verse and takes the reader through the process of getting dressed in the morning and undressed at night. Gives an opportunity to talk about clothes for different times of the day as well as the self-help skills that young children learn at this age.

Let's Make Latkes. Illustrated by Sally Springer. Rockville, MD: KAR-BEN Copies. 1991.

> Shop, mix, fry, and eat these favorite Hanukkah treats.

Little Bunny Follows His Nose. Katherine Howard. Pictures by J.P. Miller. Racine, WI: Western Publishing Co. 1971.

> To release the non-toxic fragrance labels in the rose, the strawberry jar, the pine needle, the peach, the dill pickle, and the chocolate mint cookie, scratch vigorously. This book can be used over and over and the fragrances last a long time. Great for extra sensory input for any child who could benefit from the additional stimulation. Especially good for children with visual impairments.

The Little Engine That Could. Watty Piper. Illustrated by George and Doris Houman. New York: Platt and Munk. 1954.

> Children enjoy the refrain in this delightful story and get the message that they should continue to try even when they think they can't do the job. This may be especially inspiring for children with special needs who continually need encouragement to try difficult things.

The Little Fur Family. Margaret Wise Brown. Illustrated by Garth Williams. New York: Harper. 1946.

> Classic tale that is redone and covered with a soft fake gray fur. A wonderful day in the life of a little fur family. The Little Fur Child explores through the day and then comes home to his mom and dad, who tuck him in bed. Told in lovely half rhymes.

Mouse Paint. Ellen Stoll Walsh. San Diego: Harcourt Brace. 1989.

> Three little white mice discover three jars of paint—red, yellow, and blue. As they jump in and out of each jar, they discover how to make new colors.

My First Kwanzaa Book. Deborah M. Newton Chocolate. Illustrated by Cal Massey. New York: Scholastic. 1992.

> A young boy and his family celebrate the seven days and principles of this African-American holiday with love and pride.

My Very First Book of Numbers. Eric Carle. New York: T. Crowell. 1974.

> This is a board book which is spiral bound and pages turn from top to bottom so that the child can match the top and bottom halves of the pages. The top has the pictures of a certain number of objects and the bottom has the number.

My Very First Book of Colors. Eric Carle. New York: T. Crowell, 1974.

> This book is the same as the number book, except that the concepts being taught are colors. Fine illustrations by this talented artist.

No Nap. Eve Bunting. New York: Clarion Press. 1989.

> It's time for Susie's nap but Susie isn't tired. "No Nap," she says. So Dad makes plans to tire Susie out. A fresh and humorous approach to a real-life situation.

Noisy and Quiet. Illustrated by Lorraine Calaora. New York: Grossett and Dunlap. 1976.

> The entire book only talks about "noisy" and "quiet" scenes. There are lovely pictures of all kinds of indoor and outdoor scenes with many examples of noisy and quiet on each page. Plenty of opportunity for conversation starters here.

Numbers: A First Counting Book. Robert Allen. New York: Platt and Munk. 1968.

> Clearly illustrated book showing the correct number of objects, one concept to a page. There are pages with one kitten, two eggs, three dolls, four pictures, five cars, six buttons, seven flowers, eight candles, nine blocks, ten cookies. An opportunity to talk about numbers and also to name familiar objects.

On Mother's Lap. Ann Herbert Scott. Illustrated by Glo Coalson. New York: Clarion. 1992.

> A very important story which shows older brothers and sisters that Mom will still have room for them in her life after the new baby arrives. Involves a Native American family.

Push Pull, Empty Full. Tana Hoban. New York: Macmillan. 1972.

> Black and white photographs showing opposites. A great "talk about" book for naming as well as to introduce the concept of opposites. The concepts shownare: Push/pull, empty/full, wet/dry, in/out, up/down, thick/thin, whole/broken, front/back, big/little, first/last, many/few, heavy/light, together/apart, left/right, day/night.

The Snow. John Burningham. New York: Harper and Row. 1975.

> Nice illustrations of all of the fun things there are to do in the snow and then coming indoors and warming up with hot chocolate. A warm book to read while you are curling up with hot chocolate after playing in the snow.

The Snowy Day. Ezra Jack Keats.New York: Viking Press. 1962.

> Another fine book with beautiful illustrations and no text about activities to do in the snow. This one ends with a warm bath after the chilling fun day.

Sunshine. Jan Ormerod. New York: Lothrop. 1981.

> Each moment of a typical day is pictured as the little girl wakes up and gets ready for her day at the day care center. Teaches the concepts of sequencing and the routines of everyday life. The sunshine moves from the little girl's pillow and moves up the wall as the day's events unfold.

Talkabout Clothes. Ethel Wingfield. Illustrated by Harry Wingfield. London: Ladybird Books. 1974.

> Talks about all different kinds of clothes for all kinds of weather and people. How we make clothes, colors of clothes, repairing clothing. Opportunities for the child to be involved with matching different clothing as well as finding simlarities and differences in items of clothing.

Vehicle Books: *Boats, Cars, Trains, Trucks, Fire Engines,* and *Big Wheels.* Anne Rockwell. New York: E.P. Dutton. 1982, 1984, 1988, 1989, 1986.

> Simple text and bright illustrations teach preschoolers about all of the vehicles they may see in their world. A rich array of language opportunities in this series.

The Very Quiet Cricket. Eric Carle. New York: Philomel Books. Division of the Putnam and Grosset Book Group. 1990.

> A multi-sensory book which tells the story of a very quiet cricket who wants to rub his wings together, and make a sound as many other insects do. He finally achieves his wish. Listen for a great surprise at the end of the story! Great self-esteem builder for your child if he is not talking as others his age are at this time.

Where's Spot? Eric Hill. New York: Putnam. 1980.

> A lift-the-flap book which teaches prepositions as Spot's mom looks all over the place to find him.

SUMMARY OF YOUR CHILD'S THIRD YEAR (24–36 MONTHS)
LANGUAGE

Developmental Milestones	Date Achieved	NOT YET	PROGRESSING
uses plurals			
uses noun phrases with articles a ball an apple the door			
uses three-word phrases Mommy bye-bye car			
uses possessive nouns which ones?			
uses pronoun "I"			
asks simple questions who? what? when? where?			
adds "ing" to verbs			
uses past tense for verbs			
uses 4–word sentences			
can say whole name			
can respond to questions with choices			
uses social phrases thank you please			
sings along with music			
outsiders understand his speech			
knows 800 words			

PHYSICAL

Developmental Milestones	Date Achieved	NOT YET	PROGRESSING
Can walk backwards			
can walk up stairs alternating feet holding hands or rail			
can run without falling			
can jump; both feet off floor			
can bounce and catch a large ball			

Developmental Milestones	Date Achieved	NOT YET	PROGRESSING
can pedal a tricycle			
can build a tower of blocks how many?			
can hold crayon not fisted			
can make snips with scissors			
can hold a glass with one hand			
can hold fork in fist			

COGNITIVE

Developmental Milestones	Date Achieved	NOT YET	PROGRESSING
can point to body parts hair tongue teeth hand ears feet head legs arms			
can name body parts mouth eyes nose hair hands ears head			
can match colors orange purple brown black			
can identify colors give me the red car blue yellow green			
can match shapes circle square triangle			

Developmental Milestones	Date Achieved	NOT YET	PROGRESSING

can follow directions that include prepositions
    put the doll in the box
    put the doll under the box			

can demonstrate knowledge of opposites
    little/big
    short/long			

can demonstrate knowledge of use of common objects
    What do we do with beds?
    Why do we have coats?			

develops imaginative play more fully			
able to express feelings			
understands math concept of "just one" Give me just one block			

The Fourth Year

Thirty-Six to Forty-Eight Months

You may be relieved to discover that this can be the "calm after the storm" age. The "terrible twos" has ended and magically your child doesn't seem to have tantrums the way he used to. At the developmental age of three, your youngster has graduated from toddlerhood. He is now quite steady on his feet. And he is much more ready to consider other people's points of view, not just his own. All of these things will happen gradually, not overnight.

Now he can look at books for quite a long period of time. Since he may be in a transition time with his daytime naps, you may have some bedtime difficulties. This is an excellent time to establish a bedtime routine. We suggest a bath after dinner, followed by a quiet game or toy activity. Then bathroom routines are completed, and you end by reading a story to your child, or having him "read" to you. State the number of stories to be read beforehand and then stick to that number. A firm good night with permission to "read" to himself for a few minutes will end your evening with your youngster. Do not be drawn back into the room with pleas of "one more story" or "one more drink of water." Your firmness and consistency are important in order for him to learn limits. Being allowed to "read" for a few minutes gives him the idea that he is in control of when he actually falls asleep. So many of the arguments about bedtime are really "control" kinds of arguments. This compromise solution will avoid many of these arguments.

If your child is not in a preschool program, you might want to consider organizing a play group in your neighborhood so that he can have the opportunity to interact with other children and learn about sharing toys and playing together. You should be within earshot when they are playing together but resist the temptation to step in and solve every problem that comes up. Children need to argue things out. They learn to reason, defend their position, assume leadership, and abandon control through their play at this age.

Your child will have a better idea of the larger world outside his home and may begin to develop some fears. He may be afraid of monsters, or of having you leave him, or of death. Since this is the age when he develops an ability to fantasize, the combination of fantasy and fear can be a potent one. You may have to address some of his fears in your play situations.

Encourage him to share his activities and especially his feelings. You may need to ask questions to spur him on and keep the conversation going. "Then what happened?" "Can you tell me more?" "How did you feel when he said that to you?" Sharing his feelings and his experiences helps him realize that you enjoy listening to him and are eager to discuss things with him.

Now you can begin teaching him how to play games. Waiting for your turn, moving only a certain number of spaces, "reading" the directions, winning and losing are all skills you can teach through games. He'll take great pride in hearing you say, "Daddy likes the way you're sharing your toy with Jodie." If he plays games with other children, keep the number of participants small so that they really have a chance to practice these skills and are not spending a lot of time waiting for their turn.

Board Games

Typically, board games lend themselves to having a winner and a loser. Instead of emphasizing this aspect of the game, encourage playing the game for the fun of it. This way, winning and losing will take on their proper perspective. Once you have taught your child how to play the games and have used them for your language teaching, she will enjoy playing them with friends. In the beginning, it will be helpful for you to be involved in the games to keep things moving along smoothly and to ensure that your language delayed child has all of the vocabulary that she needs to play the game.

Candyland

Candyland is a classic and your child will love the bright, sturdy, and colorful board, cards, and playing pieces. Allow her to handle the playing pieces freely at first because the game is new and she will want to touch all of the pieces. As she is doing this, name all of the playing pieces for her:

"See all the bright cards we need for the game. There are blue, yellow, red, green, purple, and orange. Can you put them all together in a pile? Watch me shuffle the cards and mix them all together. This is the board that tells us where to go when we pick a card. We'll move our little marker around the board and match the pictures on the cards we pick. Which color marker would you like? I'll take red. On your mark, get set, go . . . pick the first card!"

Candyland is a wonderful play opportunity to review colors with your child or to introduce them if you have not done so already. Also, you can reinforce the incidental counting that you taught earlier as you two count together the number of squares you must move. When you play the next game that we discuss, Hi-Ho-Cherry-O, you will be teaching more about numbers.

"Let's count how many squares you need to go before you get to the candy cane: one, two, three, four, five . . . great!"

In addition to teaching colors and counting, Candyland helps your child practice the social skills of sharing and taking turns. You may find that she is able to handle sharing and taking turns well when she is playing with you but will be unable to do this yet with friends. Help her by playing with her once or twice and if she cannot share with her friends, then use the game only for teaching times with you.

Hi-Ho-Cherry-O

This is another classic favorite made by Parker Brothers for this age group. The board for the game has four cherry trees and each one has holes for ten cherries. Next to each tree is a hole for the bucket to fit in. The buckets are red, yellow, green, and blue. The object of the game is to be the first one to pick all the cherries off the tree and fill the bucket.

The spinner has pictures of one, two, three, or four cherries as well as a picture of a spilled bucket. When you spin, you can pick the same number of cherries as the number you landed on. When you are first playing this game, you and your child can put the cherries from your tree onto the spinner so that you can actually match the cherries to each other. You can count them out loud as you do it.

"Let's see how many cherries you can pick. Good. Put one of your cherries on each of the cherries on the spinner. That's one, two, three. You get to put three cherries in your bucket. Good job. . . ."

If you hit the "dump the bucket," then all of your cherries must go back into the tree. You will enjoy playing this game with your child and might consider some of the language you can use.

numbers - one to four	take it out
colors - red, green, blue, yellow	pick up the cherry cherries
ordinal numbers - first, second, third tree	bucket
put it in	

Because these games require only short explanations, they are excellent for children with language delays. If your child has a visual impairment, you can put pieces of Velcro on the cherries on the spinner so that she can feel them as she matches her cherries to them. You may want to put Velcro on the little cherries also so that they can stick to the ones on the spinner and will not roll out of touch for your child. This will also be helpful if she has physical difficulties and cannot keep all of the pieces from rolling about. With these modifications, this game will help to promote eye/hand coordination and finger dexterity.

Remote Control Car

We have talked a lot about "control" with young children. These issues of who is in control are true for *any* preschooler. When you add in the factor of a physical, mental, or sensory challenge, you may find that control becomes a "larger than life" issue. In earlier sections, we have mentioned toys that can benefit children with disabilities by giving them control of the environment. This toy, the Remote Control Car made by Hasbro, Inc., is just such a toy that will give a child complete control over where it goes, with very little physical effort on his part. The control button is very large, very easy to push, and

can be used by a child who is in a wheelchair, a standing chair, or freely running about the room.

To first activate the car, your child will probably need adult help. You must push on the white space between the flashing lights. This gives the message to the inner electronic circuitry of the car that it will now be controlled by the remote. Then it is a simple matter to push anywhere on the wheel of the remote and the car will turn in a circle. When it is facing the direction you want it to go, you let go of the button, then push it again and the car will go in the direction you have chosen. Remote control vehicles are a lot of fun for most children because of the feeling of power it gives them. We know of adults who still enjoy more sophisticated versions of remote control vehicles!

Your input of language will help your child learn how to work the toy as well as teach him the beginnings of directions.

"Oh, Jonathan, look at this new toy we just bought. It's a fire chief's car. He needs to go to the fire and help people put out the fire. Here we go! Push this button and watch him go around and around. Which way should he go? Straight ahead—good. Okay, stop pushing the button now while he is facing straight ahead; now push again. There he goes—off to the fire. Ooops! He made a wrong turn. He needs to turn around. Push the button. See him going round and round. Now he is facing you again. Stop pushing the button. He is facing the right direction. Now push the button again and here he comes back towards you again. Can you make him go to the left? to the right? You can make him go any way you want. . . ."

Place and Trace™

Even though your child is very active at this age, it is nice to have some quiet kinds of activities for her to do. The Place and Trace™ game combines elements of puzzles as well as creativity with drawing, which will help with her fine motor skills. This set is made by Discovery Toys and has three plastic boards in the set. One board represents transportation, another dinosaurs, and a third zoo animals.

Your first activity with this toy should be to name all of the objects on the board that you will be using. You want to make sure that your child has the receptive vocabulary of the words that you will be using. Towards the end of this developmental age, she should know all of the vocabulary on all three boards and then you can play a

"lotto" type game with all three boards. Let's talk about how to do this.

"Gabrielle, we have three boards to play this game, so let's ask Barry to play with us. Okay, now let's dump all of the pieces into a bag. Who wants to go first? Okay, Barry, you can go first since you are our guest today. Let's see, which board do you have, Barry? Right—you have the one with different forms of transportation. I have the dinosaurs. Which do you have, Gabrielle? Right—you have the zoo animals."

"Okay, Barry, reach in the bag and see what you get. What is that? Oh, it's a Stegosauraus. Is that on your board? No—then you can put it back in the bag. Now it's your turn, Gabrielle. Reach in and pull out an object. What did you get? A zebra! Do you have space for a zebra on your board? Yes, you do—okay, you can put it on your board. Okay, now it's my turn. You are doing a good job of waiting for your turns. . . ."

Continue with everyone taking turns until one person's board is filled up.

As the name of the set implies, you can trace around the figures themselves or the inserts in the puzzle board. Your child can make a large picture of the zoo with all of the animals that she might see there. The boards themselves have raised areas that represent the environments these animals might be in—trees, grass, water—which your youngster can do a rubbing of to add to her picture. Once the scene is complete, you can talk about the animals (or dinosaurs or transportation vehicles) and, of course, hang the picture up for visitors to see.

The pieces can be used to press into playdough or play clay and used over and over again to create new play figures. You can even use them as cookie cutters to make dessert for dinner tonight.

The play variety of this toy is vast and your child should get enjoyment from it for many months to come. She will continue to find new ways to play as her fine motor skills continue to develop.

Count and Match Pegboard™

There are several of these large pegboards on the market today and essentially they all have the same play value. The one we will be describing is made by Battat and has the additional feature of a lace for stringing so that we can talk about the value of stringing beads for fine motor control practice.

The pegboard has five sets of different-colored and different-shaped pieces. There are the familiar shapes of square, triangle, and circle but now we can add heart-shaped and star-shaped to the growing vocabulary of your youngster.

Of course, the first activity will be to make sure that your youngster knows the vocabulary associated with this toy. You can review the color names, go over the shape names, and add the new ones he doesn't know.

He can stack the pegs on top of each other and match all of the colors. Or you can have him imitate a pattern— for instance, by stacking one pile with alternating colors and asking him to match your pile by making alternating colors. Being able to match sets of things that are the same is a good readiness skill for reading and for math work later on.

The pegs in this toy are large and easy for a young child to handle. If your child has a visual impairment, you can help him with the colors by associating them with the shapes: all of the stars are orange, all of the hearts are green, all of the triangles are yellow, all of the circles are red, and all of the squares are purple. Always use color names when talking with your child with a vision loss because he will begin to develop a sense of what those colors represent. Later on he can associate an apple with red or green, a cantaloupe with orange, and grapes with green or purple.

This pegboard game also comes with a lace for stringing. This is a very good motor activity for little hands to practice. You have the chance to practice vocabulary such as "put the string *through* the peg," or "*pull* the peg through." Some children really enjoy tying the string together when they have several pegs on it and wearing it as a necklace.

For our dialogue with this toy, let's play a stacking game.

> "Here we go. Here's our fun pegboard. Let's see how high we can stack them up today. Howard, here are some blocks for you. You stack yours up and I'll stack some of mine. Let's say the color names as we do that. Wow—you knew all of those colors. You really know a lot, Howard. Let's dump them all out. Now let's stack them up again. This time let's count. One, two, three, four, five, six. Uh oh—mine is getting wobbly. How about yours? Do you think they will fall? Whew—you have ten pegs on your stack. You can stack them pretty high. Count with me— let's see how many you have now. One, two, three. . . ."

Timothy and Amanda's Closet™

Up until now, we have not talked about the language of clothing, but we hope that you take the opportunity during the day to talk with your child about the clothes that he is wearing. With young children, you often have this opportunity several times during the day, but for sure you will be able to talk about his clothing in the morning when you help him to dress and in the evening when you help him to undress. Be sure to label all of the clothing and parts of the clothing with accurate language. Every "shirt" is not the same. Talk about the different materials, the number of buttons or other closures, the collar, and the sleeves. Enriched vocabulary input will give your child exciting vocabulary output.

These two puzzles that are made by Ravensburger and distributed by Discovery Toys help you talk about the language of clothing in a fun and challenging way. Each puzzle features girls' or boys' clothing. To make things even more fun, you can use the clothing interchangeably on the two puzzles. The language on the girls' puzzle is:

four different types of hats	a dress-up outfit
six different types of tops	sneakers
two kinds of pants	high heels
a skating outfit	cowgirl boots
a dance outfit	a jacket

The language on the boys' puzzle is:

three kinds of hats	sneakers
a superhero outfit	sport shoes
a cowboy outfit	cowboy boots
a baseball outfit	slippers
pajamas	denim jacket and pants
shorts and shirt	

The pieces are easy to handle and your child will quickly learn where they go in the puzzle. Your language activity for this game might be as follows:

"Let's play with Timothy's and Amanda's closet puzzle, John. Which one do you want to play with? Amanda or Timothy? Okay, let's dress Amanda up. Where does she want to go today? Oh—she has her ballet class at 2 o'clock. Okay, let's find her ballet outfit. First we have to take off the play outfit that she has on. Okay, now you can put on the ballet top. Look, it has a scoop neckline and long sleeves. Does your friend Sara have a ballet top like that? Hers is different?"

"Okay, now let's find the bottom part of the ballet outfit—the skirt. Right, that's it. It's very short because she wears those purple tights underneath. Say, John, look at all the colors in her ballet skirt. Can you tell me all of them? Great job. Now finally we need to put on her ballet slippers. The straps on the slippers are the same color as her skirt. Okey doke—now she's ready to go to ballet class. You helped her to get ready. . . ."

Fun to Talk Phone™

All little children love to play talking on the phone. There are telephones that are pull toys, pay phone type phones, princess type phones, cordless or cellular phones, and even phones your youngster can make at home. (We will talk about making phones in the four- to five-year-old age group.) Your youngster will enjoy playing with any of these. You also may want to have just a plain play phone around so you can sit back and enjoy her "conversations." This will give you a chance to hear how her speech and language are progressing and perhaps give you some ideas of the kinds of language she might need some help with.

The phone that we will introduce here is one of the line of VTech Electronic Toys. This particular toy gives a lot of language input to your child while you play with her and when you are not with her. One unique feature on this toy is a volume control. Your child can make the sound louder or softer as she likes. This toy may not work well for a child with a profound hearing loss, but would work for one with a moderate and perhaps even severe loss. You can try this out in the toy store before you buy it so you will know if your child can hear it or not. The voice quality is excellent; so, if your child has a visual impairment, this phone offers excellent practice in following auditory verbal directions. The toy is easy to handle, the buttons push very smoothly, and do not require a lot of effort; so, your child with a physical limitation should have no trouble operating this toy.

An informative booklet explaining all of the possible play opportunities comes with the Fun to Talk Phone so you can learn more and more ways to play with this toy.

There are nine characters on the touch pad dialing area: a daddy, a mommy, a little boy named John, a little girl named Mary, a baker, Grandma, a firefighter, a nurse, and a police officer. When you touch any of the keys it will identify itself and then tell the caller to call someone else. "This is Daddy, call the baker."

There is a phone book with numbers to dial. When the phone is off the hook, you can dial one of the numbers in the book. For example, if you dial 012, the voice says the numbers out loud as you dial them, there is a ringing sound, and a voice answers and says, "This is the operator, please call the baker. Bye bye."

When the phone is on the hook, and you press the numbers, the number names are repeated out loud.

Additionally there is a piano keyboard on the bottom of the phone desk. When the phone is on the hook, you can use the piano like a piano keyboard and create your own songs. When the phone is off the hook, each key plays a different nursery rhyme. The words to the nursery rhymes are in the little booklet; so, you and your child can sing along.

You have no doubt heard stories of young children using the phone to call 911 during an emergency. It is never too soon to teach your child how to do that. You can use this phone to teach this valuable lesson. Even if your child cannot speak intelligibly or cannot hear what the person on the other end is saying, she can learn to leave the phone off the hook and the rescue department will respond with a call. Make sure you discuss how serious calling 911 is so that your child does not do this routinely in play. Here's what you might say:

> "Sallie, I know you really like using your telephone to play and hear different people talking to you. I want you to know that if you or someone in the house is very sick or hurt and needs some help, you can dial three numbers and someone will come and help you. Find the nine—right—now find the one—good. Now dial 911. Great—you found the right numbers. Try it again. Dial 911. (If you do this with the phone on the hook, the numbers will be repeated out loud for reinforcement.) Okay, after you dial 911, you say "I need help" and put the phone down. Someone will come and help you very soon. Remember, you only do this when you know that someone needs help very quickly. Let's practice that again. . . ."

Little People® Airport

We have talked before about how much children enjoy playing with toys that are miniature representations of their real worlds. Your child's imagination will soar when he plays with the people and objects that come with this toy made by Fisher Price.

He will delight in taking on the role of the passengers (playing himself or Mom or Dad) or perhaps he would like to play the pilot role. He can decide where the plane will go. With this toy, the "sky's the limit" when it comes to learning new language. With your help, your child can plan and carry out an entire trip to Grandma's house.

"Okay, let's pack your suitcase before we get on the plane. Which clothes and toys would you like to pack? You want to take your goldfish, 'Swimmy?' No, he can't go with us! You'll need pajamas, shorts, and some shirts. (You can even get into weather differences if Grandma lives in a different climate than you do.) Now it's time to drive to the airport. Get your money ready to pay the toll on the highway."

"Look, Jim, there's the airport. See how gigantic it is! It's as high as the clouds. We need to find a parking spot. Be patient. Here we are. This person is called the attendant. She collects all of the passengers' tickets. Can you give her your ticket? Now let's find our seat. See this little cabin in front of the plane? That's where the pilot sits. It's called the cockpit. The pilot is the person who flies the plane. Look, he has on headphones. . . ."

Once you're into your airplane ride, your child can be the pilot, steward, or passenger. You can then choose another role. You can talk about loading the luggage onto the trailer, which is then loaded into the airplane. You can talk about the meals that are served on the plane.

Best of all, you can take a trip out to the airport even if you're not planning an airplane trip. Sometimes you can arrange for a pilot to take your child into the cockpit of the plane and show him all of the controls and how the plane goes up and down. Often there are tours of the control towers during quiet parts of the day. Call ahead and find out what accommodations they will make for you and your child.

Action Sounds Garage™

The garage is also a familiar place for your child. One or more times a week, you may go for a gas fill up or perhaps some repairs on your car. Your little mechanic can play out these activities with the Action Sounds Garage™ made by Fisher Price, Inc. The two cars that come with this set have removable wheels and removable body chassis. There's an "electric" drill that runs on batteries that can power assist in removing the chassis and the wheels.

Here's some dialogue you might use when playing with your child with this garage.

"Uh oh, it looks like my car has a tire that is pretty low. We'd better take it to the garage right away and get the tire fixed or maybe buy a new one. Let's go! (Let your child be the mechanic.)

Child: Yes, it looks like your tire has a hole in it. If you can wait I can fix it for you.

Driver: Yes I can wait. Thank you for fixing it for me.

Child: Okay, first I will put it up on the lift so it will be easier for me to see. Then I will use my "electric" screwdriver to take off the tire. Now I can put a new one on. There you go—it's as good as new. Do you need any gas today?

Driver: As a matter of fact, I do need some gas. Can you help me?

Child: Yes I can. Let's get your car down from the lift and you can drive it over to the gas pump. I will show you how it works and you can pump it yourself.

Driver: Thank you for fixing my tire and for all of your help today. I will come back to your garage anytime I need some help with my car."

Representational toys are great fun for you and your child and provide practice with language that is useful in the real world outside of play. When you visit the real places, make sure that you include your child in the conversations so that he will remember the language that he learned at home when he was playing with you.

Puppets

You can use puppets at earlier developmental stages, especially when you want to elicit language from your young child. Sometimes having a puppet who pretends to talk will encourage your youngster to talk as well.

The puppets that we will include in this developmental age are made by Creative Education and called **Pick a Puppet**™. There are two puppet bodies included in the set and eighteen different accessories that can make your puppet into a boy, a princess, a clown, or a dog. This will

certainly spark the creativity in your child. And think of the language involved here as she makes her choices about what she wants this puppet to be! For our language play, let's make our puppet character become a boy.

"I see that you are going to play with your puppets now. What character would you like it to be today? A little boy? Okay, that's super. What will you put on him? Right—first he needs some eyes. His eyes are black. What color are yours? Yours are brown—right! And of course, he needs a nose. What do you do with your nose? Smell things—right! What's your favorite thing to smell? Chocolate! Me, too—I love chocolate! So, if he's going to eat some chocolate, what does he need? That's right, a mouth. So now we have his eyes, a nose, and a mouth. What else do you want to put on him? Some hair? Great. Okay, now he needs some clothes. There is a bow tie and some shorts. Now he is ready and dressed for play."

You can take the other hand puppet and dress it the way you want and then the two of you can have a play dialogue with each of you providing voice for one puppet. This is especially useful for children with speech difficulties. Talking through a puppet reduces stress and performance anxiety and gives your child the practice she needs to help develop good speech production.

You: "I have a dog puppet today and you are my master."

Child: "Okay, my puppet is a girl like me. Let's go out and play."

You: "Arf, arf! Will you throw a ball for me?"

Child: "Sure, let's go!"

Linky Rinks™

These nontoxic Linky Rinks™ by Forecees Co. can be used for many years for many different purposes. When your child is an infant, you can use them to attach his toys to his crib, highchair, or carseat so that when he drops them, they can be retrieved. When he is in school, you can use them to teach beginning math concepts. We will introduce them to you at this age and you can find new and creative ways to use them all through the developmental ages of your child.

The links require some motor coordination to get them to hook together. A child of this age should be able

to do it himself, whereas a younger child would need your help. When you use them with a younger child, however, they are safe because she will not be able to get them undone by herself.

At this developmental age, you can use the links to talk about colors, counting, sorting, and comparing, and making patterns. You could go on with an older child to talk about addition, subtraction, and graphing. The possibilities are limitless.

For our discussion here we will talk about making links to match to number cards. You can start with matching links to pictures of links. Use 4 x 6 index cards and draw a number of links on each card. For example, on one card, draw one link; on the next card, two links, and so on up to the number five. Make sure that you leave one card blank so that you can talk about the concept of "zero."

Take out your bucket of links and invite your child to play with you in this matching game.

> "Jason, come and see what I have for us to play with today. Do you remember these links that used to hold your toys on your high chair? I am going to show you a new game we can play with them. Here's a card and it has a picture of some links on it. How many do you see? Let's count them.
>
> One, two, three. Great. Can you get three links out of the bucket? One, two,three. Okay—let's match them to the links on the card. Here we go—one, two, three. Very good. Pick another card and we'll see how many links there are on it. . . ."

Once your child can match the picture of the link to the link itself, you can make new index cards and put dots on them. Again, make the number of dots up to five. Have him match the links to the dots as you count them out. The final step will be to make index cards with the numerals zero to five on them and have him match the correct number of links to the numerals on the card. You will find that this activity can go on for several weeks or even months. Don't push too hard but keep the activity at a fun level.

HOMEMADE TOYS

Playdough

Another classic toy that you can make easily at home is playdough. There are many recipes for this mixture. We include a few below.

Nonedible Playdough (non-toxic)

- 1½ cups flour
- ¼ cup vegetable oil
- ½ cup salt
- liquid food colors
- ½ cup water

Mix the food color with the water before adding to the flour mixture. The color will be more even this way. You will want to talk about the colors as you decide which color to make the playdough. When your child is four or five, you can talk about how you can mix colors together to make different colors. For example, red and blue mixed together make purple, and blue and yellow mixed together make green.

Mix flour and salt together. Add water and oil and knead the dough well. If you leave your finished product out in the air, it will harden. If you do not want your dough to harden, put it in the refrigerator in a covered jar and it can be used again.

Baker's Clay

- 4 cups flour
- 1–2 cups salt
- 1 1/2 cups water

Mix dry ingredients, add the water slowly. Knead for five minutes. (You will have to take turns with your child because she will not want to continue this for long.) Then cut or mold shapes or objects and bake at 350 degrees for 45–60 minutes. Decorate with paint or markers. If you think you will want to put a string through your creation to make a necklace, make a hole in it before you bake it.

Peanut Butter Playdough

- 2 cups peanut butter
- 2 cups powdered milk
- 1 cup honey

Mix all of the ingredients together. Add more powdered milk to make it less sticky. You can roll and form this playdough like any playdough, but you would not want to make too much or keep it too long. Once you have played with it and eaten as much as you both want, put it in the refrigerator to keep it cool. You can keep it in covered containers for several days without it spoiling.

Making playdough together with your child is a wonderful time to introduce measuring concepts. She can help you measure, pour, and mix.

> "Oh, Jamie, it's raining out today and we won't be able to go to the park. I have an idea. Would you like to help me make some playdough? Let's see if we have what we need. Let's look in the cupboard. We need flour. Do you see the flour? Right, there it is. Okay, can you find salt? Good! We need salt also. Now where is the oil? Oh, I see it—way in the back. Can you carry the salt? Good! Bring it to the table. Up you go—come on up where you can see and help.

> "I'll measure the flour and you can dump it in the bowl. Good job! We have flour in the bowl. Now we need the salt. I'll measure the salt. Can you dump that in the bowl? Now you can mix it up with this big spoon. Good. Now we're ready to add the liquids. We need water and oil. What color should we make the playdough? We have red, green, yellow, and blue. . . ." (Point to each color as you name it. Your child probably can tell you the names of the colors at this developmental age.)

> "Okay, you want to make yellow playdough today. Yellow is a good color for today because the sun is not shining and we can still make it a sunshiny day. What a good idea you had. Now we can pour the water into this small bowl. Then we can add the oil. You did that very well. Do you want to squeeze the yellow food color? Oops, that's a lot of yellow in there! Okay, we will have a very bright playdough. Now we can add the liquid to the flour and then mix up our playdough. . . ."

There is no limit to what you can do with playdough. Most children enjoy the squooshing and squeezing of the material. Do not interfere with this, but you can have your own plan in mind for what you are going to make with yours. We have always had fun making balls out of the playdough and rolling them across the table to the child to roll back to us. Another favorite activity which encourages new language concepts is rolling out *loooooong* snakes and short snakes.

> "Jamie, would you like to make something with your playdough now? Can you get it from the shelf? Here's some for you and I'll play with some. . . ."

It's important that you follow your child's lead here and be ready to comment on whatever she's making without making her do what you are doing. Comment on what she is doing and then add comments about what you are making.

> "You like to squeeze the playdough. It feels so good when you are squooshing it between your fingers. I'm going to roll my playdough. Oh, look, I made a long rope. Now I can make a short one. This one is long and this one is short. Did you make a short rope too? Good work. Let's see what else we can make. I made a small ball. Shall I roll the ball to you?" (This is a great time for an impromptu 'roll the ball' game.)

Anticipate when your child is tiring of playing with playdough, so that you can leave enough time for her to participate in clean-up with you.

Another time, you may want to use a rolling pin and cookie cutters to make different shapes to discuss and perhaps even create a story about. You can match the cookie cutters to whatever vocabulary you want to work on. For example, there are cookie cutters in animal, toy, and holiday shapes. Many plastic toys such as the Place and Trace™ we talked about earlier can also be used as cookie cutters for playdough since the playdough washes off easily. Let your imagination run wild with this wonderful, expandable toy.

Sunflower House

Children love to garden! They enjoy pulling weeds with you, planting vegetables and flowers, and harvesting their crop. Take advantage of this joy by involving them in your summer gardening and winter care of indoor plants.

There is a wonderful book called *Sunflower Houses: Garden Discoveries for Children of All Ages* by Sharon Lovejoy which gives beautiful descriptions of unique and interesting gardens to plant with children. One that intrigued us was the planting of a sunflower house.

You can make this house as large or as small as you would like. If you have no back or front yard garden area, perhaps you could try this in a large cardboard box and watch it grow. Sunflowers grow very large! The directions we will give are from the book mentioned above and are given for a backyard garden area.

Use the flattest and sunniest spot in your garden area. Mark off a rectangular area as large as you would like your house to be (this might depend on how many children you think will be playing in there). You and your child make a trench a few inches deep around three sides of your rectangle. Plant your seeds in the trench. Alternate sunflowers and heavenly blue morning glory seeds. Put the earth back over the seeds and water all around your rectangle. (Be sure to leave one side open for the door.) When the sunflowers have grown as tall as you want, tie a string around the top of one sunflower neck and wind it back and forth across the top of your "house." In just a few days, the morning glories will cross the string and your sunflower house will have a roof of blue. Your child can play in and out of the house for the rest of the summer.

Additionally, you will have created a natural bird feeder for many of the birds in your area to feed from. They love the seeds and yellow petals of the sunflower.

The language you will use in planting and watching your sunflower house grow will be the same as for other types of planting you may want to do. It is great fun to have your own vegetable garden and you and your child can go out each evening and pick some fresh vegetables for dinner that night.

> "Amy, would you like to make a sunflower house with me? Come, I'll show you what we need to do. These are some sunflower seeds. See how long and black they are. They will grow into sunflowers after we plant them. They will look like these flowers on the package. These other seeds are called Morning Glories. When they are grown, they will be blue just like the picture on the packet.

> "Let's go out back and find a special place to plant your sunflower house. This looks like a spot that will be sunny for a lot of the day. Can you make a trench with your little trowel? Good job. Now let's put in the seeds. Boy—you did that very well. Okay, now we need to cover them up with the warm earth and then give them lots of water to drink. The seeds need earth, sun, and water to grow. Tomorrow we will have to give them some more water. Now the hardest part is to wait many days for them to grow. . . ."

Another excellent resource for gardening with small children with disabilities is the book *Accessible Gardening for People with Disabilities* by Janeen Adil.

TOY SUMMARY FOURTH YEAR

The following is a list of toys that we have worked with in this developmental year. The * indicates a homemade toy.

Board Games
Candyland
Hi-Ho Cherry-O
Remote Control Car

Place and Trace
Count and Match
   Pegboard
Timothy and Amanda's
   Closet

Fun To Talk Phone　　**Linky Rinks**
Little People Airport　　***Playdough**
Action Sounds Garage　　***Sunflower House**
Pick a Puppet

VOCABULARY AND CONCEPTS

The following list will give you an idea of the vocabulary and concepts your child should be familiar with by the end of the fourth developmental year.

- action words: shuffle, mix, match, spin, pick, spill, put it in, take it out, trace, draw, color, stack, squeeze, roll, go, stop, plant, take turns, pull, push, dial
- body parts
- colors: blue, yellow, red, green, purple, orange
- clothing: buttons, collar, sleeves, hats, pants, leotard, tutu, sneakers, boots, shirts, skating outfit, dress-up outfit, high heels, jacket, cowboy outfit, pajamas, superhero outfit, baseball outfit, shorts, sport shoes, cowboy boots, jeans, jacket, slippers, scoop neckline, long sleeves, short sleeves
- dinosaurs: stegosaurus, tyrannosaurus, triceratops, dimetrodon, camarasaurus, pterandon
- directions: straight ahead, left, right, round and round
- emergency number: 911
- feelings: angry, happy, worried, afraid
- matching: same/different; bigger/smaller
- measuring words: cups, half, quarter
- negatives: don't, won't, can't
- nouns: cherries, bucket, airport, pilot, suitcase, toll, tickets, parking lot, cockpit, steward, passengers, luggage, control towers, wheels, body of the car, drill, screwdriver, hex wrench, tires, gas, lift, flour, salt, oil, sunflowers, morning glories, trench, trowel, seeds, packets, earth, water, sun, rain
- numbers: zero through twelve
- nursery rhymes
- ordinal numbers: first, second, third
- opposites: long/short; forward/backward; day/night, light/ heavy; first/last
- people names: mommy, daddy, little boy, little girl, baker, grandma, firefighter, grandpa, nurse, doctor, police officer, fire chief
- questions: how many, who, what, when, where, how much, why
- shapes
- tenses: past, present, future

- time words: today, tomorrow, tonight, yesterday, last night
- transportation: hot air balloon, rocket, airplane, truck, train, car
- weather words: sunny, rainy, cloudy, cool, hot, cold, warm
- zoo animals: hippopotamus, giraffe, elephant, zebra, lion, kangaroo

BOOKS

There are many wonderful books which help teach preschoolers such invaluable skills as counting, recognizing shapes and letters, and distinguishing colors.

Bears in the Night. Stan and Jan Berenstain. New York: Random House. 1971.
> A story of the adventure of little bears which uses very few words on each page. The emphasis is on prepositions. The prepositions are: in, out, to, at, down, over, under, around, between, through, up.

Bible Heroes I Can Be. Ann Eisenberg. Illustrated by Roz Schanzer. Rockville, MD: KAR-BEN Copies. 1990.
> A first introduction to favorite Bible heroes and heroines.

Brown Angels: An Album of Pictures and Verse. Walter Dean Myers. New York: Harper Collins. 1993.
> Shows the author's collection of over 30 pictures of African-American children with original poems that celebrate the life and pride that shines out of their faces.

The Carrot Seed. Ruth Kraus. Illustrated by Crockett Johnson. New York: Harper, 1945.
> Simple pictures show a little boy's faith in the carrot seed that he plants. No one else believes that it will grow. What a surprise for the grown-ups.

Cat in the Hat. Dr. Seuss. New York: Random House. 1957.
> A well-loved favorite for many years. The children's mother goes out on a rainy day. The Cat in the Hat moves in, makes all kinds of messes, but nearly cleans up before Mom walks in the door. A fun story to tell and retell.

Circles, Trangles, and Squares. Tana Hoban. New York: Macmillan. 1974.
> An excellent book of photographs of everyday objects that are in the shapes mentioned in the title. Great conversation starter for talking about shapes in our environment and learning to identify them.

Come to the Doctor, Harry. Mary Chalmers. New York: Harper and Row. 1981.

> Harry hurts his tail and is scared to go to the doctor, but all ends well for him.

Count and See. Tana Hoban. New York: Macmillan, 1972.

> This photographic study of objects focuses on numbers. The numbers one through fifteen are represented and then the numbers are by tens to fifty and from fifty to one hundred. The highest numbers may be too difficult for this age, but this is a good age for exposure to the idea.

Curious George. H.A. Rey. New York: Houghton Mifflin. 1941.

> Curious George is like a child in a fur suit. He is always getting into scary situations and being rescued by his protector—the man in the yellow suit. Children enjoy all of the books in the series which involve this little monkey.

Eric Needs Stitches. Barbara Pavis Marino. Photographs by Richard Rudinski. New York: Addison-Wesley Publishing. 1979.

> Eric cuts his knee and needs stitches. Medical terms and procedures are clearly explained. Many children will have the experience of needing stitches. This is an excellent book to have on hand.

Frances Series. Russell Hoban. Illustrated by Lillian Hoban. New York: Harper and Row. 1968.

> This series features Frances, a bear who experiences many of the situations that children of this age experience. In *Bedtime for Frances* we see her posing all of the protests that young children make when faced with bedtime. Her parents handle it in a very calm way and Frances learns. In *Bread and Jam for Frances,* Frances will only eat what she wants, which happens to be bread and jam. Her mother and father give her that for every meal of the day until, of course, she gets sick of it and begins to see that variety is more fun when it comes to food.

> These stories are amusing to young children and also show them in a nice way that these problems can be handled and that other children feel the same way they do.

Freight Train. Donald Crews. New York: Greenwillow Press. 1978.

> A train moves along next to the highway, going through tunnels, crossing different railroad tracks, and going in both the dark and in the light. Each com-

ponent of the train is shown and then linked together to show the entire train. Beautiful pictures. Excellent vocabulary.

Going to the Doctor. Fred Rogers. Photographs by Jim Judkis. New York: Putman. 1986.

Clear photographs of what children experience when they go for a regular check-up. Excellent resource to use before your child's check-up.

Golden Sound Story Books™ . Golden Books. Racine, WI: Western Publishing Co., Inc. 1993.

Electronic story books which talk, play music, and create sounds. Replaceable long-life batteries are included. Your child can follow the story, press the matching sound picture, and hear the sound. Look for popular titles such as: *Aladdin, Bambi, Beauty and the Beast, Dumbo, 101 Dalmations, Peter Pan, Pinnochio, Snow White and the Seven Dwarfs,* and *Winnie the Pooh and Tigger Too.*

Hey, Look At Me, I Can Be. Merry Thomasson. Illustrated by Valerie Poole. Charlottesville, VA: Merrybooks. 1987.

Children will be delighted as they become everything they ever wanted to be through the magic of "Look at Me Windows."

If You Give a Mouse a Cookie. Laura Joffe Numeroff. Illustrated by Felicie Bond. New York: Harper and Row. 1985.

Relating the cycle of requests a mouse is likely to make after you give him a cookie takes the reader through a young boy's day.

Into the Napping House. Audrey Wood. Illustrated by Don Wood. San Diego: Harcourt, Brace, Jovanovich. 1984.

A cumulative story of a sleepy grandmother, grandson, dog, cat, and mouse, who pile on a cozy bed to nap on a rainy day. What happens when a wakeful flea joins them is startling and hilarious.

Is It Red, Is It Yellow, Is It Blue? Tana Hoban. New York: Greenwillow Books. 1975.

Another excellent photo essay, this time emphasizing colors. These concept books are an excellent addition to a child's book shelf.

It's My Body. Lory Freeman. Illustrated by Carol Deach. Seattle, WA: Parenting Press. 1989.

This book will help young children learn how to communicate their feelings about their bodies.

I Want to Sleep in Your Bedroom. Harriet Zirfert. Pictures by Marie Smith. New York: Harper and Row, Publishers. 1990.

> It's nighttime and everybody says good night. But when the lights are out, Susan goes to her parents' door and says, "I want to sleep in your bed." Here's a gentle lesson for bedtime that will delight young listeners and their parents!

Jamberry. Bruce Degen. New York: Harper and Row. 1983.

> A bear and a young boy are joined by a variety of farm animals as they ramble down streams, through fields, and into a village, picking mouth-watering berries of all kinds along the way. The story is written in a lively verse.

The Ladybird Box of Books is a series of books that is available through Discovery Toys. The book titles in this series are:

> *A is for Apple*
> *Colors and Shapes*
> *I Can Count 1, 2, 3*
> *Nursery Rhymes*
> *Tell Me the Time*

> All of the books in the Ladybird series are bright and clear with excellent photographs and printed text. Reading these books together will help you teach concepts to your child in a fun and meaningful way.

Loving Touches. Lory Freeman. Illustrated by Carol Deach. Seattle, WA: Parenting Press. 1986.

> A book that teaches children the difference between loving touches and those that make them feel uncomfortable. It is a reminder that loving touch is necessary to a productive life.

Madeline Series. Ludwig Bemelmans. New York: Viking Press. 1939.

> A classic in children's literature. These lovely stories written in captivating rhyme have charmed children and adults for many years. Madeline is the smallest of twelve orphans under the care of Miss Clavell, and each story tells of the mischief that Madeline gets into. A delightful series.

Martin's Hats. Joan W. Blos. Illustrated by Marc Simont. New York: Morrow Press. 1984.

> Using his imagination and a variety of hats, Martin goes on a whirlwind of adventures. A great springboard for developing imaginative play with your young child.

Moonlight. Jan Ormerod. New York: Lothrop, Lea, and Shepard. 1982.

Follows a little girl as she gets ready for bed. Each event, which is pictured in its own panel, helps teach the concept of things happening in sequence.

My Five Senses. Aliki. New York: Crowell. 1989.

This book helps children become more aware of how they learn through all five of their senses. Particularly important for children who are delayed in one of these areas. It makes them aware that the area exists.

Nobody Asked Me If I Wanted a Baby Sister. Martha Alexander. New York: Dial Press. 1971.

A lovely story just right for this age when new babies come into the family. Oliver decides that he doesn't want his baby sister and carts her down the street, offering her to a variety of people. During this walk, Oliver discovers how much his baby sister wants him and decides that being a big brother may not be so bad after all.

One Fish, Two Fish, Red Fish, Blue Fish. Dr. Seuss. New York: Random House. 1960.

Always a favorite with children, this book emphasizes counting and color with Dr. Seuss's usual delightful rhythm and rhyme. This is one you will read and read again many times.

Over, Under, and Through. Tana Hoban. New York: Macmillan. 1973.

A photo essay showing children illustrating all of these prepositions. A very nice conversation starter and perhaps an encouragement to have your child imitate actions.

Peter's Chair. Ezra Jack Keats. New York: Harper and Row. 1967.

Peter is upset when he sees all of his things being refinished for the new baby. So far, his special chair has not been touched, so he takes it and a few other priceless possessions and runs away to the outside of his house. He finds that he is too big for the chair and when his mother convinces him to come inside and join his parents at the table in a grown up chair, he decides that he really is grown up now.

The Polar Express. Chris Van Allsburg. Boston: Houghton Mifflin, and Co. 1985.

A magical Christmas Eve train ride takes a little boy to the North Pole to receive a special gift from Santa Claus.

The Red Balloon. A. Lamorisse. New York: Doubleday. 1978.

> No words in this elegant picture story. Tells the story of a lonely little boy who is teased by his friends, but finds a friend in a red balloon who is always around to help the little boy and take him on beautiful rides high above Paris. Photographs are excellent.

The Rose in My Garden. Arnold Lobel. Illustrated by Anita Lobel. New York: Greenwillow Press. 1984.

> Written in a pleasant rhythm, making it an ideal read aloud book, this tale tells a cumulative story starting with a single rose in the garden. The young listener will soon be adding the words that he has learned by listening to this story.

Rosie's Walk. Pat Hutchins. New York: Macmillan. 1968.

> Rosie is totally unaware of the danger when a fox follows her on her walk. The emphasis is on the prepositions in the story, but you will not miss the humor of something always happening to the fox and nothing happening to Rosie. The prepositions included are: around, under, through, over.

The Runaway Bunny. Margaret Wise Brown. Illustrated by Clement Hurd. New York: Harper Collins. 1991.

> A little bunny imagines all kinds of ways to run away but his mother assures him that she will follow him. The mother bunny's calm and steadfast love gives children a feeling of safety and security.

Sammy Spider's First Hanukkah. Sylvia Rouss. Illustrated by Katherine Janus Kahn. Rockville, MD: KARBEN Copies. 1993.

> Sammy watches longingly as a little boy lights another candle and gets a new dreidel every night of Hanukkah. On the last night of the holiday, Sammy gets his own spinning surprise.

School Bus. Donald Crews. New York: Greenwillow Press. 1984.

> An excellent book to introduce the school bus to your child. This may be the first year that he is going to ride the school bus and you can begin his adventure for him with this wonderfully illustrated book.

Sesame Street Book of Shapes. Eleanor Feltser. Boston: Little, Brown and Co. 1970.

> Shows shapes in everyday objects and includes pages for matching shapes, finding the ones that are the same and different. Shows how to make different pictures with shapes. A fun book to follow up with a cut and paste activity to make some of the pictures shown.

Seven Candles for Kwanzaa. Andrea Davis Pinkney. Illustrated by Brian Pinkney. New York: Dial Press for Young Readers. 1993.

> Follows the sequence of Kwanzaa week, describing the symbols and their meanings. A realistic look at the way many African American families today celebrate Kwanzaa.

Shapes. Gwenda Turner. New York: Penguin USA. 1991.

> Learning shapes, squares, circles, triangles, and stars is fun with this clever cut-out book.

Starting School. Janet and Allan Ahlberg. New York: Viking Kestrel. 1988.

> Warm and humorous book about a preschooler just starting to school. Should help to reassure your child about being away from Mom and Dad.

Tale of Peter Rabbit. Beatrix Potter. New York: Warner. 1902.

> One of the first books ever to use animals acting like little children. The story is well-known and the drawings are exquisite. Should be added to your child's personal bookshelf.

Ten Nine Eight. Molly Bang. New York: Greenwillow Books. 1983.

> A different slant on counting and a lovely way to say goodnight. Pictures are charming. Counting backwards from ten little toes to one big girl who is ready for bed. A sleepy-time favorite.

The Tomorrow Book. Doris Schwerin. Illustrated by Karen Gundsheimer. New York: Pantheon. 1984.

> A very different calendar-concepts book for young children because their world is oriented to the present. This simple book shows that tomorrow begins when you go to bed and talks about all the new things that tomorrow might bring. In addition to helping to teach this concept, this book is handy to have around when the day is not going well and your child needs to look forward to a new beginning tomorrow.

Too Many Tamales. Gary Soto. Illustrated by Ed Martinez. New York: Putnam. 1993.

> Maria tries on her mother's ring while her hands are sticky with the "masa" she is kneading to make tamales. Panic ensues when she discovers the ring is missing. A look into a tender and funny Mexican American celebration.

Truck. Donald Crews. New York: Greenwillow Press. 1980.

As the truck winds through town, it goes over, under, across and through. Additionally, many traffic signs familiar to young children, such as "STOP," "ONE WAY," "ENTER," are shown. Other vehicles are pictured as well.

A Turn for Noah. Susan Remick Topek. Illustrated by Sally Springer. Rockville, MD: KAR-BEN Copies. 1992.

Things have been going wrong for Noah all week in nursery school. Soon the holiday of Hanukkah will be over. When will it be his turn? There is a series of Noah stories for several holidays, including *A Taste for Noah* and *A Holiday for Noah.*

We Can Do It!! Laura Dwight. New York: Checkerboard Press. 1992.

Five special children show what they can do—and they can do just about anything. Fun and inspiring, children will love the words and beautiful photographs.

Whistle for Willie. Ezra Jack Keats. New York: Harper and Row. 1973.

Peter wants very much to learn to whistle so that his dog will come to his very special whistle. With much practice and persistence, Willie is successful. A wonderful boost to children with special needs who have to work a little harder and practice a little harder to get some things done.

William's Doll. Charlotte Zolotow. Illustrated by William Pene du Bois. New York: Harper and Row. 1972.

William loves all of his "boy" toys but he also wants a doll. Finally his grandmother helps to explain to William's parents why he should have a doll so that he can learn to take care of the baby when he is a Daddy.

You're My Nikki. Phyllis Rose Eisenberg. Illustrated by Jill Kastner. New York: Dial Books for Young Readers. 1992.

A beautiful story which reassures children that love has no boundaries. Particularly good for young children whose mothers may be just starting to work away from home.

Your New Potty. Joanna Cole. Photos by Margaret Miller. New York: Morrow Jr. Books. 1989.

Tells the story of two toddlers, Steffie and Ben, who are both learning to use the potty. Written in a simple reassuring style which is perfect for young children.

SUMMARY OF YOUR CHILD'S FOURTH YEAR (36–48 MONTHS)
LANGUAGE

Developmental Milestones	Date Achieved	NOT YET	PROGRESSING

uses negation
    don't
    won't
    can't			

uses plurals			
asks questions			
can tell of experiences in sequence			
can say age and sex			
uses 5–word sentences			
can deliver a simple message			
can respond to conversation of others			
knows some songs			
knows 1800 words			

PHYSICAL

Developmental Milestones	Date Achieved	NOT YET	PROGRESSING
can walk downstairs alternating feet			
can climb low ladder			
can run smoothly			
can jump several times in a row how many times?			
can hop how many times?			
can catch a large ball bounced by someone else			
can bounce a large ball two or three times			
can wind up a toy			
can build a tower of blocks how many?			
can do puzzles of 3–5 pieces			
can put on clothing			
can pull a wagon			

COGNITIVE

Developmental Milestones	Date Achieved	NOT YET	PROGRESSING
can point to body parts fingers thumb toes neck stomach chest back knee chin fingernails			
can name body parts legs arms fingers thumb toes neck stomach chest back			
can match colors pink gray white			
can show colors when asked orange purple brown black			
can name colors red yellow green blue			
can show shapes when asked circle square triangle			
can match shapes hexagon rectangle star			

Developmental Milestone	Date Achieved	NOT YET	PROGRESSING

understands time concepts
    today
    tonight
    last night			

can point to opposites
    tall/short
    slow/fast
    over/under
    far/near			

can sort objects by color			
can sort objects by shape			
can count to 4			

understands ordinal numbers
    who goes first?
    whose turn is second?			

can tell about the use of household objects
    What do we use a stove for?
    What are dishes for?
    Why do we we need houses?			

Can tell what part of the day is for certain activities
    When do we eat breakfast?
    When do we go to sleep?			

plays with friends own age			
can express feelings			
develops more fantasy play			
can match letters			

The Fifth Year

Forty-Eight to Sixty Months

As you look back over the earlier developmental stages, it is hard to believe how far your infant has come. From total helplessness, she has emerged as a sturdy individual capable of carrying on long conversations with you. If she has no physical disabilities, she should be able to walk up and down stairs alternating feet on the steps even while carrying things in her hands. She may be able to ride a bike with or without training wheels. She will enjoy coloring and can often draw simple round objects such as balls or apples after you show her how. She will be interested in letters and may be able to trace them and perhaps write some on her own. We have included some school-oriented toys in this category because she may be going to nursery school during this time. If she has older brothers or sisters, she will enjoy doing "homework" while they are doing theirs.

As you have been for the last four years, you are still your child's model and her teacher. Continue to build her receptive language and give her new and wondrous words for everyday things. She can learn that "huge," "gigantic," and "humongous" are fancy words for "big." Children this age just love to play around with multisyllabic words. We are sure that their love for dinosaurs at this age is largely because they get to say neat words like "diplodocus" and "tyrannosaurus rex." Continue to talk about all of your daily activities when you are together. Building an enriched vocabulary will pay major dividends as your child moves along in school and reads and writes. Her knowledge of language will be a valuable asset for her.

While you are continuing to bolster her receptive language skills, you may want to add some idiomatic expressions. Examples of these are "It's raining cats and dogs today"; "My eyes are bigger than my stomach"; "You look as cool as a cucumber." Your child will enjoy learning about these different ways to use and understand words.

We do not recommend a lot of high pressure teaching at home, but you can begin getting your child interested in school types of activities. Having lots of paper, crayons, and other art materials around will help her develop the fine motor skills for beginning writing next year in kindergarten. Coloring books help with learning how to stay within lines. Be sure to also provide plenty of large paper and let her choose whether to color within or without lines. Our favorite coloring paper is a huge roll of white shelf paper from the grocery store. It is inexpensive and lends itself to borderless pictures which can become wall murals or a painting that can be added to over a period of time.

Your play with your child can include some basic concepts related to numbers, letters, and prepositions which will be fun for her to learn. Resist having her "recite" her letters and numbers for friends and family, however. She doesn't need the stress of performing at this age.

Action Figures

Action figures provide the opportunity to teach our children tons of rich language as they play. Practically all children we know enjoy playing with them. Although their names and packaging may change over time, their function and value remain the same. Your children will love them.

Four-year-olds are the center of their own universe. They are sorting out all that makes their life tick. Their role with their family, friends, school, hobbies, and environment is taking on meaning in a new and grown-up way. They have become more interested in trying out adult roles they see such as parents, teachers, healthcare professionals, firefighters, and a myriad of other community helpers.

By representing the people in your child's life, action figures give your child the freedom to act out her life experiences in the comfort and safety of her own living room. They present opportunities for creative play, problem solving, and practicing language skills.

Children especially love playing out the themes of their own lives via dolls and action figures because they can be in total control. When they write the script, there are no surprises and no anxiety. What may occasionally be a stressful experience for your child (a trip to the doctors' office, physical therapist or speech pathologist) can be acted out at home before or after the actual episode to help dispel any fear or anxiety on your child's part.

Children at the age of four often talk out loud to themselves while they are playing. The reason they have these dialogues with themselves (essentially carrying on a two-way conversation by themselves) is children's words are tied closely to their actions. Often, as a child is doing something, he automatically verbalizes what his play characters or toys are doing. ("I'm going to give you a bath now, Dolly.") Although this is true for adults as well, it is much more intensified or pronounced in young preschool children. Speaking in a monologue style allows your child to create a play situation, then change and alter his actions with words, even if hypothetical or absurd in nature.

Action Figures:
Multi-Ethnic Little Tikes Family Members and Van™

Multi-Ethnic Mattel Dolls™: Barbie, Ken, Skipper, Todd, and Stacie

Little Tikes manufactures wonderful pretend people and action sets, as does Mattel, with its ever-popular family dolls: Barbie™, Ken™, Skipper™, Todd™, and Stacie™. We love all of these kinds of dolls because they are made of easy-to-clean plastic; they can be dressed and/or posed, and they are just the right size for four-year-old hands. Another nice feature about these dolls is that they are multi-ethnic and can be found in dark or light skin tones. We recommend them equally for boys and girls.

There are no set guidelines here. You can combine dolls and pretend people, settings, and accessories from either set. Small children do this routinely. Just follow your child's lead. Encourage creativity. There is no one right or wrong way to play with these toys. Your child is in charge during his playtime with action figures. Acting out real-life scenes with action figures will help your child attain a feeling of mastery and control over his environment.

You may want to help him act out a scene where this eclectic cast of characters includes professionals such as a doctor and nurse, a physical therapist, speech pathologist, and/or audiologist, as well as a patient, representing your child. Help provide the necessary language to make the scene work, but follow your child's lead as far as where he wants the scene to start, where he wants it to go, and how he wants it to end. Taking the mother and father and a child from either set, say:

> "Do you have an appointment today? What kind of an appointment do you have? Oh, you need to go to the doctor for a check-up? OK, let's get in the van and drive to see Dr. Jones. Let's put on your seatbelt. . . ." (Pretend to drive the Little Tikes Van™ to the doctor's office.)

> "We're here! That was a pretty quick ride. Let's tell the receptionist your name and that you're here to see the doctor. . . . She says you won't have to wait too long. You can go into the waiting room and look at a book while you're waiting for your turn. . . ."

As 50 percent of all graduating seniors from medical schools are women today, do not be at all surprised if your child's physician is a woman. Help your youngster dispel outdated sterotypes that doctors will necessarily be men by offering a Barbie Doll or a Little Tikes woman figure to portray your child's physician. In fact, look for a Dr. Barbie™ in your nearby stores. Likewise, many men are entering the healthcare profession today as nurses, office assistants, or lab technicians. Use male action figures to portray these roles if that is what may occur in your child's life.

> "Hi, Dr. Jones. We're here for a physical exam. I want to make sure Leila is healthy and growing the way she should. Could you check her height and weight? Oh, the nurse will come in to do these measurements and to take Leila's blood presssure? . . . Hi, Nurse Fred. How well has Leila grown since her last check up?"

Fisher-Price Baseball Set™

As your child's physical coordination improves and her social world begins to broaden outside the home, she'll be interested in trying out sports like the "big kids" in the neighborhood play, and just like the pros she see her parents watch on television. This toy helps your child learn to hit a ball and practice playing the game of tee-ball, a precursor to baseball. The white plastic ball sits on a plastic,

bounce-back tee. This tee can be adjusted to perfectly fit the height of your child, whether she is standing or sitting in a chair or a wheelchair.

A plastic bat, ball, helmet, and bases are included in the set. If your child is blind you might want to use a beeper ball (available from the American Print House; see Resource section). If she is partially sighted, you may want to use brightly colored or fluorescent balls instead. This toy helps fine motor control (grasping the bat) and gross motor control (swinging the bat), and eye-hand coordination (having the bat meet the ball according to where the eye sends the message).

This is a great toy for practicing the skill of hanging onto the bat once it's been swung, a vital skill for playing the real game of baseball. It is also a great toy for helping your child improve her powerful swing. Once she can successfully hit a ball from a still target, she can graduate to hitting a pitched ball and throwing accurately; two skills that are needed for the real game of baseball.

Playing with the Fisher-Price Baseball Set™ will also give your youngster a great opportunity to learn the appropriate sports-related language concepts that go with the game.

"Step up to the plate. Now grasp the bat with two hands. Here, let me show you. Your right hand goes on top and your left hand goes on the bottom. Turn sideways so your left shoulder is facing the pitcher. Now bring your right shoulder up behind you so that the bat goes up behind your right ear. Your hands should be at the height of your shoulders. Keep your eye on the ball. Now, swing the bat. Try to hit the ball as hard as you can. Great, you did it. You hit the ball, just like a pro!"

Last, and probably most important, this toy is a great self-esteem booster once your child successfully meets the goal of hitting the ball. The broad smile on her face will tell you how proud she is of herself as she learns new skills and all the language that goes with them.

Art Materials

Your child has been enjoying and experimenting with basic arts and crafts materials for some time now. When he is four, you will really begin to see a vast improvement in his fine motor skills, and he will have the desire to create all sorts of exciting pictures and designs with his new-found skills.

Children at this age have vivid imaginations which you can encourage and stimulate by providing the right materials and asking the right questions. At this age, offer oversized paper so your child can draw and print freely. He's still working on improving his fine motor skills! Because large muscles develop first, it is easier to draw on large surfaces. Your child will still appreciate being allowed to outline shapes with stencils and to trace pictures with tracing paper. He now can take a great deal of time to work on an artistic masterpiece and will feel a great sense of pride on its completion.

Tremendous language can be pulled from your child's experimentation with art supplies. We have listed the "basics" that we'd recommend having in your household as well as a list of language concepts that can be introduced.

We recommend that with any of these toys, you let your child create the ideas for the pictures and designs. Rather than asking, "Can you make a happy face?" ask, "What can you think of to draw?" If he "draws a blank," which happens to even the finest artists from time to time, then offer a few ideas for him to choose from. Once he begins to draw, paint, or create a three-dimensional object, begin to stimulate his imagination even further.

"What will you make today? A puppy . . . what a good idea. What color will you make him? I see your puppy has ears, legs, and a tail. How many ears? How many legs? Where does your puppy live? At your house? Can you draw a picture of yourself next to your puppy? Will you decorate your picture with a lot of colors?"

If your child is not ready to create pictures, encourage him to experiment with the basic properties of each of the materials and create designs.

"What will you use to make a collage today? You need paper, pictures from the magazines you cut out, and glue. Would you like to make a collage about animals?"

For a child with a visual impairment, make collages using materials that provide a tactual experience—dried beans, corn, pasta, old puzzle pieces, sandpaper of varying coarseness, ribbons, string, and items from nature such as leaves, pinecones, shells, pebbles, and so on. Let your imagination soar.

Handling art materials involves using fine motor skills of hands and fingers to coordinate their movements with what you see. For a child who may not be able to hold a crayon well, we suggest that you insert the crayon through a small stryofoam ball two and a half inches in diameter. The easy-to-grasp styrofoam ball (which can be purchased in craft stores) now becomes the handle. This easy and inexpensive adaptation makes it less frustrating for your child to hold the crayon and also allows him to concentrate on the large motor skill involved rather than the finer motor skills he may not have yet.

Your child can refine these perceptual motor skills by drawing, painting, molding clay, and cutting with scissors. Painting pictures, coloring within lines, tracing, and copying shapes and designs are all precursors to writing and reading, the developmental milestones your child is working on. If your child has a visual impairment, you can use Elmer's™ glue on an outline of a drawing. When the glue dries, there will be a raised edge which will help him stay within the lines when he is coloring. If your child has partial vision, use colored glue or dark markers to make the outline.

While using art materials such as crayons, markers, or paints, you can help your child learn about working from left to right, top to bottom, and making straight and curvy lines. Moreover, the strokes he makes in his art work will provide practice for making the same basic strokes that form letters and numbers.

To begin practicing letter writing, you will need to demonstrate to your child how to use the correct strokes. Again, we recommend offering a large piece of unlined paper. Precision is not paramount at this stage. It often helps if your child can trace the letters first with his fingertips or pencil point to get a feel for the shapes and direction of each letter. Making the letters out of sandpaper adds texture for children with visual impairments and children who benefit from the extra sensory input.

If you haven't offered your child an opportunity to create a masterpiece on your driveway or front sidewalk with colored chalk, we recommend this highly. We bet you'll start a new trend with the neighborhood children in no time flat. Thick, one-half-inch to one-inch sticks of chalk are recommended when drawing on sidewalks or driveways as they will not break as easily as thinner pieces. Offer your child several colors and suggest that he draw a welcome home picture for Daddy on the front sidewalk of the house. Rest assured, your child's picture will eventually wash off in the rain.

Art Materials List

brushes	string
stickers	yarn
clay	stencils
crayons	paper
colored pencils	plates and cups
tracing paper	toilet paper rolls
construction paper	paper towel rolls
magic markers	pastels
scissors	old greeting cards
tissue paper	magazines to cut up
chalk	glue/paste
chalkboard	tape
eraser	paint
stapler	

Vocabulary Concept List

create	right
trace	across
glue	top
tape	bottom
attach	diagonal
cut	up
draw	down
color	dark
erase	light
decorate	shape
paint	names
names of colors	collage
left	

Magnetic Letters

Magnetic letters on the refrigerator can provide a lot of entertainment for your child as well as more teaching time for you. If your child is more stable in a wheelchair or special seat, this activity can still be a lot of fun. You can use a cookie sheet on the tray of her chair or wheelchair. This way, she can still play with the unbreakable letters and provide hours of fun. You can ask her to tell you the letters as she takes them on and off the refrigerator. You can play a game where she asks you a word and you tell her the letters that she needs to spell that word. Your child will especially enjoy spelling the names of members of your family and her very own name!

Avoid problems and buy two or more sets of letters so there will be enough letters for those indispensable words with double letters such as "Daddy" and "Mommy." You can be sure that these will be on the list of things that she is interested in learning to spell. You may want to make some cards for her with some special words on them so she can match the letters and "spell" the words herself.

When she is ready, you can begin to talk about the difference between the names of the letters and the sounds that they make. For example, the letter "b" says its name of "bee" but has a sound of "buh." Or the letter "m" says its name of "em" but has a sound of humming—mmmmmm. Follow your child's lead and give her what she is ready for and interested in.

"What word would you like to spell with your letters?"

(Child) "Dog."

"Okay. Listen while I say the word 'dog.' What sound do you hear first?"

"Bee."

"Listen again. 'Dog.' The first letter is 'Dee' and it sounds like 'Duh. Can you find the 'Dee' letter?"

(Child holding up the "D" letter) "Is this one 'Dee?'"

"That's right. That's the letter 'Dee.' Do you remember how it sounds?"

"Duh."

"Good job! You did a fine job of listening."

Continue with all the letters for the word "dog." Help your child with the sounds and with finding the letters. This activity should be fun and not stressful. Remember, you are playing and not actually "teaching" her the alphabet. She will be able to learn them better if you make it fun for her.

Dominoes

Dominoes can be played on a very simple matching level or on more complicated levels. Of course, we suggest the matching level at this time. At this level, dominoes is an excellent game for learning to take turns as well as to observe details. There are many types of picture dominoes as well as number dominoes available. We'll tell you a little about each and how they expand into other matching activities for learning purposes.

The picture matching sets are usually made of cardboard and have a picture of a familiar object or animal on either end of the rectangular piece. The simplest form of

play is to put all of the pieces face down in a pile. You and your child each take turns picking one to see if it matches either end of the piece(s) that are face up on the table. As you turn over pictures, you have lots of opportunity to talk about what is represented. Talk about the color, size, and use of the object. If they are animal dominoes, talk about the characteristics of the animals pictured—how they look, what they eat, how they make sounds. This is another opportunity to remind your child of his visit to the zoo, the farm, or whatever excursion is appropriate here.

"We're going to play with the dominoes now. Can you help me turn all of the dominoes over? These dominoes have pictures of animals on them. Can you tell me their names as we turn them over? Good, you know a lot of animal names. Okay. You can go first and pick one of the dominoes. Let's see. That one has a horse at one end and a duck at the other. I'm going to choose a domino from the pile and see if it matches the horse or the duck. I picked a sheep. It doesn't match the horse or the duck. I'll have to pick another domino. Oh, good, I got one that has a horse on one side and a fish on the other. I can match the horses.

"Now it's your turn and you need to find either a duck or a fish. Do you know that both a duck and a fish can swim in the water? The duck uses its feet to swim and the fish uses its fins. Can you see the fins on the fish? That's right. Those are the fins. . . ."

If you are ready to move into simple counting you can "deal" out a certain number of dominoes to begin the game. For example, start with three each and count aloud deliberately as you "deal" out the pieces. If you think he is ready, have your child imitate the counting with you. If he is able to count to three alone then give him a turn to be the "dealer."

If your child is taking an interest in counting and you feel he is ready, you can use the dominoes that have the dots on them. The numbers only go up to six so it is an excellent beginning counting game. Some of the number sets are also color coded so that each piece that has one dot on it is red, whereas six dots may be yellow. This gives your child an additional way to recognize the piece that he needs to add to the dominoes. These sets of dominoes

Single Concept

▼ "Let me deal the dominoes. Here are *three* for you. *One, two, three*. Now I'll deal *three* dominoes for *myself. One, two, three*. Can you count with me? *One, two, three*. Great, you counted *one, two, three* with me."

which have a contrasting color on a black background are excellent for children with low vision. To enhance this effect, use a playing background that has no competing visual information such as an empty table top or a flannel board. If you use a flannel board, you can add pieces of Velcro to the backs of the dominoes. This will help to steady the placement of the dominoes for children with low vision or physical challenges.

When you begin counting, have your child put his finger on each dot as he says the number. If he is not ready for counting himself, you can take his finger and point to each dot as you say the number names.

It may be difficult at first to explain the idea that the first one who uses up all of his tiles is the winner, so you may want to play until the pile is used up and then see who has fewer pieces left. The concepts of *fewer, less,* and *more* are some of the very early concepts that your child will need when he starts school. This is an excellent game for teaching those concepts. You don't have to wait until the end of the game to teach them. As each piece is put down, you can ask about the two numbers on the piece: which number is more and which is less? Keep varying the way in which you ask him so it doesn't turn into a boring exercise in counting.

As with all of the language that you have taught so far, your child will understand the concepts before he is able to accurately express them. Your job is just to keep putting the information in.

Train Set

A train set is an excellent language-enrichment toy for both boys and girls. Although there are many to choose from, the one we recommend here is made by Brio. It is durable, well made, and will stand up over time. There are less expensive copies of the Brio Wooden Railway™ with less detail.

Your four-year-old will enjoy playing with his train set by himself and should be given plenty of opportunity to do so. A child this age is also quite capable of cooperative play with another friend. For this reason, we suggest purchasing one of Brio's more advanced railway systems so that your child and a friend could take on different roles during their playtime.

At times, you might consider starting off your youngster's playtime with his trains by introducing new words and ideas with which he may be unfamiliar. Once he hears you use these words a number of times, don't be surprised if these same words suddenly begin to appear as a part of his own vocabulary.

"Adam, are you and Cody going to play with your trains today? Which one of you is going to be the engineer, and which one will be the passenger? You could take turns and both of you could get a chance. You need to figure out which tracks you need for your layout. The curvy ones, the straight ones, or some of each?"

Children plus trains translate into opportunities for problem solving and creativity. All tracks, trains, and accessories in the Brio sets are compatible and expandable. As your child progresses in his development, you can add more sophisticated accessories. Be sure to provide him with the correct words to help him expand his vocabulary and provide words for his actions and ideas.

"Hey, Zachary, how many bridges and tunnels do you need for the layout you're making? You'll need the right number of supports to hold up the bridges. Let's figure out together exactly how many you'll need. Do you need help fastening them onto the track? Let's attach them together. . . ."

Purposely add words into your dialogues with your child that you feel will expand his vocabulary at this point. He is ready for more grown-up ideas than he was a year ago. Furthermore, he is interested in solving more complex problems. Whereas one year ago, he may have been challenged by building a single loop with his basic track system, now he'll want to link more trains together and learn the fun, new names of the trains he's playing with, like locomotive, caboose, and passenger train.

Be sure to discuss the unique magnetic coupling of one train to another.

"Can you find the side of the black steam engine that matches to the next train? Try turning the second train around in the other direction. Now does the magnet attract or stick to the next train? Experiment and you'll find out. . . ."

At age four, your youngster will be interested in acting out real-life situations with the people, farm, and circus characters and animals, and railway trains, cars, and signals that can be added onto this modular set. His creations will be limited only by his imagination. When he temporarily runs out of ideas of what to build, you can offer him some of yours.

One extra benefit from this language-rich toy is that it will add to your child's emotional well-being by building confidence and self-esteem. As your child sets progressively more challenging goals when building his playscapes and then follows his goals through to completion, he will have a great sense of "I did it!"

HOMEMADE TOYS

My Letter Book

We are strong proponents of children creating their own books of pictures and words. Out of life's personal experiences come great discovery and learning for your child. Making a book is a terrific activity for helping your child develop auditory discrimination skills—recognizing and distinguishing between sounds of letters. At this age, the focus is on the initial consonants of words: P = "pee" and B = "bee." A child with a mild to moderate hearing loss will be able to hear the difference in most of these sounds with repetition and a child with a more significant loss may benefit from the visual input of signing or cuing.

A good foundation in the visual discrimination skills needed for reading can also be established by using this toy book. Why call this letter book a toy? Your child will approach and cherish it with the same enthusiasm (if not more) than her other playthings because it holds an extra personal meaning for her.

To help your child discover letters and their sounds, we recommend introducing the beginning sound of no more than one new letter each week. Throughout the week, plan activities around one letter. On "P" day, for instance, you could choose a *p*urple shirt for your child, take a trip to a local *p*et shop, plan for *p*otato chips or *p*ickles as a side dish for lunch. At the end of each day, record the letter you emphasized, as well as words that begin with that letter on a separate sheet of paper. Ask your child to draw a corresponding picture or help her find a picture in an old magazine, newspaper, or greeting card, and glue it in her book. Eventually, help assemble your child's book in alphabetical order. This is a special keepsake your child will enjoy playing with over and over again.

Let's Make Music

We have not talked very much about music with your child. You can include it from the very beginning of your child's life through lullabies and baby songs that lull him into a peaceful sleep. You can keep music on during the

day. Perhaps you like classical music, show music, or pop music. Whatever brings you pleasure will bring him pleasure. So, too, will the many recordings available for children. Singing with him, doing finger plays to songs such as "Eensy Weentsy Spider," and just dancing about the room with him are marvelous fun activities.

At this age level, we suggest musical instruments that your child can make with you. If you want them around at earlier ages, then you can make them and just have your child join you in playing with them. At this age, however, he can be an active participant in making them.

Drum

Any pot will do with a wooden hammer or spoon for a drumstick. Give your child an old pot that he can keep for this purpose. Another type of drum can be made from an empty coffee can with a plastic lid. Once again, a wooden spoon can be used for the stick. You can make different sounds with different sizes of containers.

Single Concept

▼ "Let me hear you *strike* the drum. Take your stick and *strike* the drum. Boom, boom. *Strike* the drum. Can you *strike* the drum fast? Now, can you *strike* the drum slowly? Can you *strike* the drum loudly? Now, *strike* it softly. Very good."

Castanets

Juice cans make great castanets. After they are opened, cleaned and dried carefully, put in some beans or rice. Seal the top very thoroughly with paper and tape. Shaking the cans will produce different sounds depending on what you put in them. Rice will make a very soft sound while beans will be much louder. Your child will be able to feel the objects moving in the can, which will add another sensory input to his play.

Single Concept

▼ "*Rattle* your castanets. *Rattle, rattle.* Listen to the pretty sound when you *rattle* your castanets. Can you *rattle* them loudly . . . hard . . . slowly . . . fast?"

Rhythm Sticks

Any two wooden rods that can be banged together can be used as rhythm sticks. You can purchase dowels at a hardware store or use your old faithful wooden spoons.

Single Concept

▼ "Hold a *wooden rod* in each hand. That's right. One *rod* in your left hand and one *rod* in your right hand. Now beat the *rods* together. Rat-a-tat-tat. Good. Can you beat the *wooden rods* fast . . . hard . . . slowly . . . softly? What great rhythm you have."

Tambourine

Use two aluminum pie pans. Fill one with metal bottle caps. Put one pan on top of the other to make a container. Punch holes around the edges with a pointed scissors and then string them together. You and your child will enjoy doing this project together but be safe and do the hole punching yourself. The sound that this toy makes when tapped is similar to a tambourine.

Single Concept

▼ "*Listen* to what happens when you shake your tambourine. *Listen* carefully. It is very soft now. I am *listening* too. Can you shake it hard? *Listen to* that! Boy, is that loud. It is easy to *listen* to loud sounds."

Bells

Bells of different pitches can be purchased in a craft store. You can sew the bells to a piece of leather or other material. Your child can shake the bells in rhythm to music.

We're sure you can think of other musical instruments that you can make with your child. When you play with him, you will be teaching him listening skills. If you play a record, have him play along but when the music stops, he must stop also. This is difficult for small children because they so enjoy making the music, but it is an excellent listening skill for them to learn to develop. When you are first teaching him this skill, you will want to start with him seated on the floor with you, watching as you turn the music on and off. If he is sitting near you on the floor, you can reach out and stop his hand from making the sound.

After he has the idea of the activity and is able to stop making music when the music stops, you can get up and move about the room, marching while playing the musical instruments. You can add galloping and skipping to the rhythm of different music.

When you are teaching him this listening activity, your conversation might sound like this:

"I'm going to turn the tape on now. I want you to keep your bells quiet until I turn the music on. When the music stops, then you stop playing your bells.

Single Concept

▼ "Let's listen to the *music*. Listen, the *music* is very soft now. Can you shake your bells softly with the *music*? Ooooops, the *music* stopped. Listen. It's very quiet. When we hear the *music* you can shake your bells again. Your *music* is nice to listen to. I like it. Can you shake your bells hard? The *music* is very loud. Great job. You made *music* with your bells."

Okay. Here's the music. Good—you're playing your bells. You can make pretty music too. Watch, now I'm turning the record off. Stop playing your bells. Good job—you stopped when the music stopped. . . ."

If your child doesn't get the idea at this point, you can hold his hand and stop the bells and tell him that the music has stopped and the bells have to stop too. Then try it again. Most children catch on quickly to this idea.

Public libraries often have excellent collections of recordings for young children. Ask your librarian about them. Having a source such as this makes it possible to vary the types of music your children listen to.

There are excellent musical stories on CDs and tapes that you can listen to with your child. Often there are story books that you can get to go along with the listening activity. In some areas, there are "lollipop" concerts which introduce children to classical music early in their lives.

Special Considerations

Listening to and appreciating music is a marvelous activity to share with your child. If he has a hearing loss, do not automatically deprive him of the fun of music. We are never quite sure exactly what sound is like for a deaf or hard of hearing child, so go ahead and expose him to the activity. Begin with music that has actions or finger plays to go along with it and you may be pleasantly surprised to see how much he enjoys this activity. You might also adjust the controls on your stereo to see if he hears more with the treble accentuated or the bass accentuated. Some types of music, such as orchestral music or country music, may be easier for him to hear. Enjoy the fun of playing with music and see what your child enjoys the most.

Playing Cards

Playing cards are a wonderful source of activities for counting, sorting, and putting numbers in order. Not only that, but most children enjoy playing with them.

"Here's a deck of cards. Can you help me find all the red hearts? Let's put all the red hearts in this pile over here. Okay, now let's find all the red diamonds. This shape is called a diamond. Can you find all the red diamonds? Okay. Now we have a pile of red hearts and a pile of red diamonds. How about this one now? This is a black spade. We can find all the black spades. Put them in a pile over there. Now all the rest are black clubs. What is this shape called? It is a club.

"Can we put all the hearts in the right order? What comes first? This one with the "A" on it is called an ace and it is the same as number one. So the ace is

first. Now can you find the two? Good, that's the number two. See, there are two hearts and the number two. That comes after the ace, which is the number one. Now can we find the next one? What comes after two? . . . ."

Continue through all the numbers and face cards for each of the suits. This will give your child lots of practice in counting either by imitating you or actually counting the correct number of hearts, clubs, diamonds, or spades. Children will enjoy learning the names and values of the face cards as well.

There are many card games that children of this age enjoy. The one most trying to your patience is the seemingly never-ending game of "war." You may want to set a time limit for this game rather than playing until someone wins. To play, divide the deck in half. Each of you places the top card from your pile face up in front of you. The card with the higher value is the winner. This is excellent for helping your child with the concept of "more" or less."

"This game is called 'war' because one of our cards will win over the other. You put down your top card. You have a five and I have a four. Which one is more? Is five more than four? Yes, five is more than four so your card is the winner. . . ."

As the numbers get higher, you may have to help your child with knowing which is more or less. If this is too difficult, you can sort the deck and use only the lower numbers. This will also shorten your game time. Add in the higher numbers one at a time until your child is comfortable with all of them.

If your child has a visual impairment, you can put a little dot of glue on each of the numbers of hearts, diamonds, clubs, or spades. When they dry, they will be raised and your child can feel and count the number. Put a different textured piece of material on the different suits to help her identify the hearts, clubs, diamonds, or spades.

TOY SUMMARY FIFTH YEAR

The following is a list of toys that we have worked with in this developmental period. Asterisks indicate homemade toys.

Action figures:
    Little Tikes: Multi-ethnic families and van
    Mattel's Barbie, Ken, Skipper, Todd, and Stacie dolls
Art Materials
Dominoes
Brio Train Set
Baseball Set
Magnetic Letters
Playing Cards
*****My Letter Book**
*****Let's Make Music**

VOCABULARY AND CONCEPTS

The following list will give you an idea of the vocabulary and concepts that your child should be familiar with:

- adjectives (huge, gigantic, tiny, humongous)
- art materials (markers, pastels, tissue paper, construction paper)
- children's songs
- counting 1–20
- dinosaur names (diplodocus, tyrannosaurus rex, stegasaurus, triceratops, etc.)
- fairy tales
- feelings
- fewer
- health care and community helpers (doctors, nurses, audiologists, speech pathologist, physical therapist, teacher, dentist)
- idioms (It's raining cats and dogs)
- last week
- letters of the alphabet
- musical instruments (castanets, drum, rhythm sticks, tambourine)
- nursery rhymes
- opposites:
  higher/lower
  more/less
- prepositions:
  above/below
  behind/in front of
  by the
  beside
- safety rules (never talk to strangers, children don't touch matches, look both ways before crossing the street)

- ships and boats
- sounds of letters
- spelling of words
- tee ball rules (keep your eye on the ball, swing the bat, don't throw the bat, touch the plate)
- telling time (big hand, little hand)
- things in space (stars, planets)
- tomorrow
- train names (steam engine, locomotive, caboose, engine, passenger train, train tracks, bridges, tunnels, engineer)
- transportation vehicles (cement truck, dump truck, steam shovel, jeep, taxi, race car)

BOOKS

Books which focus on special interest areas are fun for children of this age. They are interested in a variety of topics and can get heavily into books about dinosaurs, rocks, or trucks.

Airport. Byron Barton. New York: T. Crowell. 1982.
Clear, beautiful pictures tell what happens on an airplane trip, from arriving at the airport to the take-off of the plane. A great prelude or follow-up to an actual visit.

Big Truck Book. Janet and Alex D'Amoto. New York: Renewal Products, Inc. 1968.
A board book which shows the following kinds of trucks: farm truck, moving van, gas tanker, delivery truck, cement mixer, steam shovel, dump truck, milk truck, mail truck, car carrier, sanitation truck, ice cream truck. Great for vocabulary and discussion.

The Car Book. William Dugan. Racine, WI: Golden Press. 1968.
All different kinds of cars are pictured here: big cars, little cars, police cars, campers, homemade racers, ambulance, fire chief car, taxi, jeep, sports car. Great for vocabulary and discussion.

Dinosaur Days. David C. Knight. Illustrated by Joel Schick. New York: McGraw Hill. 1977.
Many children at this age are interested in these prehistoric monsters. This book has simplified drawings with a general description of dinosaurs and the times they lived in. Fun to practice saying those incredibly long names.

Each Peach, Each Pear, Each Plum. New York: Viking Press. 1978.

> Familiar nursery figures such as Jack and Jill and Mother Hubbard are hidden in the pages of this book. The rhyming words continue from page to page. A fun book for learning to look for clues and details.

Fire, Fire. Gail Gibbons. New York: T. Crowell. 1984.

> A nice book to precede and follow a trip to the station. Talks about how firemen handle fires in the city, country, forest, and waterfront. Lots of new vocabulary and opportunities for discussion about fire as a safety issue.

The Freight Train Book. Jack Pierce. New York: Carolrhoda Books. 1980.

> Black and white photographs show locomotives, boxcars, tank cars, auto carriers, hoppers, flatcars, refrigerator cars, and cabooses. Good for vocabulary building and discussions. Take a trip to a train museum or freight yard to see the real things.

Harbor. Donald Crews. New York: Greenwillow Books. 1982.

> Colorful pictures of activities in and around a harbor with different kinds of ships and boats.

The Jolly Postman or Other People's Letters. Janet and Allan Ahlberg. Boston: Little, Brown and Co. 1986.

> Open this book, take out the letters, each from its own envelope, and you'll discover what well-known fairy tale characters have written to each other.

Leo The Late Bloomer. Robert Kraus. Illustrated by Jose Aruego. New York: Windmill Press. 1971.

> Leo, a tiger, is slow to talk, read, write, and draw but when he is ready, he does learn. An excellent story for a child who may be a little slower than her friends in learning new things.

Little Toot. Hardie Gramatky. New York: Putnam Books. 1939.

> A classic tale of a playful tugboat who didn't like to work until he was faced with a dangerous situation.

Mike Mulligan and His Steam Shovel. Virginia Lee Burton. New York: Houghton Mifflin. 1939.

> Another story similar to *The Little Engine That Could* and *Little Toot,* of a smaller and less able steam shovel beating the more modern fancy equipment. An excellent example for children who may have to work a little harder to achieve their best.

Mommies at Work. Eve Merriam. Illustrated by Eugenie Fernandes. New York: Simon and Schuster. 1989.

> Simple clear pictures and text describe many of the jobs that mommies can do.

Rain. Peter Spier. New York: Doubleday. 1982.

> No words in this lovely story of two children exploring the rain.

The Shopping Basket. John Burningham. New York: Thomas Crowell. 1980.

> Tells the story of a young boy going to the store to buy six eggs, five bananas, four apples, three oranges, two donuts, and a package of potato chips. Counting and naming as well as preparation for trying out a shopping list with your child when you go to the store.

A Special Trade. Sally Wittman. Illustrated by Karen Guntersteiner. New York: Harper and Row. 1978.

> A special book for children with special needs. Old Bartholomew pushed Nelly in her stroller when she was a little girl. As time passes and old Bartholomew needs a wheelchair, Nelly is happy to push him.

The Story about Ping. Marjorie Flack. New York: Penguin Books, 1977.

> The little duck, Ping, does not hear the call from Mother to come home and when he finally realizes it, everyone else has left. Afraid of being spanked, he hides and ends up in many frightening adventures. After being caught and almost cooked for dinner, he is set free and finds his way home again, happy to be safe and secure.

Swimmy. Leo Lionni. New York: Pantheon. 1968.

> A story with beautiful pictures that tell a tale of a little fish who is different from the others. He is the one to save his friends in the story. Nice for children who may feel different from their friends.

The Truck and Bus Book. William Dugan. Racine, WI: Golden Press. 1972.

> This is a paper shape book with pictures of a tank truck, moving van, dump truck, mail truck, coal truck, garbage truck, telephone truck, cattle truck, tow truck, fire truck, school bus, motor bus for trips, and ice cream truck. Good for vocabulary and discussion.

The True Book of the Mars Landing. Leila Boyle Gemme. New York: Children's Press. 1977.

> Full-page photos of the planet Mars taken by the spacecrafts Mariner and Viking. There is a clear and simple text for youngsters who are interested in space.

Walt Disney Series. New York: Random House.

This series is comprised of stories and adventures and special adaptations of the Disney Classics. Donald Duck, Mickey Mouse, Dumbo, Peter Pan and all of the other Disney favorites will be along to assist every youngster in exploring the wonderful world of reading. Some examples of titles are: *Peter Pan and Wendy* (1972); *Cinderella* (1974); *The Sorcerer's Apprentice* (1973); *Lady and the Tramp* (1981).

Where's Waldo? Martin Hanford. Boston: Little Brown and Company. 1987.

Follow Waldo in this series of detailed picture books as he travels through the world and takes on various roles. Requires clear attention to little details.

The following books can be used for "problem solving" discussions with your child.

A Birthday for Frances. Russell Hoban. New York: Harper and Row. 1968.

One of the hardest things for young children is to not be the Birthday person. This book helps a young child to understand those feelings.

My Mama Says There Aren't Any Zombies, Ghosts, Vampires, Creatures, Demons, Monsters, Fiends, Goblins, or Things. Judith Viorst. New York: Atheneum. 1973.

Explores some of the fears of night creatures that some children have.

When I Have a Little Girl. Charlotte Zolotow. New York: Harper and Row. 1965.

It is difficult to understand why there have to be so many rules when you are young. This book helps with those feelings

SUMMARY OF YOUR CHILD'S FIFTH YEAR 48–60 MONTHS

LANGUAGE

Developmental Milestone	Date Achieved	NOT YET	PROGRESSING
asks for definition of words			
can define more common words and tell how used book, shoe, table			
almost complete use of correct grammar			
uses 6–8 word sentences			
knows town or city			
knows street address			
uses social phrases excuse me			
can carry on a conversation			

PHYSICAL

Developmental Milestone	Date Achieved	NOT YET	PROGRESSING
can walk down stairs carrying object			
can skip, alternating feet			
can do a broad jump how far?			
can hop how far?			
can throw a ball how far?			
can play rhythm instruments in time to music			
can ride small bike with training wheels			
can do puzzles that are not single pieces how many pieces?			
can hold a pencil in proper position			
can color within lines			
can cut with scissors			
can use knife for spreading			

COGNITIVE

Developmental Milestone	Date Achieved	NOT YET	PROGRESSING
can identify all body parts			
can name all body parts			
can name all colors			
can name all shapes			
understands directions			

uses prepositions
    by the
    beside
    below
    behind
    above
    in front of			

understands time concepts
    yesterday
    tomorrow
    tomorrow night			

understands opposites
    bottom/top
    go/stop
    low/high
    off/on
    inside/outside
    closed/open			

The Sixth Year

Sixty to Seventy-Two Months

Five-year-olds step out into the world! At this age, your child's world expands far beyond your house and neighborhood into school. It is most likely that your child has been in a day care setting, a play group, a nursery school, or a special-needs placement by this time, but regardless of his early exposure, age five is his introduction to the formal world of school. He no longer is "a preschooler" but is "school age." He is required by law to attend school.

Going to school with age-appropriate peers and curricular expectations presents new opportunities and places new demands on your child. If his developmental delay has been mild, this may be when you start to see differences in your child compared to others his age. If you have been working on his developmental needs for some time, you may find he has "caught up" with his peers at this point.

By the end of this year, your child should have a full command of the English language with very few errors of articulation or grammar. If he does not, and you have not done so to date, you will want to have his speech and language evaluated by a speech and language pathologist. The Resource Guide at the end of this book lists some references that may help you. A general guide to follow is that if your child is easily understood by the end of his sixth year by adult friends, new acquaintances, and friends of his own, then a visit to the specialist is probably unnecessary.

During this year, it is a good time to help your child's language continue to become more precise and specific. Instead of saying, "Look at the beautiful flowers you drew," say "Those look like long-stemmed roses!" Remember to use language at, or slightly beyond, your child's level of comprehension.

Compared to a four-year-old, the five-year-old expresses a much keener interest in learning letters and words. The written word has taken on a real personal meaning and the child now conceptualizes that the written word is a symbol for the receptive and expressive language he has mastered so far.

The five- to six-year-old often resembles a "kid in a candy shop"—a word candy shop, that is. Your child suddenly begins to notice, and be fascinated by, words all around him: "EXIT" signs, 35 mph signs, McDonald's logos, street signs, tee shirt logos, words in TV commercials. The five-year-old can't seem to get enough of them, and constantly tries to sample as many new words as possible. Pointing to a restaurant logo, he will ask, "Does it say McDonald's?" And then of course, "Can we stop here?" Children at this age are attracted to these things because they are now developmentally ready to take on mastery of the written word.

For a child with a language delay, the interest in learning letters and words may be just starting to blossom. Remember, the rate at which your child develops language is not as critical as the fact that he is moving steadily along in learning more complex skills. Many five-year-olds begin to relate the written word to their experiences, and need lots of repetition to remember and retain new information. For example, the word m-o-m stands for the object, mom or mother. The red sign on the street corner stands for the action to stop, and so on.

There is a direct correlation between the five- to six-year-old's developing fine motor skills and developing cognitive skills. Along with his increasing ability to identify and copy shapes accurately (a zero, a square, a diagonal, and a cross) comes his interest in the written word. You could say that for most age five is when the spoken word meets the written word. Cognitively, five is the age when children can developmentally start to understand this relationship. Why does this happen at this age?

As you may remember, all children go through fairly predictable, hierarchical stages of development—with each more advanced skill building on the previous skill. Now that speaking, (signing, cuing) skills are developing, many five-year-olds are ready for the next complex skill: developing *readiness skills* in reading and writing. By five and a half, some children will recognize all upper and lower case letters of the alphabet. A wide range of pre-reading and reading skills can be seen at this age. There is such variation because every child is a wonderful and unique individual.

Most parents of five-year-olds tend to compare their child's reading ability or lack thereof with others the same age. This is a bad trap to fall into. Remind yourself that learning to read is a developmental process. It takes time and practice. You, as parents, can help by providing play activities that will enrich your child's language development and your child will learn to read when he is ready.

Parents ask us whether their child's language development can be accelerated. The answer is yes! An enriched language and experiential environment can increase the rate at which your child learns to read and write. We, as parents and teachers, *do* have the ability to influence our children's development. Research shows us that toy play can contribute to the development of reading/writing readiness skills.

Children with a developmental lag need more time and more experience to develop more complex language. A larger vocabulary (spoken, signed, cued, or pointed to with the use of a communication board) as well as longer and more complex sentences must be developed before any sort of formal reading readiness program is attempted.

The key to helping your child develop necessary tools for reading and writing is to help him associate the written word with meaningful experiences he has in his life. In effect, you're helping to make the printed word come alive for him. We therefore recommend a language experience approach to teaching reading in which all language (listening, speaking, writing, and reading) is woven into your child's personal experiences. For example, if you take a trip to the zoo and visit the Panda bears, you may want to come home and write a little story about the trip. Have your child give you the language as you write it down. Then he can illustrate the story with his own pictures. This makes the written word much more meaningful to him.

The toys and activities in this chapter provide a language experience approach to helping your five-year-old learn necessary skills to read and write. Simultaneously, they will also help your child improve his receptive and expressive language. You will see that all of these activities are fun for your child. He can learn and practice new language concepts in a way that will sustain his interest and challenge him to a higher level of thinking.

Remember to use the simple language dialogues as a guide. Use your playtime to challenge your child and always try to stay one step ahead. Introduce new words. (Would you like to *borrow* a book from the library? If we go there, you can get a library card and they will *lend* you a book for free. After you've *borrowed* it for three weeks, you'll have to *return* it.)

Besides making great strides in language skills, children between the ages of five and six also take off in other areas. Usually there is a rapid and tremendous increase in muscle and bone growth. Your child looks suddenly slimmer, taller, and stronger by the time he turns six! All large motor abilities such as walking, hopping, running, throwing, catching, and jumping are done with much greater ease and precision compared to one year ago. Five-year-olds are a constant whirlwind of motion. Children with no physical delay love to jump and run and are extremely flexible.

Fine motor skills such as eye-hand coordination also improve greatly during this year. Five-year-olds can grasp and release objects more easily and more accurately and aim at a target more precisely compared to when they were four. That's why any type of ball play is enjoyed more. This is a great time to provide space and an opportunity to practice motor skills.

As a precursor to organized team sports, solo physical activities such as running, climbing, throwing, catching, bicycling, roller skating, and jumping rope all help build physical strength and endurance and are just plain fun for the five- to six-year-old. The child who is in good physical condition will more likely want to play sports on a team because he will be a better team player and enjoy being part of a social group.

As we have mentioned before, a big difference between age four and five is that the latter begins to take a big step away from family and into the larger community. This can be seen many ways. Strong friendships outside the immediate family circle begin to intensify at this age because children at this age become more interested in cooperative play. For the first time, parents may notice that their child's friends and shared activities may take on as great a significance as those relationships within the family, and are tied to the child's sense of self-esteem.

Child development research indicates that there is a strong relationship between motor skills and competence among peers. Starting at age five with the onset of formal education in kindergarten and with participation in organized sports, five-year-olds are beginning to be cooperative and helpful members of a social group.

One way to help many language-delayed children foster friendships with peers is through organized games and sports. We have seen many children increase their self-esteem, and develop friends by enrolling in extracurricular sports beginning at this age. The language delay that separates the child from his peers fades in importance as he shares his love and abilities in physical activities with the other children. For children with mental, visual, or physical disabilities who are not comfortable participating with their nondisabled peers, we recommend the Special Olympics or other community sports programs designed for children with these special challenges. Consider starting your own group if none are available, as specialized sports teams such as these give *every* child a chance to excel. Look for the reference for Special Olympics in the Resource Section.

It is no secret why sports and organized games such as soccer and basketball are offered in school and in the community for children this age. Such activities tie together the emerging physical, cognitive, and social interests of five-year-olds in physical activities, organized games and rules, and peers.

Cognitively your child is much more advanced than he was at age four. Your child's attention span lengthens and he can memorize and retain rules necessary for playing cooperative games. In fact, the five-year-old loves rules. They are the standards which govern his play.

Socially, the five-year-old is able to play much more cooperatively, compared to a year before. Five-year-olds play together quite well when they have a common goal in mind. They can understand and even relish the notion of teamwork. They can really dig their heels in and accomplish the learned tasks of sharing and taking turns. It is not uncommon for a leader to emerge who gains the respect of his peers and who assigns the rules of the game to the others.

As teachers and parents, we feel it is far more valuable to stress the cooperation aspect of team sports than the competitive aspect. Children benefit a great deal more from feeling that they are a valuable and contributing member of the team than they do from worrying about whether they are winning.

To introduce sports-related vocabulary words and rules of the games, picture books are helpful. For example, *The Young Soccer Player* by Wayne Holder presents all the rules and vocabulary of the game in simple words and pictures. This is expecially helpful for language-delayed children who need the extra clarification and repetition an introductory sports book can offer.

Ball Play

Start simple. Choose the sport or game which most appeals to your child (not the sport which is necessarily your favorite!). Go to the store and buy a ball. We like the ones made by Franklin Sports Industries. They're durable, colorful, and just the right size for most children. Go to the library and select an introductory book on your child's favorite sport. Read through the book together, emphasizing rules of the game and positions of the players. Explain key terms and new language concepts such as time out, coach, overtime, foul throw, goalie, forward, field goal, and shin guards.

If your child is going to play on an organized team, brief her ahead of time. Discuss what to expect and clarify terms. Ask your child questions such as, "If such and such happened, what would you do?" Do not simply enroll your child in a league and send her to the first practice with her soccer team, hoping for the best. Repetition is the key.

"Rebecca, time for soccer practice. This is your first real scrimmage. Grab your gym bag and let's make sure all of your equipment is in there. Do you have your soccer ball? Your shin guards? Your soccer shoes with cleats on them?

"Let's review the important things you learned from that book on soccer we took out of the library the other day. Cooperation is the key—right? Remember, you're part of a whole team where you all have to work together. You have to kick the ball to your teammates to give everybody a chance to score a goal. One person helping out the next means success for *everyone* on the team. . . ."

In basketball, for another example, it is important to stress to your child that making baskets and scoring points for her team is only one aspect of the game. Not all children are great at throwing foul shots or scoring points! It is equally important to stress defense, getting a rebound, or blocking an opposite team member from scoring a point.

General team sports etiquette like learning how to be a humble winner and a good loser should also be taught beginning at this age. Most important of all is to teach the child that what is most important is not whether she wins or loses but how she plays the game. Is she courteous to her fellow team players and to those on the opposite team? Does she encourage her team players to say things like "Good try" when a teammate's shot doesn't go in the hoop? Does she learn to evaluate her own performance based on how hard she tries and how much she improves since the last game rather than on whether she is the star player of the game? Does she understand that every member of the team is an important person? All for one, one for all. This goes for the score keeper, cheerleader, or equipment carrier, too, in the event your child chooses this sort of team responsibility instead of being an actual player on the field.

Parents and team coaches must both learn to praise and reward effort rather than performance. Understanding concepts such as good sportsmanship, effort versus performance, and learning the necessary rules and terminology of the game all are part of the complex language of sports and organized games. For the five- to six-year-old with no language delay, it is a huge task to learn all the required language. For a child who has difficulty with language, learning the ins and outs of sports and games takes even more practice and hard work. All of this requires cognitive and social maturity, which are continuing to develop hand in hand.

Playing a sport can be such great fun and a wonderful physical outlet for the language-delayed child. But remember: because there is such a great deal of language involved in individual or team sports, your child must be familiar with the sports terminology before her skills and activities in sports can flourish.

🖐**A NOTE ABOUT SAFETY:** A child kicking around a soccer ball or dribbling a basketball on her own front lawn or driveway must do so with safety in mind. Kneepads, helmets, and elbowpads can be introduced early as safety gear.

The five- to six-year-old can be taught to watch for cars and to look both ways before riding out into the street. Along with increased independence and need for explanation, safety must continue to be stressed.

Playmobil Action Figures and Systems: Classroom Setting and Schoolbus

We have discussed the value of using make believe or representational toys starting at age two, and have made specific recommendations on role-playing toys in each age range. Your child's desire and need to act out real-life situations using pretend people continues to be strong between age five and six. Not only is make believe a great opportunity for language enrichment, it gives you the chance to help your child express his emotions about his life experiences.

Some of our favorite role-playing toys, especially suited for the five-year-old, are activity systems made by Playmobil. Bright colored, detailed, and realistic, Playmobil sets will captivate your five-year-old's imagination, and provide a great opportunity for language enrichment. The small, high quality, colorful plastic figures can be used to represent the real people in your child's life. Figures can sit or stand; move their heads, hands, and feet; wear a variety of hats, backpacks, or purses; or carry props which help recreate reality.

For your five-year-old, we highly recommend the Playmobil Classroom system and Schoolbus, complete with teacher, students, school desks and chairs, easel and blackboard, schoolbus, driver, and passengers, road signs, and traffic light. These two sets—the classroom and school bus—are sold separately. While playing with these sets, your youngster can act out his whole experience of riding the bus and entering school for the very first time.

"Chris, time for school. Grab your backpack and let's head down the street to the bus stop together. Be careful when you cross the street. Look at the traffic light. Red means stop, so we'll have to wait until the light turns green. It's still important to look to see if any cars are coming. First look to the left. Then look to the right. No cars—now you can cross. Hurry, here comes the big yellow schoolbus. Say hi to your new bus driver. Her name is Freda. Can I have a great big hug? It's time to say goodbye. I love you. Hope you have a great day. I'll be waiting for you here at the bus stop when you get home. . . ."

You, as the adult interested in enriching your child's language abilities, can help move the conversations along. In the beginning, you'll provide the language for your child's role playing with his action figures. We would like to add for emphasis that we recommend ample time for your child to play alone to come up with his own dialogues. However, during some of his playtime, you could sit down with him and interject new, exciting words and ideas into his play. For instance, you could continue the playscene described earlier by asking:

"What will happen when you get to your classroom? Can you take the little (Playmobil) boy and teacher, and show me what you're supposed to do when the bus drops you off at your school? Oh, you walk with the other kids in your class to your classroom, I see. Then what's the first thing you do when you get to your room? Hang your coat up on a hook and find your desk? Does your teacher then take the attendance? Will you say the Pledge of Allegiance to the Flag? What will you be learning about in school today? It looks like your teacher has a lesson planned about dinosaurs. They ruled the earth millions of years ago. . . . Raise your hand if you know the answer to some of your teacher's questions about dinosaurs and she will call on you."

Little Smart Writing Alphabet Desk™

This toy made by VTech is a colorful, sturdy, electronic "talking play desk" that a five-year-old can sit at comfortably. Your child can even carry it from room to room because it is so lightweight.

This toy is extremely versatile and user friendly. Different activity modes built into the desk will reinforce pre-reading skills such as letter recognition, beginning sounds, alphabetic order, numbers, and musical notes as well.

Another nice feature of this toy is that there is a repeat button which allows a phrase to be heard again and again. This is especially helpful for a child with a hearing loss or one who benefits from extra input. Moreover, the sound resolution on this toy is extremely clear. A clear, friendly "desk teacher" built into the playdesk encourages your child to answer questions and instructs your child during her playtime.

Another terrific feature for the hard of hearing child is a volume control knob that allows your child to easily regulate the volume. If your child has an accompanying physical delay, you may have to help her push the desired buttons, but all buttons and an activity choice lever on this toy are easy to push with simply a light touch.

This toy is well designed to be played with by your child at progressive stages of difficulty. The child playing at a pre-reading level can practice singing the alphabet song as she touches each letter on the board. You can slow the pace of the song to match her ability to point to each letter in order. Several rounds of this and she'll be singing her ABCs in no time at all.

Another pre-reading skill this toy can help your child acquire is letter recognition. You can help encourage your child by asking her to push any letter on the desk.

It might say, "Show me the letter P. Good, you pointed to the letter P." "Show me the color green." "Show me the number two," etc.

This toy is completely self-correcting. As soon as your child responds to the command by pushing a letter, the activated voice in the toy will either acknowledge a correct response or ask your child to try again. Your child will enjoy this positive reinforcement and will want to continue progressing to more difficult levels of play.

More advanced skill level opportunities include putting letters together to spell words and practicing printing on the special letter board on the front face of the desk. Directional arrows are provided to show the child which way to move her pencil. However, at least in the beginning, we recommend you help your child learn where to place her pencil or crayon and how to configure the letters.

> "Cara, can you find the little number one at the top of the letter A here? Good, this is where you start making the letter A. Now, keep the pencil on your paper and draw straight down to number two. Now let's look for number three. There it is. Great. That's where you'll bring your pencil next. . . ."

If your child is just starting to write letters at this time, it is best to start with upper case letters, which are easier to read and write than lower case ones. Move on to lowercase letters once your child feels comfortable with uppercase ones. This toy provides an opportunity to practice both.

The idea here is to present an opportunity to explore letters, shapes, numbers, and musical notes in a fun way. The exploration will come naturally to your child and she will enjoy learning this way. Reading is definitely made fun when your child can master it at her own pace.

Easy Bake Oven™

This popular toy by Kenner, which is now in its thirtieth year of existence, is included here because of its language value and plain FUN appeal for the five-year-old.

Unlike the family kitchen where your child may sometimes help Mom and Dad with meal and snack preparation, this toy is made to scale specifically *for* the child, *with* the child chef in mind. Children enjoy the completely self-contained, child-sized unit, including child-sized baking pans and cake and cookie mixes. Being able to say, "I can cook" or "I made it all by myself" is what children like best about this toy.

What parents like best is the chance to teach their children rich language skills, including the language of math, while having fun doing so. This includes reading the instructions together; discussing the sequence of steps involved before, during, and after baking; assembling the necessary ingredients and utensils ahead of time; and following directions. So much language can be introduced during the play session: "Pans, cake mix, frosting, measuring cup, spoons, water, spatula, oven timer, oven mitts or pot holders, apron, recipe, ingredients, utensils, oil the pan, plug in the oven," etc.

Some beginning readers can help "read along" as the adults read through the recipes. Other children can be encouraged to pick out familiar letters or words on the back of each mix (perhaps ones that match the familiar letters in their name or other family members' names). Children can help Mom and Dad or the adult in charge identify the written numerals signifying the sequence of steps involved as they bake together. Ordinal numbers can be introduced—which step is first? second? and third? Children can also be taught to read the numbers on the oven timer. Some five-year-olds can count up to twenty; others up to one hundred. The overriding fact is that the typical five-year-old's interest in numbers is beginnning to peak. Parents can capitalize on this by providing lots of enriching language activities which would utilize these math skills. Remember that children learn best from direct experience in the present. All children, but especially children with a language delay, need more time and experience to develop language concepts, including the language of mathematics.

Many people think of math as plain old-fashioned adding and subtracting, but it is so much more. For young children, math is problem solving; it involves quantifying and understanding relationships between things, cause and effect.

> "What happens when we add *three teaspooons* of water to the cake mix? We can then stir it until it's creamy. If we only add *one teaspoon*, it will be too lumpy. If we bake the cake for exactly *ten minutes*, it will be firm, light, and fluffy on the inside. . . ."

Try an experiment with your child. Bake two different cakes: one for the correct number of minutes, and the other one ten minutes too long. Discuss the quality of the overbaked cake once it is cooled:

> "The outside is too dark in color, especially around the edges. The edges are crispy and taste burnt. Even the inside of the cake is too hot. . . ."

Your child will learn from her own personal experience about some important properties of mathematics, the importance of accurate measurement, and cooking time, and the necessity of following directions.

For a quick beginning lesson in fractions, you can have your child figure out how she wants to divide her cake when it's done. Does she want to eat the whole thing? (Remember one of the greatest joys of this toy is that the child can say afterwards,"I ate the whole cake myself!") Each whole cake weighs only a couple of ounces, complete with frosting.

For the child who can't be persuaded to share, she can be told: "You can eat one half of the cake now, and the other half after dinner—two halves equal a whole." Or perhaps you helped supervise a cake baking session with your child and two friends. Demonstrate how you can cut the cake into thirds or three equal parts. Ask the children, "Are the slices equal, or is one of them bigger than the others?"

Children enjoy learning math skills when they solve problems that have personal meaning for them. Realize that all of these math skills and terminology contribute to more highly developed language learning. First, your child learns the language of math by using actual objects (e.g., in this case, baking materials). By using these manipulative materials, she can begin to progress to using pictures of objects and finally from pictures to numerals.

Children in kindergarten learn math best through play situations and real-life situations. Teaching situations must be varied but repetitive for five-year-olds to grasp mathematics concepts involving numbers. The next toy described is another fun toy for fives that will allow you to introduce or review and reinforce earlier knowledge.

✍ **A NOTE ABOUT SAFETY:** Although this baking toy is designed for children, they must be supervised closely by an adult because of the heated electrical bulb and the hot metal baking pans.

Motorized Money Mill Coin Bank™

Up until this point, children are generally happy merely to receive a few coins and classify all of them together under the general category "money." Around the age of five, however, children begin to be genuinely interested in money for the first time. They like to collect it, learn the names of the different coins and bills, and spend or save it, depending on the day.

The keen desire to learn about money which develops around this age is so pervasive we recommend spending some of your child's playtime helping him learn the language of money. Children learn about money best when they can actually handle money on their own. For children with a learning challenge such as low vision or developmental delays, you can add the tactile sense when teaching about the coins because their sizes are different and children can learn to tell the difference between the coins that way.

Most people do not think of a toy bank as a play toy, but your child will love to play with his bank and all of the money he stores in it again and again. He'll want to fill it up, empty it out, and fill it up all over again. He will want to get the feel of the money this way, understand the classification system involved, sort the coins by color, size, material, weight, even shape (in some other countries, for instance, two silver coins can be about the same size and weight but one is round and one is hexagonal.) He'll want the pleasure of sorting his coins, seeing his bank fill up, and feeling how heavy his bank becomes. The heavier and fuller, of course, the more the cries of "I'm rich!"

For all of the reasons above, we recommend purchasing a clear, plexiglass bank such as the one made by Mag-Nif, Inc. This company makes a number of different models of banks but we especially like their Motorized Money Mill Coin Bank, which quickly sorts, stacks, and counts up to two hundred and fifty coins a minute. Your child will have great fun watching his see-through bank automatically carry out these functions as he drops in his

coins. The storage compartment in the bank even comes with sample coin wrappers to make deposits to commercial banks easy. Sorted coins can be removed easily from their tubes at the base of the toy bank so that the process of collecting, sorting, and saving can be done over and over again.

"Hugh, do you want to put the coins you got for your birthday in your new bank? Drop a handful of coins into the top coin chamber and watch them go down through the hopper. See how they get divided into separate piles? All of the pennies go together down one chute; all of the nickels go together through another chute; all of the dimes stay together; and all of the quarters stay together like magic. They automatically get sorted by size and weight—almost like the machine has a brain of its own. See how they finally end up in neat stacks in the bottom of the bank? When the chutes get entirely full we'll wrap them up in the wrappers here and bring them to the bank to deposit them into your account. . . ."

Single Concept

▼ "Let's see how much money you've saved in your bank. We'll count all your *pennies* first. *Pennies* are the small, brown coins. They're made of copper and zinc. Each is worth one cent. Now let's count each *penny* to see how many cents you have. (Help your child carefully count each penny by demonstrating how you touch each penny, then move it into a separate pile as you count. After all the pennies have been moved to a separate pile and counted carefully, say . . .) Great, you have five *pennies*. Five *pennies* is the same as five cents." (This is teaching the math concept of sets and assigning a numeral "5" to a set of five pennies.)

Single Concept

▼ "Now let's see how many *nickels* you have saved in your bank. Nickels are the large silver-colored coins. *Nickels* are made of copper and nickel. Another name for a *nickel* is five cents. A *nickel* is worth more than a penny. If you wanted to buy a piece of gum from the gumball machine, you could pay for it with a *nickel* or five cents. . . ."

Children at this age also like the idea of having their very own money for the first time, money that they can save or spend as they wish. To learn the real value of money, however, they must be taught how to count to higher numbers, how to understand the mathematic value of each coin, and how to do some simple addition and subtraction.

Math skills that can be reinforced with toy banks are:

- classifying—identifying objects by noting differences
- sorting—likeness and difference
- ordering—more or less
- counting

Learning basic math principles can be fun because it is learned naturally out of your child's play experience. The symbols for money (1 cent, 5 cents, 10 cents, 25 cents, $1.00) make no sense until they become a direct part of your child's concrete experience.

Continue this game with dimes, quarters, and dollar bills.

Checkers

Capitalize on your child's developing cognitive interest in playing games "by the rules" as well as her interest in counting by teaching her the game of checkers. Like ball play, it involves cooperation, playing by the rules, and learning how to be a gracious winner or loser. Again, we recommend stressing the process and fun involved in playing, rather than whether you win or lose!

By the time your child is five, she can play this game with a friend without adult supervision, once you help her get the hang of it. The concepts introduced in this game are learning to remember and stick to the rules, taking turns, colors (red and black), directions (forward, backward, and diagonal), and counting. (The object is to see how many of your opponent's checkers you can collect by *jumping over* an opponent's checkers and trying to move to the back line to *get a king* (which then allows the player to move forward or backward as well as diagonally). These

---

> **Single concept**
>
> ▼ "Try to *jump* your opponent's checker when he leaves an opening on the board. Once you *jump* a player's checker, you can take away his checker and keep it. See how many checkers you can *jump*. The person who collects the most checkers is the winner."

---

concepts of forward, backward, and diagonally may be new vocabulary for your child.

To begin, introduce the checker game board and the playing pieces and explain that the object is to move to the farthest line and capture the other player's (opponent's) checkers.

"There are only three ways you're allowed to move your checkers. You can move them forward, backward, or diagonally on the board (demonstrate). An easy way to remember what square you can move to is that you must always stay on your *own color*. If you are red, you can only move to the red squares. If you are black, you can only move to the black squares. . . ."

The first few times you play this game with your child, you'll need to remind her to stay on her color squares only. The concept of moving diagonally is complex at first but can be mastered with practice.

This game is wonderful for teaching language skills and can be played on a magnetic board, making the pieces easier to physically move across the board. Likewise, we have seen checkerboard sets made with Velcro so that people with physical disabilities can manipulate the pieces with greater ease. Additionally, you can put little knobs onto each checker which make them easier to pick up. Small knobs that are used for a variety of purposes can be purchased at a craft store.

Child's First Clock

A great birthday gift for your five-year-old is his first clock. He will like the sense of ownership, that an "adult thing" like a real clock belongs to him alone, and that he is old enough and responsible enough to begin to take care of some "adult things." Your child has an increasing sense of independence but enjoys modeling adults.

Like a toy bank, you may not think of your child's first clock as a play toy, but your child will! He will love to play with it and will spend a great deal of time paying attention to it. With a captivated audience, you as a parent have a great vehicle for teaching language.

Although there are many fine children's clocks on the market, the one we like is called the Teaching Clock, distributed by Lillian Vernon Mail Order Catalogue. It's bright colored, lightweight, and sturdy so your child can handle it freely without fear of harming either the clock or himself.

What makes this battery-operated quartz clock especially useful is that it has two sets of numerals around the outside face of the clock. Like standard clock faces, on the outer edge the numerals one through twelve are written in large, easy-to-read print.

Within the outer blue ring of numerals one through twelve, there is an inner contrasting white ring which marks each five minute delineation with the following words: 5 past, 10 past, quarter past, 20 past, 25 past, half past, 25 to, 20 to, quarter to, 10 to, 5 to, and finally o'clock.

There are also two more clear labels on the face of this cheerful clock: a bright yellow semicircle on the left which spells out the word "TO" and a bright red semicircle on the right which spells out the word, "PAST." This offers a clear way for you to explain:

"When the long minute hand sweeps past the red semicircle on the right side of the clock, you always read the number of minutes PAST whatever hour is on the clock. Likewise, when the long hand sweeps past the yellow semicircle on the left hand side of the clock you always read the number of minutes TO whatever hour is on the clock. Let's look at the clock together and actually practice moving the hands around to get the hang of it. . . ."

When your child is five, we recommend starting to familiarize him with the hour hand and the minute hand. Set the clock by adjusting the hands where you want them.

"See, if you have the long hand, called the minute hand on the number twelve, and the short hand, called the hour hand on the number six, your clock says six o' clock. Let's try it again. Let's keep the long hand on the 12 and move the short hand onto the number 7. What do you think your clock says now? Seven o'clock—yes, you're right!"

This is a toy your child can grow with. At this point, you are just beginning to teach him about the numbers and hands on the face of the clock and the basic language involved in learning to tell time. Your goal is to help him understand that telling time has significance to him personally and that specific times of the day are directly related to his actions.

"It's seven o'clock, time to wake up; 12:00 p.m., time for lunch; 6:00 p.m., time for dinner; 8:00 p.m., time for bed."

Your child will begin to recognize these times on the clock and remember which activities correspond to these times.

Your child will not be able to fine tune his time-telling skills until he is around eight years old. At the age of five, however, it's important to begin to lay the foundation for more complex thinking that will occur in the not-so-distant future. Hanging up a wall clock in your child's room tells him that you believe learning to tell time is important, and that it has very personal meaning for each member of the family.

Bug and Insect Catcher/Holder™

Catching fireflies in the summer when the cool night sky invites both young children and insects to roam about and explore their environment is thrilling.

Curiosity about the natural world becomes a springboard for language exploration, for learning new vocabulary, for collecting, counting, and classifying (sorting) objects, and for working either independently or as part of a team.

Your five-year-old typically will not be content just to read about scientific creatures like bugs and insects. She'll want to discover them for himself. This toy will allow her the opportunity to do so.

The bug and insect catcher we like is made by Exploratory, a division of Educational Insights. It has a colorful plastic base with an easy-to-lift lid. The see-through lid allows your youngster to easily study the bugs and insects she catches by peering through on all sides. There are ample airholes all around so that bugs and insects can continue to live within their new home.

Your child, filled with scientific curiosity and wonder, will naturally want to touch and even take apart and inspect the bugs and insects she finds. Now is the best time to instill in her respect for all living things, including people, animals, plants, flowers, and sea creatures. Explain that it is acceptable to study and inspect bugs and insects by handling them only if they have died. Otherwise, a "listen and look, touch, but don't harm" policy should be established early on. There is much to be learned through these modalities as well. An example of a language-enriching dialogue between you and your youngster while using this toy might go something like this:

> "Andrea, would you like to go outside and try to catch some fireflies? Grab your Bug Catcher and let's go see what we can find. Wow, it looks like Christmas time out here with all of these flickering bulbs lighting up the dark sky. Notice how the fireflies light up for just a quick second. If you listen carefully, you can hear them make a soft buzzing sound as they light up. Bzzzzzzz. See how many you can catch tonight. . . . You're as fast as lightning! Definitely faster than these lightning bugs. . . ."

Sometime shortly after your "catching session" is over your dialogue can resume and sound something like this:

"Good for you, Andrea. You collected three lightning bugs tonight. Notice how they can get air and continue to breathe through these tiny airholes in the container. All living creatures need oxygen to breathe. . . ."

Encourage your child's budding interest in classifying objects. This will help promote her desires to be a scientist so that she can better understand the world around her.

"Can you figure out if all three fireflies look alike or are they different from one another? What do you notice about them? Is one bigger? Darker or lighter than another? Does one have longer antennae than the others? Does one flicker more quickly than another? See if you can figure out which one flies the fastest. . . ."

After a firefly catching session, remember to stress cleanliness and hygiene. Remind your child to wash her hands with soap and water immediately after handling insects.

HOMEMADE TOYS

Pretend Restaurant

The typical five-year-old loves to act out the social roles of adults she sees. A highly popular play-acting scene for five-year-olds is creating a restaurant. Pretending to prepare food or being a waiter, waitress, or a customer at a favorite restaurant are all popular games. It is important to encourage this sort of play. It provides a tremendous opportunity for teaching language—spoken, signed, pointed to, written, or read—meaning that all aspects of a language experience approach are inherently

built into this play activity. Did you know that many fast food restaurants today have pictures on their cash registers so developmentally delayed adults can work there? A few small props will enable your child to carry out her playacting to its fullest. A cash register; toy money (coins and bills); basic drawing materials (paper, markers, or crayons) for writing items on menus or signs; plastic fruits, vegetables, or other foods; and a kitchen area and eating area are helpful items to dramatize play.

The following are some great reading readiness activities:

- Write out food prices on items to sell
- Label food items for sale with their names printed on a 3 x 5 card next to the item
- Advertise the restaurant and daily specials on poster or storefront
- Write out menus with pictures or words
- Add up food items purchased in the restaurant
- Describe the food served to the customers
- Take food orders

In the beginning, you'll need to help your child. Eventually, she will do this writing on her own using invented or made-up spellings by sounding out the words.

"Rachel, would you and Alexa like to play restaurant? I'll get some big pieces of posterboard and markers so you can make a sign for the front of your restaurant. What will you call your restaurant? Would you like help spelling the name of it so you can write it on your sign? How about writing the time of day that your restaurant is open so your customers know what time they can come in to order a meal? There are many other signs you could make, too. Rachel, while you're working on the restaurant sign, Alexa can start making another sign advertising the daily specials at your restuarant. Alexa, you can even draw pictures of the foods you'll be serving. Why not think of some of your favorite foods, like pizza or spaghetti or tacos and draw those for starters? Try to sound out the words and label your pictures with the names of the foods on them. I'll be happy to help you if you'd like.

"Is everyone having fun? Rebecca, you're finished with your sign? That looks terrific. I'm sure a lot of customers will want to come in your restaurant when they see your bright sign. Let's hang it up at the entrance of your restaurant so everyone passing by will notice it. Now you can get started on making the menus for your customers. . . ."

This play incorporates a thematic curriculum of social and cognitive skills. It is a perfect opportunity to test out new skills in math and language (oral skills, reading, and writing). The goal here is to help your child associate words and their meaning with experiences she has in her life. Remember: children relate words to their experiences and need lots of varied repetition to test out all the words they are learning.

Playacting using a restaurant theme naturally lends itself to your child developing what's called a sight vocabulary: recognizing printed words and their meaning without necessarily being able to sound them out by their letters. Help your child label in clear print on a 3 x 5 card the word associated with the item she's using in her play scene. Cards can be taped to label play items such as "cash register," "restaurant," "kitchen," "menu," "fruit," or "vegetables," etc. With frequent exposure, your child will begin to associate the written word with the actual item. This way, written words take on a real personal meaning and will therefore be recognized and retained more easily by your child. Your child can clearly see that writing is speech (sign or cues) written down and that the two are integrally related.

Yet another way you can use this playacting scenario to enrich your child's language is to focus on mathematical concepts. Encouraging your child to establish her own prices, to buy and sell her own foods at her restaurant, and to make change for customers are all fun ways to help improve language skills.

> "Alexa, Rachel, I think your customers need help figuring out the prices of the dinners you're serving tonight. Why don't you go over the different costs of each of the entrees on the menu? Spaghetti is $3.00 and comes with salad and garlic bread. Soda is fifty cents extra. You say you have $5.00 to spend? That will be plenty! You'll even have plenty of money left over to give the waiters a tip. . . ."

Homemade Journal

One of your goals as a concerned parent, caretaker, and teacher is to help your child develop interest in the written word. One way to do this is to help your child understand that the written word is a symbol for his experience. To help build this understanding, we recommend having your child write and illustrate an experience book. This is in keeping with the language experience approach to reading we described earlier. Remember, the backbone of a language experience program consists of the written story developed by the child himself.

Five-year-olds love books and stories about other children, and enjoy seeing how other children act. They also enjoy stories in which children are portrayed by animals. The famous Berenstain Bears stories are favorites.

Above all, however, five-year-olds love stories about themselves. At this age, children are still rather egocentric: the center of their own universe and present-oriented (focusing on the here and now). What better book for your child to read than one that was written by him and about him? Your child can be the author and illustrator all rolled into one. Perfect spelling isn't necessary; rather your child should get turned on to language and continue to develop *confidence* in mastering language. Developing a feeling of mastery and success is key.

Your child can write or dictate a story about one of his experiences. In the beginning, he will need your help. Open-ended questions (questions that cannot be simply answered with a "yes" or "no") invite your child to expand his thinking and language development. In effect, you, the adult, will help him with what he can say, sign, cue, or point to but cannot yet write.

After he adds some illustrations to his book, your child will be delighted to read what he has written. It is especially fun for your child to read his book to other family members and friends. With practice, you can help him increase his reading ability as letters and corresponding sounds become more familiar. Eventually, he may develop phonic skills—the ability to sound out the letters and syllables of words. At this point, he will be able to write and read whatever he can say.

Here are excerpts from a five-year-old's journal, written on different days with help from her mother:

We flew to grandma's house.

Today is Easter.

I went roller skating.

My babysitter came over. Her name is Jodi.

We went to dancing class.

We realize that we first recommended making a homemade experience book in the nine to twelve month section. However, because this is by far one of the greatest language enriching experiences for your child at every age, we are including it again for emphasis here. Moreover, while the experience book in the nine to twelve month developmental section was, of course, written and illustrated by an adult, now your child will be capable of writing and illustrating his own journal. Compared to the book you made before your child's first birthday, this journal will be much more sophisticated and complex. There will be a theme and a full story line, rather than just a picture labeled with a printed word on each page.

My Own Calendar

At this age, a homemade calendar can come in very handy. Your child can count the days, weeks, or months in anticipation of a special event; document a special occasion (first tooth out, pizza day at school, Christmas, summer vacation, birthday, Grandma coming to visit); and improve her writing and reading skills in the process. This is also a great way to teach responsibility and initiative. Your child can learn to record any afterschool activities such as karate or gymnastics and to be responsible for packing any necessary equipment or uniform in her backpack that morning before school. For children who have difficulty organizing their lives, like those with Attention Deficit Disorder (ADD), this calendar can give them a sense of order and control.

For all the same reasons that your child will love working on a homemade journal, she will also enjoy creating her own calendar. Remember, your five-year-old is the center of her universe. Many of life's experiences revolve around her. Marking a calendar with pictures and printed words gives your child a rich language and reading readiness activity that is focused on herself. This activity also offers practice in counting, recognizing letters and numbers, knowing the sequence of the days of the week and the months of the year, and learning the actual year. There are also opportunities to discuss the four seasons and to introduce time references such as yesterday, today, tomorrow, last week, this week, next week, last month, this month, next month. Last but not least, your child can be taught to glance at her calendar each morning to figure out the day of the week and the corresponding numerical date.

Your child's homemade calendar should be large, so that the squares for each day are big enough for your child to print words or draw pictures on. To help your child make her own calendar, feel free to use any current calendar that you might have around the house as a guide. In the beginning, you may have to help her with correct spelling. She will tell you which words she wants you to write on her calendar, or how she wants you to label the pictures she draws on certain days. Or, she can dictate to you what she wants to write, and you can spell out each word letter by letter, giving her the chance to do the actual printing. When your child does the actual writing herself, it gives her a sense of the direct connection between the spoken word and the written word. You can also provide your child with stickers or magazine or newspaper pictures to commemorate an upcoming special event or activity.

> "Cheryl, here are some assorted stickers I bought for you to put on your calendar. We can mark the dates of some of the special events coming up for you this year with these stickers. Here's a birthday cake sticker to stick on the day of your birthday. Let's find March; it's the month that comes after February. January, February, March—here it is. Now, your birthday is the nineteenth, right? Let's count together to make sure we put the sticker on the right day. One, two, three, four, five . . . here it is, 19. That means the 19th of March. That's your special day. Put your birthday cake sticker on that square so you'll know exactly which day is your birthday. Can you see which day of the week the 19th of March is? Let's sound it out together. Wednesday, your birthday will fall on a Wednesday this year. Wednesday is a school day, isn't it? Maybe your teacher will let you bring in a birthday treat for all of your classmates that day."

An added touch that will help make your child's homemade calendar truly personal and special is to ask your child to illustrate it by herself. Next to each page of dates could be stapled or taped a plain sheet of paper which your child can decorate with a hand-drawn picture. Try to resist helping your youngster with her drawings by telling her that this calendar is a truly special personal one made for her and by her alone. Offering encouragement such as, "Do the best job you can," or "What colors do the leaves turn in the fall?" will help your child gain the confidence to rely on her own artistic talents.

Finally, be sure to let your child know how valued her artwork and organization of personal events is by displaying her calendar proudly in her room. It should be hung up in a place where she will easily be able to see it each day when she wakes up, and before she goes to bed so it can be a conversation piece for the two of you.

We encourage you to save your child's homemade calendars year after year as a memory of her childhood.

Homemade Address Book

At this age, attention span lengthens. Your child now has a good memory for sequences, can memorize friends' and grandparents' phone numbers, and enjoys talking to family and friends on the phone or TTY. (See below.) In addition, your child can listen and speak quite well compared to one year ago. In fact, your kindergartner probably loves to talk. Why not draw on these skills and

interests to help her make the leap from the spoken word to the written word?

Keeping a personal address and telephone book with a list of all of the family, friends, teachers, or other important people in her life will help your child perceive the relevance of the written word. This is another activity which will help your child become an enthusiastic writer and reader.

You can either purchase an address book from a store or make one yourselves. We suggest the latter so that it will be large enough for your child to comfortably write in.

Start with twenty-seven light-colored sheets of plain 8½ paper. On the top of each page, help your child print one letter of the alphabet in ABC order. Next, staple the address book together on the left-hand side so that it opens and closes like a real address book. We suggest that you ask your child to go around to neighborhood friends or family members to start with to collect information for her homemade book.

"Hi, Lauren. I would like to get your address and telephone number to put in my address book. Let's see . . . your name starts with L. I need to find the L page. Here it is. How do you spell your name? L-a-u-r-e-n? There, I wrote it in my book. What's your telephone number so that I can call you? I'm going to call you when I get home to ask if you can sleep over at my house next week. First I have to ask my mother's permission when she gets home from work to know which day you can sleep over. I'll call you later. Bye now."

Help your child first write in and then recite her friends' addresses and telephone numbers over and over until she has learned them. She will feel extremely proud of her abilities to retain a seven-digit number in her mind "just like Mom and Dad."

Encourage your child to write or call friends and family whose names are recorded in her book. She will feel encouraged to write if it has personal significance to her. Why not suggest that your child send a picture she made at school to Grandma or Grandpa? Offer to help her look up their address in her personal address/telephone book, address the envelope, and stamp it.

Mailing letters your child wrote by herself is a great source of fun and learning. Her new writing skills will continue to be reinforced when recipients of her mailings send letters back. One of the happiest moments in your child's day will be opening up the mailbox and finding a letter addressed to her.

Whenever your child calls one of the friends listed in her book, help her with basic conversational skills, such as how to initiate a conversation on the phone, what to talk about, and how to end a call politely. Telephone etiquette skills must be taught. They do not naturally develop on their own.

> "Mary, do you want to call Edlyn to invite her over to play this Saturday? Let's look up her name in your address book. Look under the E section because Edlyn's name starts with the letter E. (In the beginning, you'll have to help your child with this part, but eventually she'll learn the beginning sounds and their corresponding letters on her own.) Pick up the receiver and wait for a dial tone. Do you hear a dial tone? Let me listen for a second just to make sure. OK, you're all set to call Edlyn. According to your address book, her number is 555–4431. Dial each number, one at a time. Push each button on the phone with a firm, quick touch. (You might have to let your child practice a while until she gets the hang of it.) Now listen for someone at Edlyn's house to answer on that end. When you hear someone say, "Hello," you say, "Hi, this is Mary, is Edlyn there please?" Then, you'll need to hold on until Edlyn gets on the phone. . . ."

Your side of the telephone conversation that you're modeling for your child might continue something like this:

> "Hi, Edlyn, this is Mary. Guess what? I memorized your phone number! I'm calling because I want to know if you can come over on Saturday to play. We can play with some of the new toys I got for my birthday, OK? Ask your mom if you can come over Saturday and I'll hold on. Anytime after lunch is fine with me. . . . Great, I'll see you Saturday. Bye. . . ."

Finally, instruct your child to carefully hang the receiver back on the cradle of the phone and remember to praise her for a job well done. A great place for your child's address book to be kept is someplace easy to reach near the phone.

Talking on the phone and using a telephone/address book to do so ties together your child's oral expressive skills with her reading and writing readiness skills. You build upon your child's good oral expressive skills to help her learn a higher developmental skill.

TTY
(Telephone Typewriter)

As we have said, the concept of "speech written down" is becoming more and more appealing to your five- to six-year-old. Additionally, he has a strong developing desire to communicate with family and friends across the telephone wires. This need to communicate is inherent in each of us. (Thank you, Alexander Graham Bell, for inventing the telephone.)

If your child has difficulty hearing on the telephone or his speech delay inhibits phone usage, he can still participate in a telephone conversation with family and friends by using a device called a TTY (Telephone Typewriter). This device was originally designed for use by the deaf in 1963 by Dr. Robert H. Weitbrecht. It can also be used, however, by people whose speech impairment prevents them from being understood on the telephone. A TTY converts the acoustic message from the telephone into a printed format. Its basic function operates like that of a typewriter. If your child cannot use a telephone in the conventional way, he can use a TTY to read and write his telephone conversation.

There are two ways to make a TTY call. First, the two people on either end of the telphone line can have a TTY attached to their telephones. In this case, the caller dials the other person's number and when the phone is answered, he types his message onto his TTY keyboard, which resembles a typewriter or computer keyboard. The receiver reads the printed message on the display panel on his TTY.

Calls may also be placed using a TTY if only one of the people involved in the telephone conversation has a TTY. This is accomplished through a telephone relay operator. This service is offered through the telephone company in each state. When using this type of service, there are two ways to go about it. The caller may type his printed message on a TTY to a relay operator, who then transmits the message to the receiver by way of voice. Or, the caller may give a spoken message to the relay operator, who then converts it into a printed message for the receiver to read on his TTY.

If your child is just beginning to read, a parent or another adult will have to sit with him to help him pick out letters on the TTY keyboard and to help with spelling of words. An adult will also have to be available to help your child read the printed words displayed on the TTY screen. However, this is a really FUN form of beginning reading and writing for children. They enjoy the practice of the activity itself, as well as the built in pleasure of easy communication with a friend. Don't be surprised if this develops into one of your child's favorite language building activities. With practice, you will see his writing, or in this case, his typing skills as well as his reading skills, begin to grow quickly. Even if you have no access to a TTY, your five- to six-year-old will love practicing writing on a typewriter or computer keyboard. An old discarded typewriter can be brought out especially for this purpose.

TOY SUMMARY SIXTH YEAR

The following is a list of toys that we have worked with in this developmental period. The asterisk indicates a homemade toy.

Soccer Balls
Easy Bake Oven
Motorized Money Mill Coin Bank
Teaching Clock
Playmobil Systems—Classroom Setting and Schoolbus
Little Smart Writing Alphabet Desk
Bug and Insect Catcher/Holder
Checkers
*Pretend Restaurant
*Homemade Journal
*My Own Calendar
*Homemade Address Book

VOCABULARY AND CONCEPTS

There will be further improvement in many of the skills introduced in your child's fifth year:

- action words (mix, plug in, stir, bake, taste, divide, catch, explore, investigate, compare, decide, etc.)
- adjectives (tremendous, fastest, slowest, etc.)
- bugs and insects
- calendar concepts (week, month, year, last week, this week, next week, last year, this year, next year)
- computer skills and terminology (monitor, keyboard, hardware, software, computer, disk, printer)
- cooking skills (measuring, using the oven only with adult supervision, oven mitts, potholders, baking, washing the dishes, cleaning up after yourself)
- counting skills (1–100; first, second, third, etc.)
- fantasy play - role playing
- letters of the alphabet (letter recognition improves; handwriting improves; phonetic skills improve, although invented spelling dominates)
- money (names and value of coins, saving, spending, borrowing, sorting, collecting)

- moral issues (following the rules, telling the truth, learning to say, "I'm sorry," using words to explain feelings)
- safety rules (never talk to strangers, look both ways before crossing the street, wear your seatbelt, use the sidewalk for walking, wear your bicycle safety helmet)
- school terminology and concepts (riding the bus, bus-driver, respecting the teacher and school principal, and fellow classmates, learning is fun, homework)
- self-esteem (finding a skill or area of interest your child enjoys and feels good about himself when doing)
- social skills (sharing, taking turns, taking another's point of view, cooperation)
- sports vocabulary (swing, step up to the plate, keep your eye on the ball, all for one and one for all, team spirit, equipment names, rules of the games, playing fair, etc.)
- taking initiative and responsibility (being a valuable member of a team at home, in school, or in the community)
- telling time skills
- TTY skills

BOOKS

Books that focus on special areas of interest continue to appeal to the five-year-old. So, too, do books presenting moral issues, issues about school experiences, and self-concept books about your child's special needs.

Alexander and the Terrible, Horrible, No Good, Very Bad Day. Judith Viorst. Illustrated by Ray Cruz. New York: Atheneum/ Aladdin. 1972.

This is a story every child can relate to, but particularly the child with a special need who has more challenges and, perhaps, frustrations than most others. It is an amusing story and comforting to know that this experience happens to other people as well.

All About Hanukkah. Judye Groner and Madeline Wikler. Illustrated by Rosalyn Schanzer. Rockville, MD: KARBEN Copies. 1988.

A highly praised retelling of the Hanukkah story with full- color illustrations. Candle lighting blessings, games, recipes, and songs. Everything you need for a Happy Hanukkah.

All the Better to See You With. Margaret Wild. Morton Grove, IL: Albert Whitman and Co. 1974.

> This is a clear, well-written introduction to the concept of the child with a visual impairment. Recommended reading for your child with a visual impairment or if your child has a family member or friend with a visual impairment.

Berenstain Bears Series. Jan and Stan Berenstain. New York: Random House.

> Your child will love to start collecting this series of books which tell the story of the popular bears and their family tales. Children learn great morals from these stories and can apply them directly to their own lives and similar situations. Especially recommended are *Trouble at School, Go Out for the Team, Trouble with Money, Go to the Doctor,* and *Trouble with Friends,* but each and every book is valuable and recommended.

Bob Books for Beginning Readers. West Linn, OR: Bob Books Publications. 1994.

> This delightful, color-coded paperback book series is a must for your child who is beginning to learn to read. Simple illustrations and easy phonics will help your child learn to read easily and quickly. Each book in the series is short and simple. The storyline is about everyday happenings in your child's life.

The Circus Girl. Michael Garland. New York: Dutton Children's Books. 1993.

> Alice and members of her family spend a busy day working in a circus as it travels from town to town. This is an outstanding, well-illustrated book which should be on every family's bookshelf.

Dollars and Cents for Harriet. Betsy and Giulio Maestro. New York: Crown. 1988.

> Harriet tries to earn five dollars for a kite. Your child will learn to recognize coins that add up to a dollar.

Harry the Dirty Dog. Gene Zion. New York: Harper. 1956.

> Harry gets so dirty his own family no longer recognizes him. Look for other books in this series which will entertain and lighten your spirit.

He's My Brother. Joe Lasker. Morton Grove, Illinois: Albert Whitman and Co. 1974.

> This well-told story introduces the concept of the invisible handicap, the learning disability. Clearly and compassionately told, it will give your child a great introduction to children with this special need.

Hillel Builds a House. Shosana Lepon. Illustrated by Marilynn Barr. Rockville, MD: KAR-BEN Copies. 1993.

> Hillel loves to build houses—tree houses, pillow forts, and closet hideaways. But he can't seem to find the right time to celebrate in one of his houses until fall comes, bringing the holiday of Sukkot. A fanciful trip through the Jewish year.

Howie Helps Himself. Joan Fassler. Morton Grove, Illinois: Albert Whitman and Co. 1975.

> This terrific, clearly illustrated book features a boy in a wheelchair. It is a book which will foster independence and a positive self-image.

If You Made a Million. David M. Schwartz. Illustrated by Steven Kellogg. New York: Lothrop, Lee, and Shepard Books. 1989.

> This outstanding book introduces coins, dollar bills, and how to count, spend, and save them. The story is presented by a magical wizard who will enchant you and your child.

I'm Deaf and It's Okay. Lorraine Aseltine. Morton Grove, IL: Albert Whitman and Co. 1986.

> The author portrays this boy's special needs realistically and compassionately. This is a great book for opening up a discussion with your child about his or her deafness.

Keith Edward's Different Day. Karin Melberg Schwier. San Luis Obispo, CA: Impact Publishers. 1992.

> This clear, simply told story is a self-esteem booster, explaining that every child is unique and different in his own way.

Matthew's Dream. Leo Lionni. New York: Knopf. 1991.

> A young mouse visits an art museum and is encouraged by this experience to become a great painter.

The Mitten. Alvin Tresselt. New York: Lothrop. 1964.

> In this Ukranian folk tale, the mitten becomes a warm, cozy home for many forest animals. Incredible illustrations and story that will mesmorize you and your child.

More Notes from a Different Drummer: A Guide to Juvenile Fiction Portraying the Handicapped. Barbara Baskin and Karen H. Harris. New York: New Providence, NJ: Bowker Publishers. 1984.

> Lists and describes children's fiction portraying characters with disabilities.

My Brother, Matthew. Mary Thompson. Bethesda, MD: Woodbine House. 1992.

> This illustrated story tells a realistic, compassionate tale about how family life focuses on the needs of a child with a disability and the effects that it can have on the other kids in the family. This book will encourage siblings to share their emotions and reassure them that their role in the family is very important.

Portraying Persons with Disabilities: An Annotated Bibliography of Nonfiction for Children and Teenagers. Joan Friedberg et al. New Providence, NJ: R.R. Bowker. 1991.

> This book describes over 300 nonfiction books for young people about disabilities, published between 1980 and 1991.

The Rainbow Fish. Marcus Pfister. Translated by J. Alison James. New York: North-South Books. 1992.

> The Rainbow Fish with his shimmering scales is the most beautiful fish in the ocean. But until he learns to share his most prized possession, he cannot learn the value of friendship.

The Real Tooth Fairy. Marilyn Kaye. Illustrated by Helen Cogancherry. New York: Harcourt, Brace, Jovanovich. 1990.

> Alice loses a tooth and discovers the magic of the real tooth fairy in this magnificently illustrated book.

Shelley, the Hyperactive Turtle. Deborah Moss. Illustrated by Carol Schwartz. Bethesda, MD: Woodbine House. 1989.

> The author provides clear information about the physical and emotional aspects of hyperactivitiy in an upbeat, postive tone. Your child will grasp the concept of what hyperactivity means and will feel better about himself, just like Shelley in the story.

The Story of Babar. Jane De Brunhoff. New York: Random House. 1993.

> Introduce your child to this classic story, as well as others in the Babar series. Magnificently illustrated, deeply told stories of issues involving family matters with moral lessons to be learned.

Tick Tock. Bobbi Katz. Illustrated by Carol Nicklaus. Random House. 1988.

> Movable clock hands and adjustable digital dials help your child learn how to tell time in a simple, clear way.

The Town Mouse and The Country Mouse. Lorinda Bryan Cauley. New York: Putnam. 1984.

> This lovely telling of Aesop's fable is presented in a charming way and set in the nineteenth century.

Trouble with School: A Family Story about Learning Disablities. Kathryn Boesel Dunn and Allison Boesel Dunn. Illustrated by Rick Stromoski. Bethesda, MD: Woodbine House Publishers. 1994.

> Families can benefit from this story of how one family handled the often anxiety-filled situation of identifying and understanding a child's learning disability. The mother's side of the story and the child's side of the story are presented side by side on facing pages.

Two by Two: Favorite Bible Stories. Harry Araten. Rockville, MD: KAR-BEN Copies. 1991.

> The Bible for beginners. Vivid full-page illustrations accompany simply written one-page Bible stories. Adam and Eve, Noah, Jonah, and other favorite heroes and heroines.

A Very Special Friend. Dorothy Levi. Washington, DC: Gallaudet University Press. 1989.

> This clearly illustrated, well-written story presents a special friendship which blossoms between two girls, one deaf and the other hearing. Must reading for the deaf child who would like to build friendships and be included in regular classrooms.

Where's Chimpy? Berniece Rabe. Photos by Diane Schmidt. Morton Grove, IL: Albert Whitman and Co. 1988.

> This delightful story, recommended for children ages three to seven, follows a little girl with Down syndrome as she searches for her missing stuffed animal.

Why Am I Different? Norma Simon. Illustrated by Dora Leder. Morton Grove, IL: Albert Whitman and Co. 1993.

> This is a book which will help the very young child develop a realistic self-image. The text and lively pictures help explore the theme of individualism, and that it's okay to be different.

The Young Soccer Player. Wayne Holder. New York: Dorling Kindersley Publishing, Inc. 1994.

> This highly visual, practical approach to learning soccer is written by a professional soccer player and is must reading for the beginning athlete. Detailed photographs and clear explanations illustrate basic techniques and rules of the game for a starting player. Fancy tricks are also included for the more advanced player.

Conclusion

We have traveled an interesting journey from the first sound of the birth cry to complicated thoughts of diplodoci and fungi. Your patterns of communication with your child should last throughout your lifetime together. You may be amazed that your teenager will share her thoughts with you because she knows that you have always been there to listen to her. In teaching her language skills, you have not only opened up a world of communication but helped her gain the confidence she needs in order to participate fully in the adult world. Because your child has special needs for learning language, this road to language development may be challenging for you, but spending time with her now giving her the gift of language will bring rewards later.

SUMMARY OF YOUR CHILD'S SIXTH YEAR (60–72 MONTHS)
LANGUAGE

Developmental Milestone	Date Achieved	NOT YET	PROGRESSING
Can understand full repertoire of a spoken language			
Has full spoken use of English language			
Continues to ask for definitions of more complex words (e.g.,"What does it mean to borrow a book?")			
Uses grammar with high degree of accuracy			
Can weave several sentences into a spoken paragraph			
Can tell sequence of a simple story (What happened first, next, last) into a short story			

COGNITIVE

Developmental Milestone	Date Achieved	NOT YET	PROGRESSING
Can recognize and identify all upper case letters of the alphabet			
Can recognize and identify all lower case letters of the alphabet			
Can distinguish between and recite initial consonant sounds of words			
Can distinguish left from right			
Can assemble a simple puzzle (25 pieces)			
Can notice details and patterns of a picture			
Can distinguish missing piece of picture and/or note "what doesn't belong" in a picture			
Can express feelings of real or imaginary people or animals			
Can explain in detail			
Can follow directions (three items in a sequence; "Please go into the living room, find your book, and put it away in your bedroom upstairs")			

Developmental Milestone	Date Achieved	NOT YET	PROGRESSING
Can turn on a home computer, play a familiar game, and turn off computer when finished			
Can recognize simple words and signs such as "stop," "walk"			
Can read a pre-primer with accompanying pictures as a visual cue			
Can memorize and recite a sequence of seven numbers			
Can cooperate with peers in a game involving simple rules and taking turns without adult supervision			
Can begin to be less egocentric, and take on another point of view			
Can sort out a group of coins and distinguish pennies from other coins			
Can count to 100, can write to 22			
Can recite ordinal numbers—first though ninth			
Can draw a person figure with up to six body parts			

PHYSICAL
Gross Motor

Developmental Milestone	Date Achieved	NOT YET	PROGRESSING
Can hop on one foot up to ten seconds			
Can walk on a balance beam			
Can run with greater speed			
Can throw a ball accurately at target (from how many feet away?)			
Can catch a ball (from how many feet away?)			
Can hit a whiffleball with a bat			
Can add speed to running			
Can broad jump a longer distance			
Can kick a ball (how many yards?)			

Developmental Milestone	Date Achieved	NOT YET	PROGRESSING
Can roller skate without holding on for balance			
Can ride a two wheeler with training wheels			

Fine Motor

Developmental Milestone	Date Achieved	NOT YET	PROGRESSING
Can key in letters and numbers (with increasing speed) at a typewriter or computer keyboard			
Can legibly copy letters and words			
Can copy 0, square, triangle, diamond			
Can legibly print first and last names accurately			
Can color a simple picture carefully within the lines			
Can neatly trace letters in a simple picture			
Can use child-sized scissors to neatly cut on a line			
Can tie shoes by himself			
Can button and dress himself			

Chapter 5

Teaching Language throughout the Day

Our emphasis in this book is on enriching your child's language by using specific toys, activities, and books. There are many other toys, activities, and books that you can use as successfully as the ones we chose to describe. There are also many other ways for you to teach language to your child. Basically, if you are paying attention to your child when you are with her, you will be teaching all of the time. A beautiful way for her to learn is for you to simply talk to her in short, understandable phrases about things that she is interested in. You can discuss what you are doing, try to imagine what Grandma is doing, or show her the variety of colors in the world around her. Anything will work for you if you go about it correctly.

Going on Outings

Going for a walk on a beautiful day can be an incredible language learning time if you are willing to walk at your child's pace and stop for the things she wants to explore. A caterpillar crawling on the ground, a fallen leaf, a crack in the sidewalk are all new and fasinating for her. Take your time; stroll along and let her explore and ask questions about all of the wonders that she sees.

"Look at that beautiful red leaf. Can you find which tree it fell from? I think you're right, I think it fell from that maple tree over there. Look at all the red leaves on that maple tree. Soon they will all fall to the ground. In the summer those leaves are green. But it is fall, so the leaves are turning red. They are getting ready for winter. In the winter all the leaves fall to the ground and next spring what happens? Right, they will bud again on the trees. . . ."

A trip to the grocery store can be a wonderful language learning experience if you do a little planning ahead of time. Have her participate with you in the kitchen before you go to the store. The two of you look through the pantry and the refrigerator to decide what you need to buy. As you stand in front of the refrigerator, ask her if you need to get more milk. Look at the milk container and determine if it is full, empty, or almost empty.

Whenever you can, give your child a list that she can shop for. Use the ads in the paper to clip out pictures of items and paste them on index cards. When you make your list, choose the cards that you'll need and give them to her for her list. Since many items are the same from week to week, you can re-use your index cards each week. She may be so busy looking for her list on each aisle that you will not run into the problem of screaming for candy. If she is big enough to be out of the cart and walking around, let her take the items off the shelf herself and put them in the cart. If your child has a visual impairment and cannot see the index cards, you might verbally give her a list of two things to remember and guide her with verbal language as to where she might find them. For example, you might say, "Today we need to get some ice cream and some frozen orange juice. They are both in the frozen food section. You can tell when you are there because the air will feel colder. Will you remind me when we get to the frozen food section that we need ice cream and orange juice?"

For other children your conversation might be like this:

"Can you help me find the pictures of things in the paper that we need to get at the store? Let's look at this page. We need milk. Good. Let's cut out that picture and paste it on an index card. Now we also need some apples. Do you see any apples on this page? That's right, those are apples. Let's cut that out and put it on a card. What color apples do you want to get at the store? Should we get red ones or green ones? I like green ones too. We'll look for green ones when we get to the store. What else do you see that we should get?"

Continue in this way until she has a group of cards of items that she can look for when you get to the store.

Another learning opportunity is visiting friends. This often starts out as a good idea which quickly changes into a scene of screaming and fighting because your child is not properly prepared for a new environment. Planning ahead can eliminate this conflict, as well as provide an opportunity for language learning. We suggest that you have a calendar for your child's activities such as the one we describe in the five- to six-year-old chapter. Let's say that you are going to visit Barry and his family today. Take your child to the calendar and help her find the correct day. Then take Barry's photo (which you took before) and put it on the day of the calendar. Talk about going to Barry's house this morning and the toys that you remember that Barry has. Suggest that your child take one of her toys that Barry may not have so that they can share their toys. If the worst does happen and no one wants to share, then your child will have her own toy and Barry can have his. Keep your visit short and geared to the attention span of your child.

> "Look at the calendar. What do we have that is special for today? Right! We are going to Barry's house. Do you remember Barry? He has a lot of cars that you like to play with. What do you have that you think Barry might like to play with? Do you want to take your dump truck? Maybe you can build a road and play with the cars and the truck. It's always fun to share your toys with your friends. . . ."

At Home

During the course of any ordinary day, there are numerous times for pouring language into your child. Keep

her near and talk to her as much as possible about your everyday activites. You may think that this sounds like a lot of trouble, but when you stop and think how short a time it really is and the value of what you are doing, you will agree that the long-term payoffs are great. Just think of all the things you do that you can turn into learning experiences. We have given you a few examples and you will be able to think of many more things during your day at home. Be sure to involve all of your child's senses as you talk about things—her sense of touch, sound, smell, and sight. This helps her to learn through every avenue.

Washing Dishes

"Let's wash the dishes. We need soap and water to get the dishes clean. Look at all the bubbles. Let's get the sponge and wash the dishes clean. We can even sing a song while we wash the dishes. This is the way we wash the dishes, wash the dishes, This is the way we wash the dishes so early in the morning. . . ."

Cooking

While cooking, state out loud each of the steps you're taking to put together the ingredients for the recipe.

"Let's cook some rice for dinner. You love rice. That's one of your favorite foods. We need a pot with a lid to cook the rice. Can you help me look in the cabinet for a pot? Here's one. Now we need to fill the pot with water, exactly up to here. That's two cups of water. . . . "

Vacuuming

"Time to vacuum the floor. Do you want to be my helper? We can vacuum the floors, and surprise Grandma and Grandpa when they come to visit. Everything will be so clean. The vacuum will be very loud after we plug it into the wall. We can take turns as we vacuum. . . ."

Washing the Car

"Would you like to help me wash the car? We need to do that because the car is very dirty. It doesn't get a bath every night like you do. What do we need to wash the car? Right. We need a bucket of water, some soap, and a sponge. We need all those things to wash the car. Can you help me find the bucket? We are going to make the car look shiny again. . . ."

Driving in the Car

As a parent, you probably spend many many hours driving in the car with your child. Driving to your child's school, to the store, to the doctor, dentist or speech therapist, to visit with friends . . . the list is endless. Why not make the most of this time together by building your child's language skills? Talk, point, gesture, cue, or sign about any number of different language enriching experiences. For example, if you are on your way to see your child's therapist, you can discuss with him where you are going and who you will see:

"In a few minutes, we have to get ready to see Dr. Fields. Remember we drive past the supermarket on the way? Let's count how many red cars we pass on the way. I see a red car over there. Look! I wonder how many more red cars we'll see? There's another red car ahead of us. He's making a left turn. We keep going straight to the doctor's office."

There are any number of other daily activities that can be turned into fun learning experiences, including:
- Ironing
- Cleaning the refrigerator
- Making beds
- Mowing the lawn
- Raking the leaves
- Washing the dog
- Feeding the dog or cat
- Scrubbing the bathtub
- Getting dressed
- Putting toys away

Enjoy the time with your children. You are their first and best language teacher. The relationship you establish now will last a lifetime.

Chapter 6

Computer Technology and Language Learning

It is September 1, 2005 and you are getting your child ready for the first day of school. New shoes, new backpack, new lunchbox, and don't forget the laptop computer. Yes, in the twenty-first century, many children will probably have a laptop computer to take to school.

Computers are already an everyday part of life and many children, with and without special needs, have access to a computer at school and at home. Computer technology has opened a whole new world to children with special needs. It has enabled mute children to "talk," children with physical disabilities to "move," blind children to "read," and deaf children to "hear." It has also made it easier and more entertaining for children with a variety of disabilities to learn needed skills and concepts. Your child's life will be so much easier because of computer technology.

How does this relate to the subject of this book? Is the computer a toy? Yes and no. Can computer technology be used to teach language? Most definitely yes. In the sections below, we will explain some of the ways that computers and toys that utilize computer technology can be used to teach and reinforce important concepts and language skills.

Electronic Toys

In previous chapters, we have recommended many electronic toys. Many of these computer-based toys help your child understand the very important concept of cause and effect. When your child pushes a button, flips a switch, or otherwise interacts with the toy, something happens—cause and effect. The Easy Touch Tape Player™ in our six- to nine-month-old section is a good example of a toy that teaches cause and effect. When your infant pushes the green button on this player, he is rewarded with music that he so enjoys. The buttons are light and easy to operate but you can also add a switch which will make it even easier for him to operate.

In the one-year-old chapter, we have described toys such as the Push N' Go Train™, the Listen and Learn Ball™, and the Talking Peek-A-Boo Zoo™, which also show the young child that when he activates a toy, something will happen in response. These toys are not only fun but have a long-range purpose in introducing beginning computer concepts.

One manufacturer that has made a lot of computer-oriented toys for young children is the VTech Corporation. Little Smart First Words™ and Little Smart School Words™ are geared for children as young as six months. By simply pushing a button, they receive instant responses of vocabulary words, nursery rhymes, and beginning letters and numbers, as well as shapes and objects. For the older child, VTech makes toys such as the Little Smart Driving School™ which gives your child the opportunity to hear more vocabulary with the addition of sounds in his environment such as sirens, horns, etc. In our five-year- old chapter, we also describe for you the VTech Desk™, which will provide your child with hours of learning experiences.

As we have throughout our book, we encourage you to play with your child and expand on the vocabulary offered through these electronic toys in order to enrich his language development. Remember: it is fine for him to have time alone with the toy but he should also have ample opportunity to play with you.

Computers and Software

When you actually introduce a computer to your children is a matter of your own preference and lifestyle. In some homes, a computer is standard equipment and one or both parents are familiar with how it operates. The computer can be set up so that both parents and children can use it at different times yet not interfere with each other's work. For example, a software package entitled "Kid Desk" developed by Edmark and an expanded ver-

sion called the "Family Edition Kid Desk" can allow each member of the family to access his own part of the computer. These packages can both be used on either a personal computer or an Apple product. This will help alleviate fears parents may have of their child using the adult computer and inadvertently erasing very important documents!

When you decide to purchase a computer, get a large-capacity hard drive to be sure that your computer will run the software you want; get a color monitor to maintain your child's interest; and get a CD ROM (read only memory stored on a compact disc) to open up many avenues of interactive computing for your young child. A used computer is okay, but don't compromise on desirable features for the sake of cost alone.

Some children as young as two show an interest in the computer and become quite adept at using the computer mouse to interact with the software on the screen. These children definitely need adult supervision and interaction to benefit the most from computer use. However, most software is recommended for children starting at age three. Again, you know your child the best and you know what will and won't work for him. Use your best judgement.

For children with limited physical ability, there are many adaptations for the computer keyboard. For example, there is a Muppet Keyboard, which is a keyboard with very large keys and bright colors which fits on top of a standard keyboard. There is also a board called Intellikeys, which is a flat keyboard that is used in place of a regular keyboard. This flat keyboard can be programmed to use an overlay of a keyboard or any overlay you want to create. For example, if your child is able to choose between two objects, you can make an overlay with two shapes on it—a circle and a square. When your child hits the circle he gets a response on the screen and when he hits the square he gets a different response on the screen. You can program this for any language that you are trying to teach your child.

When it comes to selecting software, it can be difficult to stay abreast of what is available. New software programs are being created daily and new editions of old software pop up regularly. One good way to find out what is out there is to subscribe to a magazine called *Club Kidsoft*, which is a very interesting software magazine for kids. It reviews the latest in software packages on disk and CDs for both Personal Computers and Macintosh Computers. There are activities and games in the magazine for older children and a catalog of "kid tested and parent tested software titles." Each issue also comes with a computer disk so that you can preview the software mentioned in the magazine. You can also download (take programs off the disk) and purchase the software via this disk. The listing for this magazine will appear below in the reference section. It is the best way we know of at this time to access the latest information.

In her book, *Kids and Computers*, Judy Salpeter gives some ideas to help parents choose developmentally appropriate software for preschool children. She says, "Developmentally appropriate software is:

- **Open ended and exploratory.** It doesn't focus on right and wrong answers but allows children to investigate and discover for themselves.

- **Easy for a young child to use independently.** It does not require reading, has easy to understand directions and only expects children to find a limited number of keys on the keyboard. Furthermore, it is flexible about input devices, allowing a child to use a mouse, the keyboard, or an alternate device—whichever is easiest for that child.

- **Focused on a broad range of skills and concepts.** It works on more than just the numbers, letters, colors, and shapes so often identified as preschool skills. In addition (or instead), it encourages children to classify, to experiment using trial and error, to create and, in general, to think.

- **Technically sophisticated.** It appeals to a child's multisensory learning style, offering attractive graphics, appealing animations, and outstanding sound. It loads quickly and does not have long delays between screens (during which time a young child can become bored).

- **Age-appropriate.** It doesn't push the child to master skills for which she's not yet ready. The images and examples it uses are from real life or are at least understandable to the young child (within her realm of experience).

- **Play and fun.** It encourages children to imagine, might involve fantasy play, and is definitely enjoyable. Furthermore, the fun is derived from the activity itself, not from some extrinsic reward given if the child succeeds at a given task.

- **Encouraging.** Children experience success when using this software; it helps build their self-esteem."*

Computers and Special Needs

During the last few decades, a great deal of exciting new computer technology has evolved, opening a world of possibilities for children with special needs. There are now computers that respond to voice commands, touch screens, speech synthesizers that talk for the user, and switches that allow the computer to be accessed by a head movement, a puff of air, or a wink of an eye.

Computers have connected the deaf to others through TTYs, Bulletin Boards, and FAX machines. The deaf are getting better use of hearing aids that are computer matched to their individualized hearing losses. There are cochlear implant devices that are surgically implanted in the child's inner ear and are programmed for the individual who is profoundly deaf to be able to respond to speech as well as environmental sounds.

For individuals with learning disabilities, there are wordprocessing programs with spelling and grammar checkers, as well as a number of programs designed to help teach reading and other problematic subjects. For the blind there are visual scanners that can "read" any book out loud for the listener. There are portable braillers as well as the devices with the capability of converting printed letters to tactile codes. The computer has the ability to display large print and output large print hard copy. For those with physical disabilities, the computer has opened the world to environmental control through electronic wheelchairs, and technology that can perform such tasks as opening and closing curtains and opening and closing the front door. Computers can also enable people with limited mobility to shop, inquire for information, and manage banking from their homes.

Making your child comfortable with computer technology is becoming more and more of a need as we move into the next century. Teaching your infant to reach and touch to control a computer switch and access a touch talker will have far-reaching benefits for him. Teaching your child words such as floppy disk, hard drive, and mouse is important for him to maximize the use of computer technology.

The following resources will help you access the newest technology in hardware and software. Make use of them. Get on the mailing lists so as new devices are developed, you will be among the first to know. Enjoy exploring these new avenues with your child. Although computer

---

* *Judy Salpeter, Kids and Computers: A Parent's Handbook (Englewood Cliffs, NJ: Alpha Books - A Division of Simon & Schuster, 1991), p. 43.*

technology will ease the daily living needs of your child, you are still a very important component. You must be a part of this learning experience with him.

Resources

BOOKS

Lindsey, Jimmy D., ed. *Computers and Exceptional Individuals.* Austin, TX: Pro-Ed, 1992.

Salpeter, Judy. *A Parent's Handbook: Kids and Computers.* Englewood Cliffs, NJ: Alpha Books - A Division of Simon & Schuster, 1991.

CATALOGS

Apple Computer-Disability Solutions Group. 20525 Mariani Ave. MS 36SE. Cupertino, CA 95014. 408–974–7910; 408–974–7911 (TTY).

Cambridge Development Laboratory, Inc. 86 West Street. Waltham, MA 02154. 800–637–0047.
> Large catalog with many software and hardware options to choose from.

Chaselle, Inc. 9645 Gerwig Lane. Columbia, MD 21046–1503. 800–242–7355.
> Educational software packages.

Club Kidsoft: Software Magazine for Kids. 718 University Ave. Suite 112. Los Gatos, CA 95030. 800–354–6150; Fax: 1–408–354–1033.

Communication Aids for Children and Adults. 6625 N. Sidney Place. Milwaukee, WI 53209–3259. 414–352–5678.
> Catalog of assistive devices to talk for individuals with disabilities, communication board materials, adapted toys for children with special needs, and voice-activated materials.

Communication Skill Builders. 3830 East Bellevue. P.O. Box 42050–CS4. Tucson, AZ 85733. 602–323–7500 V/TDD; Fax: 602–325–0306.
> Computer software as well as other activities to help with language development.

Davidson and Associates, Inc. P.O. Box 2961. Torrance, CA 90509. 1–800–545–7677.
> Has a large selection of early childhood software packages.

Don Johnston Developmental Equipment, Inc. P.O. Box 639. 1000 N. Rand Rd. Building 115. Wauconda, IL 60084–0639. 800–999–4660; Fax: 708–526–4177.
> Catalog of assistive technology such as switches, adapted keyboards, and touch windows, as well as appropriate software for special needs.

Edmark. P.O. Box 3218. Redmond, WA 98073–3218. 800–362–2890.

> Early Learning Software as well as programs for all major educational areas: art, music, social studies, reading, science, mathematics.

Educational Resources. 1550 Executive Drive. Elgin, IL 60123. 800–624–2926

> Multi-media resources. Has some Pre-K programs.

Hartley: Courseware for Quality Education. 3451 Dunckel Road. Suite 200. Lansing, MI 48911–4216. 800–247–1380; Fax: 517–394–9899.

> Special section for early learning materials starting at age three.

Kapable Kids. P.O. Box 250. Bohemia, NY 11716. 800–356–1564.

> Catalog of switches and toys that are adaptable for all children with special needs.

RJ Cooper and Associates. 24843 Del Prado, #283. Dana Point, CA 92629. 714–240–1912.

> Carries software packages for special needs, switch-adapted mouse, touch windows, special keyboards for special needs.

Sunburst/Wings for Learning. 101 Castleton Street. P.O. Box 100. Pleasantville, NY 10570–0100. 800–321–7511; Fax: 914–747–4109.

> Source for software, CD-ROM, Video, Videodisc.

ORGANIZATIONS

ABLENET
Adaptive Device Specialists
1081 10th Ave. SE
Minneapolis, MN 55914

Apple Foundation
Special Education Division
20525 Mariani Ave.
Cupertino, CA 95014

Augmentative Communication News
One Surf Way, Suite 215
Monterey, CA 93940

Computability
4000 Grand River Ave.
Novi, MI 48050

Computer Users in Speech and Hearing
Attn: William Seaton, Ph.D.

P.O. Box 2160
Hudson, OH 44236

Council for Exceptional Children
Center for Special Education Technology
   Information Exchange
1920 Association Dr.
Reston, VA 22091

Don Johnson Developmental Equipment
P.O. Box 639
1000 Rand Road
Wauconda, IL 60084

Educational Software Exchange Library
c/o Stanford Avenue School
2833 Illinois Ave.
Southgate, CA 90281

EPIE Institute
Teachers' College
Columbia University
525 W. 120th St.
New York, NY 10027

Kurzweil Computer Products
33 Cambridge Parkway
Cambridge, MA 02142

- Reading machine
- Voice Writer

Prentke-Romish
1022 Heyl Rd.
Wooster, OH 44691

- Touch Talker

Special Education Software Review
3807 N. Northwood
Peoria, IL 61614

Technical Aids and Systems for the Handicapped
70 Gibson Dr., Unit 12
Markham, Ontario, Canada L3R 4C2

Chapter 7

Videotapes and Television

The video market for home televisions is a soaring industry. Almost every movie that has ever played in the theater is available for home TV and can be rented or bought. Through videos, parents can bring quality entertainment into their homes and help to minimize the amount of violence that children see on commercial television. A cool summer evening or a cozy winter evening spent watching videos can help bring families together after hectic weeks of running from day care to work and home again. It is a pleasant interlude. A family does not have to worry about taking small children to a theater, where they may be disruptive, or about incurring the expense of a babysitter to go out for the evening.

Take the time to enjoy a video with your child from time to time. Do not get into the easy habit of using the video as an electronic babysitter and leave your child unattended for long periods of time. If you do, you will be wasting valuable opportunities to bond with your child, as well as to teach language, reading, and other important life skills.

Many movies and TV programs today are closed captioned, which makes them very accessible for the deaf and language delayed child. Look on your video carton or in the TV guide for the symbol "cc," which stands for closed captioned.

Captioned television and videotapes are not just for the deaf. Caption decoders, first marketed in 1980, are an exciting breakthrough for all children learning to read, with or without a language delay. TV watching is *fun* for your child. Captioned TV and videos are especially suited for helping your child develop good reading readiness skills. Captioning makes it clear to your child that reading is speech or signs or cues written down. (In fact, we have a Hispanic friend who uses a caption decoder to help her learn to read and speak English.) In the last decade, captioned TV has increasingly been used to assist deaf and hearing children with learning disabilities develop better reading skills.

Studies conducted in Maryland public schools and at the University of Maryland found that comprehension and motivation to read also improved with captioning. Children not only learned more words, but retained more words over time. One interesting result which came out of the studies was that some students learning to read benefited greatly from being able to comprehend the story line first as a precursor to attacking the sight reading words on the TV screen. In other words, learning to read captions with an accompanying visual display and contextual study was easier than just learning to read individual letters or words with no accompanying visual display.

There are two types of captions, **open** and **closed.**

Open captions can be read without the need for a decoder. Open captions sometime appear on your television set to alert the viewing audience about weather or government emergencies, etc. They are "open" to everyone watching the TV set.

Closed captions are similar to subtitles you read on foreign films. They can be viewed only if you have a specially equipped TV or a caption decoder. A caption decoder can be purchased through stores or catalogues which feature assistive listening devices for people with special needs. Captioners generally cost under $200.

Captioned TV helps your child develop the visual discrimination skills she needs before she can learn to read. These skills include being able to recognize and name upper and lower case letters, distinguishing left from right, up from down, following a progression of words from left to right, and being able to pick out the figure from the background.

Captioned TV also provides yet another way for your child to develop good sight reading skills to correspond with the words she hears and sees. For example, we have seen the success of *Sesame Street,* which uses a visual imput system of letters, words, and numbers on the screen in a fun and interesting way. Through repetition, the child sees the letters, numbers, and simple words over and over and begins to integrate them into easily recognizable words wherever she sees them. We have seen this in families where there are deaf adults, and the children, both deaf and hearing, are exposed to captioned movies and TV. No one knows at exactly what point the child makes the connection between the words that are captioned and those that are spoken but we do know that early exposure to the printed word results in better reading ability later on. This is true for books as well as captioned TV or movies.

Captioned TV is also great for helping your child develop sound-symbol correspondence skills, or phonetics. It can help her begin recognizing the names of letters, as well as the sounds they represent. She learns at this stage that C is called "see" and stands for the sound "kuh" at the beginning of the word "cat." Your child will start to understand that the sounds of letters blend together to form a word that she sees on the TV screen.

We recommend you consider using captioned TV and films on a regular basis at home to help your child develop her reading vocabulary. Your child will think she's got the most fun reading toy of all the kids in the neighborhood.

If your child uses sign language, you should be aware that videos in sign language are available. Because sign language is a visual language, children who know the system can enjoy some of their favorite stories told through this medium.

If your child has a visual impairment, you will want to investigate videos and television programs with descriptive video—a spoken, pre-recorded description of actions on the screen that can be heard through a special simultaneous radio broadcast or directly from video. Descriptive video is becoming more available for television shows (especially on public television) and movies. Your television set may well already have the capability to decode descriptive video.

Unfortunately, there is not enough space in the book for us to recommend specific video titles. Instead, we suggest that you let your child be your guide. Stay with videos that are developmentally appropriate for him. Bear in mind that it is not necessary to view the film in its entirety in one sitting. Your child may want to watch a while, then play outside, then nap and watch again later on. She will let you know when enough is enough.

Obtaining a Caption Decoder

In 1992, a federal bill was passed as part of the Americans with Disabilities Act requiring all new TV sets 23 inches or larger to have a special chip built in to provide closed captioning at the flick of a switch. If your television was manufactured before the law went into effect in July

1992, the following stores carry captioners in stock or can order them for you:

> *In the Northeast:* Service Merchandise, Lechmere
> *In California:* Fedco
> *In the Midwest:* Highland Superstores
> *In Ohio and Pennsylvania:* The Appliance Store

For more information, contact:

National Captioning Institute
1900 Gallows Rd., Suite 3000
Vienna, VA 22182
703–917–7600

Captioned Film/Videos for the Deaf
5000 Park Street North
St. Petersburg, FL 33709–9989

Chapter 8

Toy Safety

Protecting children from unsafe toys is everyone's responsibility. Careful toy selection and proper supervision of children at play is still the best way to protect children from toy-related injuries.

We have mentioned safety all along as we discussed specific toys in each of the age categories. In this section we offer suggestions about toy safety in general. This information was obtained from the U.S. Consumer Product Safety Commission in Washington, DC. Under the Federal Hazardous Substances Act and The Consumer Product Safety Act, the Commission has set safety regulations for certain toys and other children's articles. Manufacturers must design and manufacture their products to meet these regulations so that hazardous products are not sold.

If you have further questions you can call a Toll Free Hotline at 800/638–CPSC or 800/638–2772. We encourage you to call these numbers and report any dangerous conditions that you find in any toys. This office is very interested in having up-to-date information about toy safety.

When Buying Toys

Choose toys with care. Keep in mind your child's age, interests, and skill level. Look for quality design and construction in all toys for all ages.

Make sure that all directions or instructions are clear to you, and, when appropriate, to your child. Plastic wrappings on toys should be discarded at once before they become deadly playthings.

Be a label reader. Look for, and heed, age recommendations such as "Not recommended for children under three." Look for other safety labels, including: "Flame retardant/Flame resistant" on fabric products and "Washable/hygienic materials" on stuffed toys and dolls.

When Maintaining Toys

Check all toys periodically for breakage and potential hazards. A damaged or dangerous toy should be thrown away or repaired immediately.

Edges on wooden toys that might have become sharp or surfaces covered with splinters should be sanded smooth. Paint is regulated for lead content by the Consumer Product Safety Commission. Examine all outdoor toys regularly for weak parts that could become hazardous.

When Storing Toys

Teach children to put their toys safely away on shelves or in a toy chest.

Toy boxes, too, should be checked for safety. Use a toy chest that has a lid that will stay open in any position to which it is raised and will not fall on your child. For extra safety, be sure there are ventilation holes for fresh air. Watch for sharp edges that could cut and hinges that could pinch or squeeze.

See that toys used outdoors are stored after play. Rain or dew can damage a variety of toys and toy parts, creating hazards.

Sharp Edges and Points

New toys intended for children under eight years of age must, by law, be free of sharp glass and metal edges. With use, however, older toys may break, exposing cutting edges.

Toys which have been broken may have dangerous points or prongs. Stuffed toys may have wires inside the toy which could cut or stab your child if exposed. A Consumer Product Safety Commission regulation prohibits sharp points in new toys and other articles intended for use by children under eight years of age.

Small Parts

Older toys can break to reveal parts small enough to be swallowed or to become lodged in your child's windpipe, ears, or nose. There is a small tube that can be obtained from the Consumer Product Safety Commission or through toy stores which can help you decide how safe a small piece is. The tube is the size of a child's windpipe and any toy or part that can fit into it is not safe for a child under three. The law bans small parts in new toys intended for children under three. This includes removable small eyes and noses on stuffed toys and dolls and small, removable squeakers on squeeze toys.

Loud Noises

Toy caps, noisemaking guns, and other toys can produce sounds at noise levels that can damage hearing. The law requires the following label on boxes of caps producing noise above a certain level: "Warning—Do not fire closer than one foot to the ear. Do not use indoors." Caps producing noise that can injure a child's hearing are banned.

Cords and Strings

Toys with long strings or cords may be dangerous for infants and very young children. The cords may become wrapped around an infant's neck, causing strangulation. Never hang toys with long strings, cords, loops, or ribbons in cribs or playpens where children can become entangled.

Remove crib gyms from the crib when your child can pull himself up on his hands and knees; some children have strangled when they fell across crib gyms stretched across the crib.

Propelled Objects

Your child's flying toys can be turned into weapons and cause serious injuries.

Children should never be permitted to play with adult lawn darts or other hobby or sporting equipment with sharp points. Arrows or darts used by children should have soft cork tips, rubber suction cups, or other protective tips intended to prevent injury. Check to be sure the tips are secure. Avoid those dart guns or other toys which might be capable of firing articles not intended for use in the toys such as pencils or nails.

Electric Toys

Electric toys that are improperly constructed, wired, or misused can shock or burn your child. Electric toys must meet mandatory requirements for maximum surface temperatures, electrical construction, and prominent warning labels. Electric toys with heating elements are recommended only for children over eight years old. Children should be taught to use electric toys properly, cautiously, and under adult supervision.

Equally important is to make sure that battery operated toys have safe storage compartments so that young children cannot gain access to the batteries.

Infant Toys

Infant toys, such as rattles, squeeze toys, and teethers, should be large enough so that they cannot enter and become lodged in your infant's throat.

All Toys Are
Not for All Children

Keep toys designed for older children out of the hands of little ones. Follow labels that give age recommendations—some toys are recommended for older children because they may be hazardous in the hands of a younger child. Teach your older children to help keep their toys away from their younger brothers and sisters.

Even balloons when uninflated or broken can choke or suffocate your child if he tries to swallow them. More children have suffocated on uninflated balloons than on any other type of toy.

Street Smarts

By the time your child is five, safety issues expand to toys used outside the home. Riding a bicycle, dribbling a basketball, playing tee ball, or jumping rope outside near the street must be done with caution.

As you allow your child increased independence, you must continue to stress safety. He must be taught to look both ways a number of times before crossing the street, and not to dart in the street to chase after a ball. When using a bicycle, skateboard, or even roller skates, your child should wear a safety helmet. In fact, in many states, it is now against the law to allow your child to bicycle even down a public sidewalk without an approved safety helmet.

Consider kneepads and elbowpads for rollerskating or even for the five-year-old learning to ride a two-wheel bicycle without training wheels. Protective gear such as this will soften your child's falls.

Conclusion

Most children's toys for sale today are well-constructed and safe *for their intended age group.* Still, accidents can happen. But if you choose toys carefully and supervise your child at play, you will greatly diminish the chances that your child will be injured.

APPENDICES

Alternate Sources of Toys

For many parents, the cost of continually buying new and stimulating toys for their children can be prohibitive. Fortunately, there are several low-cost alternatives to buying brand new toys. Sometimes small groups of friends swap toys for their children for short or indefinite periods of time. This, of course, instantly increases the number of toys you and your child have to work with when doing the language development dialogues. Imagine if you were to arrange to borrow or exchange a few selected toys from one friend, a few toys from a second friend, and a few more toys from yet a third friend. You would have managed to accumulate close to a dozen different toys for you and your child to play with.

On a similiar, but slightly larger scale, we have seen neighborhood groups of parents organize a toy-sharing cooperative. This can be organized on its own or as part of an already existing neighborhood organization or a community play group. Each child brings in a different toy to exchange with another child for a period of a week or two. This way, the novelty of getting a new toy never quite has time to wear off. One new toy is continually replaced by another new toy. A child's dream come true! Again, the cost of buying new toys is drastically reduced and parents have an opportunity to see which toys their child enjoys the most before purchasing them.

Now that you have the idea of this type of alternative to buying brand-new toys in the department stores, you can see why some neighorhood preschools, special education programs, and local libraries provide this service or take it even one step further. Either for free or for a very small rental fee, you and your child can choose to borrow a toy for a designated period of time. Next time you go to your local library, find out if they have such a service. You may be surprised to find a toy lending library already in your area. Another source may be your local Arc (formerly Association for Retarded Citizens), Easter Seals, or other special-needs organizations.

Be on the lookout for garage sales and consignment shops in your area. These are two other good places to locate children's toys, often for greatly reduced prices. In these cases, the toys are often out of their boxes, which gives you a chance to look them over thoroughly. You can see how interested in the toy your child is before you buy it.

One final option is to contact the National Lekotek Center at 1–800–366–PLAY. Lekotek centers offer individualized assistance in selecting appropriate toys and play materials for children with disabilities, and may also have toys available for loan. The national office can tell you the location of the Lekotek center nearest you.

   With all borrowed or secondhand toys, we recommend that you take special safety precautions before letting your child play with them. Wash the toys thoroughly with soap and water. Run your hand over them, looking for sharp or broken edges. Make sure there are no small parts that may present a danger to your child.

Materials List

Many of the materials you need to make homemade toys may already be in your cupboards, recycling bin, rag bag, or basement. To help you recognize these valuable materials before you throw them in the trash, this section lists common items useful in making your own toys. Also listed are stores and other sources of free or low-cost materials.

Materials for Homemade Toys

Arts and Crafts necessities: tape, paper clips, string, paper fasteners, pipe cleaners, wire, rope, string, staples, paste glue, tempera paint, crayons, markers, scissors, paper in various sizes and colors, stickers, paper towels, etc.

- Barrels: fruit and vegetable crates
- Baskets
- Boxes: all types; match boxes, giftboxes, jewelry boxes, candy boxes, etc.
- Cardboard Tubing: paper towel tubing, toilet paper rolls, aluminum foil and plastic wrap tubing, etc.
- Food Items: macaroni noodles, kidney beans, dried peas, cereal bits, etc.
- Kitchen Utensils: pots, pans, measuring utensils, sifters, bowls, cooking pans, wooden spoons, spatulas, etc.
- Miscellaneous Items: rubber bands, popsicle sticks, sponges, clothespins, cotton balls, cork, leaves, pine cones, small stones and shells, straws, pipe cleaners, etc.
- Paper and Cardboard Items: aluminum foil, waxed paper, wallpaper scraps, contact paper scraps, newspaper, shirt cardboards, vegetable cartons and trays, oatmeal containers, old magazines, greeting cards, gift wrapping paper, etc.
- Plastic Bottles: milk bottles, bleach bottles, dish soap dispensers, hand lotion dispensers, ketchup bottles, etc.
- Plastic Containers: egg cartons, ice cream cartons, butter containers, cheese containers, microwave dinners
- Sewing Notions: yarn, decorative tape, buttons, zippers, beads, ribbons, thread, empty spools, cloth in different colors and textures, clasps, belt buckles, etc.
- Styrofoam: styrofoam packing, fruit trays, etc.

Materials for Dramatic Play

- Baskets, grocery carts, bags—to go "shopping."
- Boxes—to represent the stove, refrigerator, a spaceship, playhouse, etc.
- Broom, dustpan—to play clean up.
- Crates and boxes—for doll or stuffed animal beds.
- Empty food storage cans and boxes—to be part of the pretend kitchen.

- Hats, hats, and more hats. Kids love them.
- Miscellaneous—glasses, aprons, pocketbooks, wallets, mittens, etc.
- Old clothes—dresses, skirts, blouses, pants, slips, hats, coats, scarves, gloves. Discarded nylon nightgowns make great formal wear for kids.
- Old jewelry—bracelets, belts, necklaces, earrings, etc.
- Play money, boxes—to play cashier.
- Pots, pans, dishes, cups, eating utensils, paper plates and cups—for restaurant play, pretending to be Mommy and Daddy, etc.
- Telephones—a great way to practice language!
- White coats or shirts—to pretend to be a doctor, dentist, etc.

Places to Find Materials

- Carpet Stores: carpet samples and scraps
- Fabric Stores: sewing notions, excess remnants, patches
- Garage Sales: an infinite variety of objects
- Grocery Stores: boxes, plastic and cardboard cartons, food items
- Lumber Yards: wood scraps, cinder blocks, etc.
- Newspaper Companies: newsprint end-of-rolls and scraps
- Paint Stores: paint color cards
- Paper Companies: paper samples, damaged sheets of paper
- Produce Markets: vegetable and fruit crates, barrels
- Tile Companies: scraps of mosaic, ceramic, or vinyl tile
- Wallpaper Stores: out-of-date sample books, swatches

Sources for Information about Children's Books

Children's Book Council, Inc.
568 Broadway
New York, NY 10012
212–966–1990

Children's Books in Print
(revised annually; available for use in
most libraries and bookstores)
R.R. Bowker
121 Chanlon Road
New Providence, NJ 07974
800–521–8110

Exceptional Parent Magazine
P.O. Box 3000, Dept. EP
Denville, NJ 07834–9919
800–247–8080

Sesame Street Magazine
Children's Television Workshop
One Lincoln Plaza
New York, NY 10023
800–678–0613

Horn Book Magazine
11 Beacon St., Suite 1000
Boston, MA 02108

Highlights for Children
P.O. Box 182167
Columbus, OH 43218–2167

A to Zoo:
Subject Access to Children's Picture Books
Carolyn Lima and Jona Lima

R.R. Bowker
121 Chanlon Road
New Providence, NJ 07974

R.R. Bowker, 1993
Seedlings Books
Twin Vision Books (books in print and braille)
P.O. Box 2395
Livonia, MI 48151–0395
800–777–8552

Resource Guide

Included in this section are national organizations that provide support and information for children with disabilities and their families. For specific information about the goals and services of any organization, call or write and request an information packet.

General

Council for Exceptional Children
1920 Association Dr.
Reston, VA 22091–1589
703–620–3660

The Association for Persons with Severe Handicaps (TASH)
29 W. Susquehanna Ave., Ste. 210
Baltimore, MD 21204
410–828–8274

National Information Center for Children and Youth with Disabilities (NICHCY)
P.O. Box 1492
Washington, DC 20013
202–884–8200; 800–695–0285

National Lekotek Center
2100 Ridge Ave.
Evanston, IL 60201
708–328–0001; 800–366–PLAY
(Information on toys and play for children with disabilities)

Special Olympics International
P.O. Box 37111
Washington, DC 20013–7111

Autism

Autism Society of America
8601 Georgia Ave. Suite 503
Silver Spring, MD 20910
301–565–0433

Deaf Blind

DB-Link: The National Information Clearinghouse on Children Who Are Deaf-Blind
c/o Teaching Research
Northwestern Oregon State College
345 North Monmouth Ave.
Monmouth, OR 97361
503–838–8756

Helen Keller National Center for Deaf Blind Youths and Adults
111 Middle Neck Rd.
Sands Point, NY 11050
516–944–8900

Deaf and Hard of Hearing

Alexander Graham Bell Association for the Deaf
3417 Volta Place NW
Washington, DC 20007
202–337–5220 (V/TTY)

American Society for Deaf Children
2848 Arden Way, Suite 210
Sacramento, CA 95825–1373
1–800–942–2732

Council on Education of the Deaf
LBJ Building, Room 2630
52 Lomb Memorial Dr.
Rochester, NY 14623

National Association of the Deaf
814 Thayer Ave.
Silver Spring, MD 20901
301–587–1788

National Cued Speech Association
P.O. Box 31345
Raleigh, NC 27622
919–828–1218

National Foundation for Children's Hearing Education and Research
928 McLean Ave.
Yonkers, NY 10704
914–237–2676

• Parents Section

c/o Alexander Graham Bell Association for the Deaf
3417 Volta Place NW
Washington, DC 20007
202–337–5220

Self Help for Hard of Hearing People
7910 Woodmont Ave.
Bethesda, MD 20814
301–657–2248

Epilepsy

Epilepsy Foundation of America
4351 Garden City Drive
Landover, MD 20785
301–459–3700; 800–EFA–1000

Facial Differences

American Cleft Palate-Craniofacial Association
1218 Grandview Ave.
University of Pittsburgh
Pittsburgh, PA 15211
412–481–1376

FACES—National Association for the Craniofacially Handicapped
P.O. Box 11082
Chattanooga, TN 37401
615–266–1632; 800–332–2373

Fetal Alcohol Syndrome

National Organization on FAS
1815 H. St., NW, Ste. 1000
Washington, DC 20006

Learning Disabilities

Learning Disabilities Association of America
4156 Library Rd.
Pittsburgh, PA 15234
412–341–1515

Council for Learning Disabilities
P.O. Box 40303
Overland Park, KS 66204
913–492–8755

The National Center for Learning Disabilities
381 Park Ave. South, Ste. 1420
New York, NY 10016
212–545–7510

Orton Dyslexia Society
Chester Building, Suite 382
8600 La Salle Rd.
Baltimore, MD 21286–2044
410–296–0232

Mental Retardation

The ARC (Formerly Association for Retarded Citizens)
500 East Border St., Suite 300
Arlington, TX 76010
817–261–6003

Division on Mental Retardation
c/o Foundation for Exceptional Children
1920 Association Dr.
Reston, VA 22091–1589
703–620–3660

Down Syndrome International
11 N. 73rd Terrace
Kansas City, KS 66111
913–299–0815

National Down Syndrome Congress
1605 Chantilly Rd.
Atlanta, GA 30324
800–232–NDSC

National Down Syndrome Society
666 Broadway
New York, NY 10012
212–460–9330; 800–221–4602

National Fragile X Foundation
1441 York St., Ste. 215
Denver, CO 80206

Physical Disabilities

Congress of Organizations of the Physically Handicapped
16630 Beverly
Tinley Park, IL 60477–6904
708–532–3566

Division for Physically Handicapped
c/o Council for Exceptional Children
1920 Association Drive
Reston, VA 22091
703–620–3660

Muscular Dystrophy Association
3300 E. Sunrise Drive
Tucson, AZ 85718
602–529–2000

Spina Bifida Association of America
4590 MacArthur Blvd., N.W., Suite 250
Washington, DC 20007–4226
202–944–3285; 800–621–3141

United Cerebral Palsy Associations
1660 L St. NW, Ste. 700
Washington, DC 20036
202–776–0406; 800–872–5827

Speech and Language Disabilities

Academy of Aphasia
University of California at Los Angeles
Department of Linguistics
Los Angeles, CA 90024
310–206–3206

American Speech Language Hearing Association
10801 Rockville Pike
Rockville, MD 20852
301–897–5700; 800–638–8255

National Association for Hearing and Speech Action
10801 Rockville Pike
Rockville, MD 20852
301–897–8682; 800–638–8255

National Center for Stuttering
200 E. 33rd St.

New York, NY 10016
212–532–1460

Visual Impairments

American Foundation for the Blind
11 Penn Plaza, Ste. 300
New York, NY 10001
212–502–7600; 800–AFB-LINE

American Printing House for the Blind
P.O. Box 6085
Louisville, KY 40206
502–895–2405; 800–223–1839

Association for Education and Rehabilitation of the Blind and Visually Impaired
206 N. Washington St. Suite 320
Alexandria, VA 22314
703–836–6060

Council of Families with Visual Impairment
c/o American Council of the Blind
1155 15th St. NW Suite 720
Washington, DC 20005
202–467–5081; 800–424–8666

Division on Visual Handicaps
c/o Council for Exceptional Children
1920 Association Dr.
Reston, VA 22091–1589
703–620–3660

National Association for Parents of the Visually Impaired
P.O. Box 317
Watertown, MA 02272
1–800–562–6265

National Association for Visually Handicapped
22 W. 21st St.
New York, NY 10010
212–889–3141

National Organization of Parents of Blind Children
1800 Johnson St.
Baltimore, MD 21230
410–659–9314

Toy Manufacturers and Catalogs

Battat, Inc.
2 Industrial Blvd. West Circle
P.O. Box 1264
Plattsburgh, NY 12901
518–562–2200
       Count and Match Pegboard*
       Learning Blocks*
       Sight and Sound Animal Puzzle*
       Simplex Transport Puzzle*
       Soft Picture Blocks*
*Registered trademark of Battat,Inc.

Brio Corporation
6555 West Mill Road
Milwaukee, WI 553218
1–800–558–6863
       Wooden Railway Set*
       Passenger and Children's train*
       Railway Platform*
       Railway Crossing Barriers*
       Trees*
       Animals*
       Tunnel*
*Registered trademark of Brio Corporation

Creative Education of Canada, Inc.
464 Christina Street North
Sarnia, Ontario N7T 5W4
519–337–1542
       Pick-A-Puppet*
Registered trademark of Creative Education of Canada, Inc.

Dakin, Inc.
P.O. Box 7746
San Fransico,CA 94120
1–800–227–6598
      Domino Babies*
      Stretch Giraffe*
*Registered trademark Designs ^c Dakin, Inc.

Discovery Toys
2530 Arnold Drive
Martinez, CA 94553
1–800–426–4777
      Amanda and Timothy's Closet*
      Hide Inside*
      Place and Trace*
      Snuggle Time Activity Book*
*Registered trademark of Discovery Toys

Dragonfly Toy Company
291 Yale Ave.
Winnepeg, MB R3M 0L4
CANADA
   Sells several thousand toys and other products appropriate for children with special needs. Produces a catalog of selected toys, and will also perform a "toy search"—prepare a list of products available to suit a special request.

Eden Toys, Inc.
812 Jersey Ave.
Jersey City, NJ 07310
1–800–443–4275
      Cock-A-Doodle Zoo*   Shake Me Dolls*
      Hot Tot*   Wrist Rattles*
*Registered trademark for Eden Toys

ExploraToy
Division of Educational Insights, Inc.
19560 Rancho Way
Dominiguez Hills, CA 90220
1–800–995–9290
      Creature Catcher*
*Registered trademark of Educational Insights, Inc.

Fisher-Price, Inc.
636 Girard Avenue
East Aurora, NY 14052
716–687–3000
>Fisher-Price* Baseball
>Activity Walker
>Creative Pegboard
>Little People* Fun Park
>Peek-A-Boo Stacker*
>Pop-Up Farm
>Action Sounds Garage*
>Rock A Stack*
>Little People* House

*Registered trademark of Fisher-Price, Inc.

Forecees Company
P.O. Box 153
Vicksburg, MI 49097
1–800–588–9989
>Linky Rinks*

*Registered trademark of Forecees Co.

Franklin Sports, Inc.
17 Campbell Parkway
P.O. Box 508
Stoughton, MA 02071–0508
617–344–1111
>Red 8½" four square ball*
>Classic soccerball*

*Registered trademark of Franklin Sports, Inc.

Hand in Hand Catalogue Center
Route 26
R.R. #1
Box 1425
Oxford, ME 04270
1–800–872–9745
>Distributor for Tyco (Tub Puzzle)*
>Rainbow Mountain (Pat Mat)*
>Forecees Co.(Linky Rinks)*
>Random House (Sign Language Video)*
>Today's Kids (Gymfinity)*

*See information on individual manufacturers and copyright permission in this reference section

Hasbro, Inc.
1027 Newport Avenue
P.O. Box 1059
Pawtucket, RI 02862–1059
401–431–TOYS (8697)
      Baby Gumballs—Playskool*
      My Very Soft Baby—Playskool*
      Busy Beads—Playskool*
      Soft Stuff-Mr. Potato Head—Playskool*
      Remote Control Car—Playskool*
      Fold'n Go Play Around—Playskool*
      Candyland—Milton Bradley*
      Easy Bake Oven—Kenner Products*
      Nesting Barrels—Playskool*
*Registered trademark of Hasbro, Inc.
Playskool, a division of Hasbro, Inc., 1–800–PLAYSKL
Milton Bradley, a division of Hasbro, Inc. 413–525–6411
Kenner Products, a division of Hasbro, Inc., 1–800–327–8264

International Playthings, Inc.
120 Riverdale Road
Riverdale, NJ 07457
201–831–1400
      Balls in a Bowl*—from Early Start Child Development Toys
*Registered trademark of International Playthings

Kapable Kids
P.O. Box 250
Bohemia, NY 11716
800–356–1564
  A catalog of toys, games, and books selected with the child with special needs in mind.

Kenner Toys Products, a Division of Hasbro, Inc.
615 Elsnore Place
Cincinnato, Ohio 45202
1–800–327–8264
      Easy Bake Oven*
*Registered trademark of Hasbro, Inc.

Lego Systems, Inc.
555 Taylor Road
P.O. Box 1310
Enfield, CT 06083–1310
1–800–453–4652
      DUPLO Basic Bucket*
      Duplo Pull Back Motor*
*Registered trademark of Lego Systems, Inc.

Lillian Vernon Corporation
Virginia Beach, VA 23479
1–800–285–5555
        The Teacher's Clock*
*Registered trademark of Lillian Vernon

The Little Tikes Company
2180 Barlow Road
Hudson, OH 44236
1–800–321–0183
        Little Tikes Family Van (Black or White family)

Mag-Nif, Inc.
8820 East Avenue
Mentor, OH 44060
216–255–9366
        Money Mill Bank*
*Registered trademark of Mag-Nif, Inc.

Mattel, Inc.
333 Continental Blvd.
El Segundo, CA 90245–5012
310–252–2000
        Barbie*, Ken*, Skipper*, Stacie*, and Todd* dolls
        Easy Touch Tape Player*
        See 'N Say*
*Registered trademark of Mattel, Inc.

Milton Bradley Company, a Division of Hasbro, Inc.
443 Shaker Road
East Longmeadow, MA
413–525–6411
        Candyland*
*Registered trademark of Hasbro, Inc.

National Parent Network on Disabilities
1600 Prince St., #115
Alexandria, VA 22314
703–684–6763 (V-TTY)
    Contact this organization for a copy of the Toys R Us "Toy Guide for Differently
Abled Kids."

Parker Brothers, Inc.
P.O. Box 10
Beverly, MA 01915
1–800–327–8264
       Hi-Ho Cherry-O board game*
*Registered trademark of Hasbro, Inc.

Playmobil U.S.A., Inc.
11–E Nicholas Court
Dayton, NJ 08810
908–274–0101
      Playmobil Play Systems-School Bus*
      Classroom Setting*
      Doctor*
      Playground*
      Black and White Families*
*Registered trademark of Playmobil U.S.A., Inc.

Playskool, a Division of Hasbro, Inc.
1027 Newport Avenue
Pawtucket, RI 02861
1–800–752–9755
      Nesting Barrels*
*Registered trademark of Hasbro, Inc.

Rainbow Mountain, Inc.
751 Frontenac Road, Suite 157
Naperville, IL 60563
708–416–7877
      Pat Mat*
*Registered trademark of Rainbow Mountain

Random House
201 East 50th Street
New York, NY 10022
1–800–726–0600
      Sign Me a Story Videotape*
*Registered trademark of Random House (Produced by Zink Entertainment, West 19th
St., New York, NY 10022, 212/929–2949)

Small World Toys
P.O. Box 3620
Culver City, CA 90231–3620
      Humpty Dumpty Comeback Roller*
*Registered trademark of Ambi products (Small World Toys is the exclusive distributor of
Ambi products.)

Step2 Corporation
10010 Aurora-Hudson Road
P.O. Box 2412
Streetsboro, OH 44241
1–800–347–8372
        Combo Climber*
*Registered trademark of Step2 Corporation

Texas Instruments, Inc.
Consumer Relations
P.O. Box 53
Lubbock, TX 79408–0053
1–800–842–2737
        Listen and Learn* Ball*
        Talking Peek-A-Boo Zoo*
*Registered trademark of Texas Instruments, Inc.

Today's Kids
P.O. Box 207
Booneville, AR 72927
1–800–258–8697
        GymFinity*
*Registered trademark of Today's Kids

Tomy America, Inc.
450 Delta Avenue
Brea, CA 92621
714–256–4990
        Push 'N Go*
*Registered trademark of Tomy America, Inc.

Tyco Playtime, Inc.
1107 Broadway, 11th Floor
New York, NY 10010
212–741–7222
        Sesame Street Tub Puzzle*
*Registered trademark of Tyco Playtime, Inc.

VTECH
380 West Palatine Road
Wheeling, IL 60090–5831
708–215–9700
1–800–521–2010
        Little Smart Fun to Talk Phone*
        Little Smart Alphabet Writing Desk*
*Registered trademark of VTECH

Wimmer-Ferguson Child Products, Inc.
P.O. Box 100427
Denver, CO 80250
303–733–0848
       Car Seat Gallery*
       Double-Feature Mirror*
       Infant-Stim Mobile*
       Pattern Pals*
       Peek-a-boo Play*
*Registered trademark of Wimmer-Ferguson, Child Products, Inc.

Wind River Products, Inc.
10507 Gravelly Lake Dr. S.W.
Suite 15A
Tacoma, WA 98499
1–800–743–9463
       Flying Wheelchair Puzzle*
*Registered trademark of Wind River

References

Almy, Millie and Genish, Celia. *Ways of Studying Children.* 2nd ed. New York: Teachers College, Columbia University: Teachers College Press, 1979.

Ames, Louise Bates and Ilg, Frances L. *Your Five Year Old.* New York: Dell Publishing, 1981.

Anderson, W., Chitwood, S., and Hayden, D. *Negotiating the Special Education Maze. Bethesda, MD: Woodbine House, 1991.*

Atack, M. Sally. *Art Activities for the Handicapped.* Englewood Cliffs, NJ: Prentice-Hall, Inc., 1986.

Bangs, Tina. *Birth to Three: Developmental Learning and the Handicapped Child.* Hingham, MA: Teaching Resources Corp., 1979.

Barber, W. Lucie and Williams, Herman. *Your Baby's First 30 Months.* Tucson, AZ: Fisher Publishing Co., 1981.

Brazelton, T. Berry. *Infants and Mothers.* New York: Dell Publishing Co., 1983.

Breger, Louis. *From Instinct to Identity: The Development of Personality.* Englewood Cliffs, NJ: Prentice-Hall, Inc., 1974.

Burtt, Kent Garland and Kalkstein, Karen. *Smart Toys for Babies from Birth to Two.* New York: Harper and Row, Publishers, Inc., 1981.

Caplan, Frank and Theresa. *The Power of Play.* Garden City, NY: Anchor Press/Doubleday, 1973.

Cary, Elizabeth and Casebolt, Patti. *Pick Up Your Socks and Other Skills Growing Children Need!* Seattle: Parenting Press, 1990.

Cary, Elizabeth. *Without Spanking or Spoiling.* Seattle: Parenting Press, 1990.

Carney, Steven. *Toy Book.* New York: Workman Publishing Co., 1972

Cole, Joanna and Calmenson, Stephanie. *Anna Banana and Jump Rope Rhymes.* New York: William Morrow and Co., 1989.

Cole, Joanna and Calmenson, Stephanie. *The Eensy Weentsy Spider Fingerplays and Action Rhymes.* New York: William Morrow and Co., 1991.

Durkin, Lisa Lyons. *Parents and Kids Together.* New York: Warner Books, 1986.

Einon, Dorothy. *Play with a Purpose: Learning Games for Children 6 Weeks to 2–3 Years Old.* New York: St. Martin's Press, 1985.

Eliason, F. Claudia and Jenkins, Loa Thomson. *A Practical Guide to Early Childhood Curriculum.* St. Louis: The C.V. Mosby Co., 1993.

Erickson, H. Erik. *Childhood and Society.* New York: W.W. Norton & Co., 1963.

Garvey, Catherine. *Children's Talk.* Boston: Harvard University Press, 1984.

Geralis, Elaine (Ed.), *Children with Cerebral Palsy: A Parent's Guide.* Bethesda, MD: Woodbine House, 1991.

Goldberg, Sally. *Teaching with Toys.* Ann Arbor: The University of Michigan Press, 1981.

Gordon, J. Ira. *Baby Learning through Baby Play.* New York: St. Martin's Press, 1970.

Gordon, J. Ira, Guinah, and Barry, Jestes, R. Emile. *The Instruction for the Development of Human Resources.* Gainesville: University of Florida.

Gordon, J. Ira. *Baby to Parent, Parent to Baby.* New York: St. Martin's Press, 1977.

Gordon, J. Ira. *Child Learning through Child Play: Learning Activities for 2–3 Year Olds,* New York: St. Martin's Press, 1972.

Greenspan, Stanley and Greenspan, Nancy. *The Essential Partnership.* New York: Penguin Books, 1989.

Hagerston, Julie and Morrill, Joan. *Games Babies Play and More Games Babies Play.* New York: Pocket Books, 1981.

Heins, Marilyn and Seiden, Anne. *Child Care/Parent Care.* New York: Doubleday, 1987.

Hendrick, Joanne. *The Whole Child: Developmental Education for the Early Years.* New York: Macmillan, 1991.

Holbrook, M. Cay (Ed.), *Children with Visual Impairment: A Parents' Guide.* Bethesda, MD: Woodbine House, 1996.

Houghton, Janaye Matteson. Homespun Language. Whitehaven Publishing Co., Inc. 1982.

Ilg, L. Frances, M.D., Ames, Louis Bates, Ph.D., and Beeker, Sidney M., M.D. *Child Behavior.* New York: Harper and Row, 1981.

Johnson, Doris McNeely. *The Creative Parenting Toy Guide.* Self-published, 1980.

Jones, Claudia. *Parents Are Teachers Too.* Charlotte, VT: Williamson Publishing Co., 1988.

Kaban, Barbara. *Choosing Toys for Children from Birth to Five.* New York: Schocken Books, 1979.

Karnes, B. Merle. *You and Your Small Wonder. Book 2: 18–36 Months.* Circle Pines, MN: American Guidance Service, 1982.

Kumin, Libby. *Communication Skills in Children with Down Syndrome: A Guide for Parents.* Bethesda, MD: Woodbine House, 1993.

Markun, Patricia Maloney. *Play: Children's Business.* Washington, DC: Association for Childhood Education International, 1974.

Maryland State Department of Education. *Parent Helper-Handicapped Children Birth to Five: Communication.* Baltimore, MD: Division of Special Education, 1982.

McConkey, Roy and Jeffree, Dorothy. *Making Toys for Handicapped Children.* Englewood Cliffs, NJ: Prentice-Hall, 1983.

Miller, Karen. *Things to Do with Toddlers and Twos.* Chelsea, MA: Telshare Publishing, Inc., 1984.

Miller, Karen. *More Things to Do with Toddlers and Twos.* Chelsea, MA: Telshare Publishing, Inc., 1984.

Millnard, Joan and Behrmann, Polly. *Parents As Playmates: A Games Approach to the Preschool Years.* New York: Human Sciences Press, 1979.

Monsees, K. Edna. *Structured Language for Children with Special Language Learning Problems.* Washington, DC: Children's Hospital of the District of Columbia, Children's Hearing and Speech Center, 1972.

Moore, Cory. *A Reader's Guide for Parents of Children with Mental, Physical, or Emotional Disabilities. 3rd edition.* Bethesda, MD: Woodbine House, 1991.

Munger, Evelyn Moats and Bowdon, Susan Jane. *Child Play Activities for Your Child's First Three Years.* New York: E.P. Dutton, Inc., 1983.

Musselwhite, Caroline Ramsey. *Adaptive Play for Special Needs Children: Strategies to Enhance Communication and Learning.* Austin, TX: Pro-Ed, 1986.

Oberlander, June. *Slow and Steady Get Me Ready.* Fairfax, VA: Bio-Alpha Inc., 1989.

O'Neill, Mary. *Hailstones and Halibut Bones.* New York: Doubleday, 1989.

Oppenheim, Joanne F. *Kids and Play.* New York: Ballantine Books, 1984.

Oppenheim, Joanne and Stephanie Oppenheim. *The Best Toys, Books, and Videos for Kids.* New York: Harper Collins Publishers, 1993.

Powers, Margaret Hall. "Functional Disorders of Articulation/Symptomotology and Etiology," In *Handbook of Speech Pathology, and Audiology,* edited by Lee Edward Travis. Englewood Cliffs, NJ: Prentice Hall, 1971.

Powers, Michael (Ed.). *Children with Autism: A Parents' Guide.* Bethesda, MD: Woodbine House, 1989.

Pushaw, David. *Teach Your Child to Talk.* New York: CEBCO Publishing, 1976.

Schwartz, Sue (Ed.). *Choices In Deafness: A Parents' Guide.* Bethesda, MD: Woodbine House, 1987.

Scott, Eileen P., Jan, James E., and Freeman, Robert D. *Can't Your Child See? A Guide for Parents of Visually Impaired Children.* Austin, TX: Pro-Ed, 1985.

Screiber, Lee R. *The Parents' Guide to Kids' Sports.* Boston: Little, Brown, and Co., 1990.

Segal, Marilyn. *Your Child At Play. Birth-One, One-Two, Two-Three, Three-Five.* New York: Newmarket Press, 1985.

Smith, Romayne (Ed.). *Children with Mental Retardation: A Parents' Guide.* Bethesda, MD: Woodbine House, 1993.

Sobol, Tom and Harriet. *Your Child in School: Kindergarten through Second Grade.* New York: Arbor House, 1987.

Spock, Benjamin. "The Best Toys for Kids (and the Worst)." *Redbook,* November 1985, pp. 16, 18.

Stern, Daniel, MD. *Diary of a Baby.* New York: Basic Books, 1990.

Sternlicht, Nancy. *Games Play.* New York: Reinhold Co., 1981.

Stray-Gundersen, Karen (Ed.). *Babies with Down Syndrome: A New Parents' Guide.* 2nd ed. Bethesda, MD: Woodbine House, 1995.

Trainer, Marilyn. *Differences In Common: Straight Talk on Mental Retardation, Down Syndrome, and Life.* Bethesda, MD: Woodbine House, 1991.

Index

About the Authors

Sue Schwartz, Ph.D.

Sue Schwartz received her master's degree in Speech and Hearing from Central Institute for the Deaf in St. Louis, MO, and her Ph.D. in Curriculum and Instruction with an emphasis in Family Counseling from the University of Maryland. She developed the Parent Infant Program in the Programs for Deaf and Hard of Hearing Students in the Montgomery County, Maryland Public Schools, where she currently works as Provider of Family Services. Dr. Schwartz is the editor of two editions of *Choices in Deafness* (Woodbine House). Her three adult children helped her learn the immeasurable value of play in the development of language.

Joan E. Heller Miller, Ed.M.

Joan E. Heller Miller holds a master's degree in Education from Harvard University with an emphasis in Counseling and Consulting Psychology. She is a certified teacher in early childhood education and has taught and counseled children with special needs and their families. She is the author of *Living with Hearing Loss: A Lifelong Educational Process* (International Conference for the Education of the Deaf Publication Manual, 1995). An active board member of the Montgomery County Association for Hearing Impaired Children and Self Help for Hard of Hearing in Maryland, Joan has three daughters, the oldest of whom has a severe hearing loss.